Source, Sanction,
and Salvation

Source, Sanction, and Salvation

RELIGION AND MORALITY IN JUDAIC AND CHRISTIAN TRADITIONS

John P. Reeder, Jr.
Brown University

PRENTICE HALL, Englewood Cliffs, New Jersey 07632

Library of Congress Cataloging-in-Publication Data

REEDER, JOHN P. (date)
  Source, sanction, and salvation.

  Includes bibliographies and index.
  1. Christian ethics. 2. Ethics, Jewish.
3. Salvation. I. Title.
BJ1251.R395 1988   241   87–32849
ISBN 0-13-823436-1

Editorial/production supervision: Debbie Ford
Cover design: Allen Moore & Associates
Manufacturing buyer: Margaret Rizzi

Printed in the United States of America

10 9 8 7 6 5 4 3 2 1

ISBN 0-13- 8234361   01

ISBN 0-13-823436-1

Prentice-Hall International (UK) Limited, *London*
Prentice-Hall of Australia Pty. Limited, *Sydney*
Prentice-Hall Canada Inc., *Toronto*
Prentice-Hall Hispanoamericana, S.A., *Mexico*
Prentice-Hall of India Private Limited, *New Delhi*
Prentice-Hall of Japan, Inc., *Tokyo*
Simon & Schuster Asia Pte. Ltd., *Singapore*
Editora Prentice-Hall do Brasil, Ltda., *Rio de Janeiro*

For my father, the late J.P. Reeder, and my mother V. H. Reeder

Contents

Preface

Source, Sanction, and Salvation is an effort to look at familiar themes in Judaism and Christianity from a broader perspective. At one stage in this book's history, I tried to show in a comparative way how that broader perspective (expressed in the categories of source, sanction, and salvation) could help us understand some themes in non-Western traditions as well. My wise friends cautioned me against this attempt, suggesting that it would be difficult enough to develop the categories and relate them to some patterns of thought in Judaism and Christianity.

Of course, even this program will seem wildly ambitious to some. Indeed, I leap here and there for examples. The patterns in Christian thought I refer to are those most familiar to me in Protestant and Roman Catholic traditions; Eastern Christianity is alluded to only in a footnote. No attempt is made to distinguish Orthodox, Conservative, or Reform strands of Judaism. The Christian materials are better known to me than the Judaic, but I have tried not to skew the discussion in a, say, Protestant direction. I am certainly not trying to describe or propose a "Judeo-Christian" theology (although I do sometimes refer to "mainstream" positions). I am looking at what appear to be (at least on some interpretations) *overlapping* themes and issues in certain strands or strata of Judaic and Christian tradition.

Readers will also no doubt note that my categories are shaped by the concerns of particular figures. I have wrestled with the ideas of certain thinkers such as Kant and Otto. The categories also reflect recent theories in philosophy and the social sciences. But while my own perspective is inevitably limited, I hope that the categories I try to develop tell us something about the traditions themselves.

I owe a great debt to all of those who have read this book and discussed it with me at one time or another. The list is long and I run the risk of forgetting someone, but allow me to acknowledge the following: David Blumenthal, Lisa Cahill, John Carman, James Childress, Jaime M. Ferreira, John Gager, Paul Lauritzen, Michael Levine, David Little, James McDermott, G. E. Michalson, Jr., Giles Milhaven, Susan Niditch, Charles Reynolds, Frank Reynolds, Edmund Santurri, David Schenck, Donald Swearer, Sumner B. Twiss, David Wills, John F. Wilson, and Lee Yearley. Special thanks to Wendell Dietrich and Gene Outka for a final reading.

John P. Reeder, Jr.
Department of Religious Studies

Source, Sanction,
and Salvation

Introduction

THE PURPOSES OF THIS BOOK*

1.1 Understanding three connections. What does this book attempt to do? It discusses, in the first place, three sorts of connections between certain religious and moral ideas: first, the notion that a transhuman *source*—some being, force, or state—causes, communicates, and legitimates the moral order; second, the idea that such a reality operates as the *sanction* of the moral order, providing a system of rewards and punishments, righting wrongs, and assuring the fulfillment of moral goals; third, the belief that such a reality provides some form of *salvation* in which the negativities of natural and social existence are overcome and morality is no longer possible or necessary. These three types of connections seem to appear in various forms in several Western traditions; they constitute, in Peter Berger's phrase, a "sacred canopy" that links the religious reality and the moral order.[1]

*The footnotes serve two purposes. First, they introduce bibliography for further study. I have been able, however, to cite only a few articles and books; students should consult journals such as *Religious Studies, The Journal of Religious Ethics,* and *The Journal of Religion* for articles and book reviews. Second, the notes make additional points for the *advanced* student. While the text is supposed to read like an introductory lecture, the notes assume some familiarity with primary and secondary sources.

I have tried, at about the same level of generality, to refine and extend the sense of *connection* Clifford Geertz was after in his famous essays on religion:

> Sacred symbols function to synthesize a people's ethos—the tone, character, and quality of their life, its moral and aesthetic style and mood—and their world view—the picture they have of the way things in sheer actuality are, their most comprehensive ideas of order.
> . . . between ethos and world view, between the approved style of life and the assumed structure of reality, there is conceived to be a simple and fundamental congruence such that they complete one another and lend one another meaning.[2]

What I want to get at are some ways in which worldviews can be knitted together with moral convictions, a crucial part of what Geertz calls ethos, the way of life of a people.

In Geertz's theory, religious or sacred "symbols," link worldviews and patterns of life, including the moral order. In Geertz's theory it is the synthesis of views about the fundamental nature of things and views about the direction of life that constitutes a religious system of meaning. It is worth noting that Geertz could retain his concept of religion as a synthesis of worldview and ethos while not insisting that the two are *congruent;* in some traditions the basic nature of reality does not undergird but may be *opposed* to the moral order. Albert Camus' religion, it could be said, was a synthesis of his view that the universe was indifferent or hostile to human morality, and his own intensely held moral convictions. But in the traditions I will examine here the "really real" transcends but is nonetheless organically connected to morality; we will be looking at how some Judaic and Christian traditions "synthesize" worldview and moral ethos.

I assume, moreover, as I believe Geertz does, that moralities shape thought, emotion, and desire so that human, that is, social, existence is possible.[3] Roughly, by a morality or moral system I will mean: 1) a set of prescriptions addressed to agents who are self-conscious and capable of action and character traits. A prescription says, "You should be and do such and such"; to say "you" presupposes self-consciousness, and to say "be and do" presupposes the capability to be directed in character and conduct. 2) Prescriptions are governed by the laws of logic—such as, consistency—however these are interpreted in particular cultures. 3) a) The agents to whom moral prescriptions are addressed are capable of having an impact on other sentient beings who can be harmed and benefited, whose good can be affected by what they do. (Sentient beings, in my terminology, are those who are capable of consciousness and desire, of some form of satisfaction or suffering); b) moreover, a moral system will ensure that a group will not be so torn by conflicting desires that human existence is not sustainable; if to be human is to be social, to exist in a web of relationship and meaning, then that web must itself provide for its own maintenance through prescriptions, and that is what a moral system does. Given that there exist agents who have desires and who can affect others and be affected by what others do, the desires, emotions, and thoughts of these agents must be ordered through normative patterns in order that the social web be maintained. Note how broad this concept of morality is; it does not require that everyone be protected. The Nazis had a morality which treated their own group very differently than others.[4]

I present source, sanction, and salvation then as three sorts of connections that link moral structures to fundamental elements of reality which influence human life for good or ill. The transhuman reality is one conception of the "really real", the causal and structural (metaphysical) basis of existence; this transhuman reality is imaged as the ground and the guarantee of the moral order, and finally as the goal which transcends it.[5]

1.2 The critical debate. The first purpose of this book then is to try to understand these sorts of connections between religious and moral convictions. We would want to understand these links between religion and morality for intrinsic intellectual reasons, for they are an important focus for the study of religion and human culture. But there are more personal or existential reasons as well and it is these that provide the second item of this book's agenda. The notion of a transhuman being that acts as source, sanction, and locus of salvation is a model of morality that has shaped Western culture. Today, many people do not find this model believable, but others still do. We not only want to understand the model, therefore, we want to know whether it is true, or whether some other model of morality, of its nature and place in human experience, is the one we should believe.

But there are various notions of source, sanction, and salvation which appear in Western culture—variations on these themes, to use the musical metaphor—and to discuss their adequacy we have to consider specific objections critics have raised. In each of the three chapters therefore the early sections will focus on understanding various examples of the categories (source, sanction, or salvation) and the final section will be devoted to critical debate. Our society, so we are told, is torn now between advocates of traditional theistic moralities and proponents of "secular humanism." The latter presumably have discarded the idea of a transhuman being that devised the nature and destiny of humankind. The purpose of the "critical discussion" sections is to identify and to begin to adjudicate the issues that divide us. Some issues have been raised by outsiders, but others have been discussed within the traditions themselves. In the face of criticisms, believers reaffirm, modify, or reject elements of their "web of belief"; inherited traditions are constructed anew.

I have tried to get some basic issues clear and suggest some answers. Thus after exploring meanings of the concept of source, for example, I will raise critical questions about versions of this idea. There will not be space to treat all the relevant positions adequately, but I will suggest some general lines of argument.[6]

1.3 Methodology. A word about how this book proceeds. I try to *illustrate* the categories of source, sanction, and salvation by giving examples from Western traditions. This is not an attempt, however, to give historically defensible interpretations; all I can do is cite some of the examples that suggested the categories to me. Nor have I systematically reformulated or restated the examples for purposes of discussion.[7] I am actually *using* interpretations of Western religious ideas, although I do not try to do the interpreting myself.[8] I do not venture, moreover, beyond some well-known Judaic and Christian ideas; I have not felt sufficiently confident to refer to Islamic traditions. To suggest further avenues of research, I indicate along the way some other contexts where similar connections may also appear or not appear.[9]

I refer then to some general *patterns* of Western thought, or rather some familiar interpretations of those patterns.[10] But I am not merely explicating the patterns; my effort to devise categories in order to show connections between worldviews and moral ideas adds another level of interpretation. I am interpreting the patterns on the basis of my assumptions about what worldviews and moral ideas are and how they might be connected; I am looking at the patterns as an outsider who draws on philosophy, anthropology, and the history of religions. Although the sorts of connections I see have been noted and discussed in some respects by insiders, the way I put the ideas is not necessarily how they would be expressed within the traditions. I have not tried to uncover the contextual significance of the connections, but I have attempted to discuss some broad patterns that are shaped in diverse ways in particular Judaic and Christian traditions.[11] The way I state the categories or connections—source, sanction, salvation, and related concepts—and suggest illustrative examples amounts to an interpretation based on assumptions about morality and religion as parts of human culture.[12]

With the idea of *source* as a paradigm, then, here are the sorts of ideas I have tried to put together:

1. Assumptions about the role of moral and religious ideas in human culture, for example, the assumption that various traditions explain the origin and nature of the moral order in terms of their worldview
2. The notion of a transhuman being, force, or state that causes, communicates, or legitimates the moral order (the concept or category of *source*)
3. Western ideas about God as the author of the moral order.

Thus while the category of source (item 2) was originally suggested to me by Western examples, the way I formulate it is shaped by my general assumptions about morality and religion in a cross-cultural comparative context; in turn, the concept of source as an interpretative category shapes how I understand the Western examples.

The categories of source, sanction, and salvation are in fact *broader* than the Western patterns I discuss: for example, the notion of source is not limited to the model found in classic Judaic and Christian traditions of morality created in the image of God; the notion of sanction needn't refer to a just deity who rights all wrongs in the end; the notion of salvation as a transmoral goal needn't be positively related to moral striving as it often is in Judaic and Christian traditions.[13]

As far as I can tell, moreover, my underlying assumptions about moralities and religious canopies of meaning do not beg any of the critical issues. Thus my notion of what moralities are and how they function does not settle the question whether moral norms rest on a rationale independent of beliefs about the origin and destiny of humankind ("autonomous" moral kernels that could be extracted from various worldviews). This view, which I will discuss in Chapter 1, has emerged prominently in the modern West and perhaps in other cultures, but it is not assumed in my working concept of morality.[14] Similarly, my concept of religion assumes that religious convictions and practices have some bearing on ways of life, but what sort of bearing that should be is a question addressed by particular religious traditions.[15]

1.4 Categories for interpretation and critical debate. This book, then, should be seen as an introductory set of lectures; the discussion of the categories of source, sanction, and salvation is intended to suggest lines of historical investigation, and the examination of issues sets a framework for debate. My intention is that the book should signal both the difficulty of interpreting traditions and the complexity of the critical and constructive issues. I do not attempt the requisite historial work here nor do I try to present a full defense of the lines of argument I suggest. Nonetheless, I hope that the book can serve students as they seek to understand and evaluate patterns of thought in Judaic and Christian traditions.

NOTES

1. Peter Berger, *The Sacred Canopy* (Garden City, NY: Doubleday, 1969). To emphasize "belief" is sometimes said to reflect Western religion, or even just Christianity, to the neglect of traditions where practice is central and doctrine minimalized. This contrast has a point, but my interest is in how patterns of belief shape and are shaped by ways of life, how worldviews are connected to moral concepts. In traditions formal attention to worldviews may be either pronounced or minimalized, but my assumption is that beliefs and norms are intimately related.

2. See "Religion as a Cultural System," p. 89, and "Ethos, World View, and the Analysis of Sacred Symbols," p. 129, in *The Interpretation of Cultures* (New York: Basic Books, 1973). Note that Geertz uses the concept of worldview in a narrower way than other writers, who mean by worldview what he means by a set of sacred symbols. Compare Ninian Smart, *Worldviews* (New York: Scribner's, 1983). By "worldview" or the "really real" I believe Geertz means the metaphysically ultimate, the underlying structure or structures of reality. I think Geertz also suggests—or perhaps I am adding this notion—the fundamental causes or powers which affect self, nature, and society. On powers, see Kenelm Burridge, "Levels of Being," in *Religion and Morality*, ed. Gene Outka and John P. Reeder, Jr. (Garden City, NY: Doubleday, 1973), pp. 78–107.

3. Geertz claims that human nature is incomplete without patterns of meaning that order social life; see "The Impact of the Concept of Culture on the Concept of Man," in *The Interpretation of Cultures*, pp. 33–54.

4. I am indebted here to the concept of morality developed by Sumner B. Twiss and David Little in *Comparative Religious Ethics* (San Francisco: Harper and Row, 1978). But note: (1) The notion of prescription needs explication as part of a theory of normative discourse; see, for example, Neil Cooper, *The Diversity of Moral Thinking* (Oxford: Clarendon Press, 1981). (2) To say that moral systems are governed by canons of logic is not the same as saying that moral norms must apply to or be acceptable by any person or rational agent; that requirement is part of a substantive theory of the nature and grounds of the moral demand usually associated with the Kantian tradition in the West. (3)(a) The class of sentient agents to whom moral prescriptions refer can be broader than those to whom they are addressed; moral prescriptions can be about other animals or children who are sentient but not self-conscious; also note that the beings to whom the norms refer need not *be* sentient at a particular time, for the norms could refer to beings who are potentially sentient, that is, they are capable of sentience at some time; note also that this definition does not beg the question whether what is good for humans is only a function of what they desire, or whether what is "intrinsically" good can be established independent of empirical preferences; I assume in either case that we can speak of humans having desires, as capable of being harmed or benefited, as having a good; the notion of self-consciousness does not refer to any particular metaphysic of the self, but merely to the capacity to envisage oneself and others as centers of sentience and agency. (3)(b) To speak of conflicts of desires does not imply that humans somehow recognize that their desires conflict and then form moral bonds to resolve them; humans are not human without the constitutive moral bonds that provide for some form of group—that is, social—existence. The degree to which the group experiences conflicts of desires ("conflicts of interest") will be determined by the operative morality; a group could experience scarcity of resources without conflicting desires if there is some common desire for a pattern of allocation.

5. I agree with W. Richard Comstock that "definitions" of religion—and by extension, morality—are nominal, that is, they are definitions of terms, and that such definitions are not to be regarded as fixed but are established for various purposes and interpreted in wider contexts of meaning. But as such, it is worth noting, they convey theories of cultural phenomena and can be assessed in terms of criteria such as adequacy and coherence. "Toward Open Definitions of Religion," *Journal of the American Academy of Religion, LII* (September 1984), 499–517.

6. For a fully developed critical argument, see Ronald Green, *Religious Reason* (New York: Oxford University Press, 1978); see *Comparative Religious Ethics*, eds. Little and Twiss, for a work which is intended only as a descriptive analysis of patterns of thought.

7. For an attempt to show that certain patterns of moral and religious reasoning actually appear in the texts of particular traditions (descriptive ethics), see for example, *Comparative Religious Ethics*, eds. Little and Twiss. For a use of hypothetical or abstractly reformulated ideas see William Christian, Sr., *Meaning and Truth in Religion* (Princeton, NJ: Princeton University Press, 1964) and *Oppositions of Religious Doctrines* (New York: Herder and Herder, 1972).

8. What I do in this book is to interpret some interpretations of patterns of religious and moral thought. But this is *not* descriptive ethics. In struggling with how to discuss patterns of thought, I have come to the conclusion that there is no middle ground between

theoretical pieces—such as this book is intended to be—and concrete, historically responsible, case studies, whether done by philosophers or historians. On the relation between historical and philosophical description, see Reeder, "Religious Ethics as Field and Discipline," *Journal of Religious Ethics,* 6(1978), 33 ff. and passim. For a proposal of a history of religions approach to comparative ethics, see Frank Reynolds, "Contrasting Modes of Action: A Comparative Study of Buddhist and Christian Ethics," *History of Religions, 20*(August and November 1980), 128–146. Reynolds calls for historians of religion to do their own comparative work. In particular, the historian of religion would acquire a "holistic understanding of the two religions that are the bearers of the ethical perspectives to be compared." I hope that my categories may be helpful to historians (or philosophers) who attempt descriptive ethics. In particular, I want to emphasize that the "religious ethics" that I outlined in "Religious Ethics as Field and Discipline" is only one way in which religioethical materials should be studied within the general area of Religious Studies. Compare James Childress, "Methodological Issues in Comparative Religious Ethics," *Journal of Religious Ethics,* 7(Spring 1979), 4–9.

    9. I am not saying that notions of source, sanction, and salvation, much less patterns like the Western ones, appear in all traditions or have the same importance when they do appear. I am sensitive to the point of view expressed by Paul Ricoeur: ". . . a phenomenology *oriented* by the philosophical questions of Greek origin cannot do justice to the great experiences of India and China. Here, not only the contingency but the limit of our tradition become evident." See *The Symbolism of Evil,* trans. Emerson Buchanan (New York: Evanston; London: Harper and Row, 1967), p. 22. But Ricoeur adds that we must move toward a "concrete universal embracing all human experience" through "encounter and mutual clarification." The patterns and categories I discuss do not amount to a concrete universal embracing all of human culture, but they could perhaps aid in encounter and mutual clarification. Clifford Geertz, in a commentary on a paper by Tu Wei-ming, summarizes neatly the methodological problems of descriptive ethics (his point applies to Western as well as non-Western contexts):

> "First there is the classical East Asian thought of the texts—the thing on which we are trying to get some hold. Second, there is a modern historian of Chinese with access to these texts, but who lives in a world temporarally, spatially, and culturally other than that of those who, in fact, made them. Third, there are Western thinkers, approaching the historian's texts in an effort to deepen their thought about the ethical matters now concerning us. "Commentary on Prof. Tu's Paper," *Philosophy East and West, 31*(July 1981), 270; Tu Wei-ming, "The 'Moral Universal' from the Perspective of East Asian Thought," *Philosophy East and West 31*(July 1981), pp. 259–272.

Geertz urges that we look for differences between Eastern and Western patterns of thought, rather than "attempting to bridge them." I think there are some linkages, but I have only made the most tentative suggestions in the notes and text. It is interesting that at the end of his commentary Geertz focuses on the notion of a felt inability to allow others to suffer as the basis of morality; this, as he realizes, has echoes in many cultures. See Tu Wei-ming's "Further Thoughts"—in which he compares this theme with Kantian and other Western ideas—in *Philosophy East and West, 31*(July 1981), 273–277. For a theory of dialogical interpretation based on a pragmatist epistemology, see Richard Bernstein, *Beyond Objectivism and Relativism: Science, Hermeneutics and Praxis* (Philadelphia: University of Pennsylvania Press, 1983).

    10. I am using the term "interpretation" to mean historical description. Some would claim that any effort at historical reconstruction is also a normative proposal, since it proceeds from the historian's own inevitably "value-laden" perspective. If this is correct, then interpretation would refer both to reconstruction and evaluation.

    11. See Frederick Bird's warning against "ripping moral models" out of context, in "Paradigms and Parameters for the Comparative Study of Ethics," *Journal of Religious Ethics,* 9(Fall 1981), 163–164. I believe that ideas can be radically misinterpreted when taken out of context, but I also believe that it can be useful to try to identify patterns which emerge in disparate traditions. I have tried to make a contribution to what Prof. Bird calls for, the

development of "analytical concepts . . . to foster public discussions . . . , a repetoire of usable concepts and hypotheses" (p. 164). Prof. Bird is quite correct in my view to insist that comparative ethics as a descriptive endeavor must be both historically sensitive *and* informed by "general categories of analysis" (p. 165). This book does not *do* descriptive ethics; it employs analytical assumptions to make some tentative interpretations. The book also takes tentative steps toward the other task of comparative ethics which Prof. Bird identifies, namely, criticism and evaluation.

12. My working hypothesis is that scholars have already begun to accumulate a small number of useful cross-cultural categories, such as the general notions of morality and religion I assume here. But this does not mean that one must not constantly be on guard lest one construe the world (or even all the elements of one's own culture) in one's own image. For an effort to work out notions of morality and religion, which build on Geertz and others, see *Comparative Religious Ethics*, Little and Twiss ed. For critical responses, see Edmund Santurri, "The Comparative Study of Religious Ethics," *Religious Studies Review*, 6(October 1980), 296–301; Jeffrey Stout, "Weber's Progeny, Once Removed," *Religious Studies Review*, 6(October 1980), 289–295; and Donald Swearer, "Nirvana, No-Self, and Comparative Religious Ethics," *Religious Studies Review*, 6(October 1980), 301–306.

13. The notion of source as we will see need not even be imaged as an act of making or creation, and the moral order generated by the source does not necessarily reflect or mirror its nature; the sanctioning force could be an impersonal causal law which is part of the structure of things but does not exhaust ultimate reality; and salvation can be portrayed as entirely unrelated, at least in any positive sense, to moral striving. The categories link the moral order to ultimate reality, but are not intended to convey how that link is specifically imaged; the categories, in other words, are not supposed to overtly or covertly suggest Western patterns of thought where the "really real" creates the moral order in its own image and thus takes steps to make the moral enterprise succeed, even providing a final goal which builds on morality and represents its fulfilment in a transmoral mode of being. The Western patterns I discuss are only illustrations of how the categories could be fleshed out. Compare N. 11, p. 42. I am grateful to collegues in the Five Colleges Religion Colloquium for discussion and criticism of these categories in the spring of 1985 at Smith College.

14. For a view of when "morality" began to be self-consciously differentiated as an autonomous sphere of culture in the West, see Alasdair MacIntyre, *After Virtue*, 2nd ed. (Notre Dame, IN: Notre Dame University Press, 1984).

15. Compare Little and Twiss, eds. *Comparative Religions Ethics*, chap. 3.

1

Source

1. THE MORAL CONDITION AND THE CONCEPT OF SOURCE

1.1 Entry into the moral condition. When versions of Judaic or Christian tradition picture God as the transhuman source of morality, they already make the assumption that those to whom the morality is addressed are in the moral condition; as humans, they need a morality. As I noted in the Introduction, Geertz and other anthropologists assume that human nature as we know it to have evolved is social in character, and to be social, some form of morality is necessary. Interestingly enough Judaic and Christian traditions often also assume that humans need morality. So before looking at the notion of a divine source in patterns of Judaic and Christian thought, we should see first how the traditions have accounted for the human need for morality. One way this has been done is through the Adam and Eve story in Genesis: By their disobedience, Adam and Eve enter the moral condition; from that moment forward, Adam and Eve and their progeny need moral structures.

The story is subject to many interpretations, however, and some have not seen it as about entering the moral condition at all, but take it as a story about a "fall" from moral perfection to moral evil. Wendy O'Flaherty, for example, notes that Christians have often taken the Adam and Eve stories in Genesis to signify a transition from moral perfection to moral evil; before the first disobedience, the progenitors of humankind were perfectly good.[1] In classic Hindu accounts, in contrast, she says there is no original time of moral perfection; what many myths picture is a transition from a premoral time of bliss to the human, and hence, the moral condition:

> In the Hindu view, human beings caught up in the process of time are inherently, naturally inclined to fall prey to evil. The pure creatures of the original Golden Age are not a part of time at all; for them, Karma doesn't exist; they are beyond good and evil. Their "fall" consists of passing from eternity into time; once caught up in the flow of time, they are no longer immune to evil. The creatures of the Golden Age, though they may dwell upon earth, are not the first members of the human race; almost by definition, as soon as they become "human" the Golden Age must immediately disappear. The Hindu concept of the Golden Age thus lacks any vision of pristine human innocence or the corresponding belief in a separate agency of evil. To the Hindu, the original state of perfection is doomed to quick extinction from within, and there is no need for a serpent or a devil to initiate the process.[2]

But the Genesis account can also be taken as a story about the emergence of humankind into the moral condition:

> The Lord God took the man and put him in the garden of Eden to till it and keep it. And the Lord God commanded the man, saying, "You may freely eat of every tree of the garden; but of the tree of the knowledge of good and evil you shall not eat, for in the day that you eat of it you shall die." Genesis 2:15–17

One could argue that whatever else the story has meant in Judaic and Christian traditions, and we will look at some other interpretations in Chapter 2, the account could serve to picture a *premoral* state; the male and the female figures (later called Eve) on this view are not yet in the human and hence in the moral condition as we know it; their thoughts, emotions, and desires do not have to be patterned in such a way that social existence is possible; they do not *know* good and evil. There is a limitation on their existence, but they are free to eat and relate to one another without any consciousness of what is morally right and wrong.

But

> ... when the woman saw that the tree was good for food, and a delight to the eyes, and that the tree was to be desired to make one wise, she took of its fruit and ate; and she also gave some to her husband, and he ate. Genesis 3:6

Thus, one could argue, not only the delight of the food but the promise of wisdom—of moral knowledge—leads Adam and Eve from premoral bliss to the moral condition; previously, they were not even conscious of their nakedness, but now they put on "fig leaves and aprons"; nakedness could stand for a consciousness of sexuality and, by extension, other aspects of existence which require the moral structures of human culture. As John Hick argues, it is not easy to see why Adam and Eve would exchange the bliss of the garden for the world of morality.[3] But on this interpretation the story tracks the transition that inaugurates the moral condition.[4] We have seen, then, on this reading of Genesis, what the anthropologist Kenelm Burridge would describe as a transition from a premoral state of unity with the Creator to the moral condition:

> ... before culture and morality intervened man was in paradise, a free-mover not subject to articulate rules, at one with the Creator and Allbeing.[5]

On one reading of the Genesis story, therefore, these progenitors begin the moral history of humankind. The story continues through Noah, Abraham, Egypt, the Exodus, and then comes the giving of the "law" at Sinai, the event in which as the Protestant theologian Paul Ramsey once put it, Israel receives moral "garments of skin" for life east of Eden; the deity is the *source* of the moral system that is to structure the existence, the way, of the people of God.[6]

1.2 *The concept of source.* In the giving of the law at Sinai, then, Israel becomes the people of God:

> And God spoke all these words, saying,
> I am the Lord your God, who
> brought you out of the land of
> Egypt, out of the house of bondage.
> You shall have no other gods
> before me ... Exodus 20:1–3 (compare Deuteronomy 5:6ff)

Many Judaic and Christian traditions have found in this passage, where the deity proclaims itself as Lord and enunciates the ten "words" or "commandments," the answers to three basic questions that have also been asked in other cultures. Let us suppose we have a moral system or, if "system" sounds too tidy, a set of moral traditions that cohere, loosely or tightly, to form the moral structure of our culture. How is this structure *produced*? How do we *learn* it? Why is it *correct*? The first question is about causal origin: How does a moral system come into being? The second question is about learning or coming to know: How is a moral system communicated and appropriated? The third question is about justification or legitimation: Why is a moral system valid or correct, what is its rationale, what are the reasons for adhering to it? These questions are ones we would expect to have been asked in many cultures, and indeed the anthropological and historical evidence would seem to indicate that they have. The questions are not always made explicit or given the same attention in different societies, but it is natural to ask them because morality is so important. The notion of a transhuman *source* of morality is one way cultures have answered the questions: a transhuman reality in some way produces, communicates, and legitimates the moral order.

2. ORIGIN

2.1 Judaic and Christian stories of creation. The first question then is this: Where does a moral system come from? How does it come to be? One important idea in the history of religions is the notion of a transhuman source, and one important variant of that idea is the model of an act of making or creation. In contrast to other explanations of how a moral order is derived from a transhuman reality, for example, the idea that the moral order is a manifestation or outward expression of an underlying structure,[7] the idea of creation suggests a definite act of generation.[8] The notion of a divine creator appears in many versions of Judaism and Christianity, based on the biblical stories where the deity gives "laws" to Israel (for example, *Exodus 20*). A supreme deity is not only the maker of nature, but a king or sovereign. The people of God are to be subjects and to render obedience. They obey God as a debt of gratitude or justice and because they believe that what God commands is right. The sovereign establishes specific norms by which the people are to order their lives, for example, do not murder, do not commit adultery.[9] The norms of the code God establishes are morally right.

As the biblical traditions are interpreted in later generations, moreover, the idea is added that the deity not only creates a moral code but sets up the basic criteria of morality, for example, the deity lays it down that what is right and morally good is what is just and loving.[10] It is not, say these later traditions, that God merely acts according to some assumed concept of moral requirement, but the being who is loving and just *establishes these qualities* as the basic content or criteria of morality. This may seem like a "distinction without a difference," but we will see ahead how significant it is. This deity *creates* standards for how one should act (right conduct) and the sort of person one should be (morally good character).

2.2 The legislative model of making. We are dealing, then with the notion of creation and with a particular model of that, namely, creation by a king or sovereign. Perhaps it would help to diagram the categories used so far:

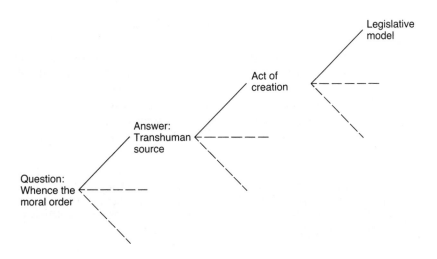

The solid lines show the route Judaic and Christian traditions usually take; the dotted ones indicate that other ideas could have been adopted. Thus the story of a divine creator suggests the idea that the moral order was made by a being at some time and place in the distant past. And the specific model of making which seems to underlie many versions of this story in Judaism and Christianity is that of a legislative action by a divine figure who resembles a political sovereign; the deity establishes a moral charter or constitution for the existence of the group, as a king establishes laws for a people.[11] Note that the model of a legislative action need not involve only a single deity; a group of gods could have been involved.[12] The crucial feature of this model is that the moral order is legislatively *constructed* by some agency or agencies and "given" to human beings.[13]

An important variation of the model, as we will see ahead, is the idea that the religious reality creates the moral order, but instead of giving it externally through some form of revelation, writes it on the mind or heart so that human beings can learn it directly by themselves. On either version of the model, a transhuman legislative agency *makes* the moral order.[14]

2.3 Patterned on ultimate reality.

Stories about the construction of the moral order often include the idea that it is somehow patterned on what Geertz calls the "really real" or what others refer to as "ultimate reality." It is often said in Judaic and Christian traditions, as I noted earlier, that the moral order corresponds to the divine nature; the deity, to whatever degree it transcends the merely human, patterns moral requirement on its own nature.

Many believers have also held that in a special metaphysical sense the moral order depends on God; the basic principles or qualities that constitute morality are not only reflections or copies of God's nature, but in some sense they continue to depend on the deity, as reflections in a mirror depend on their source for existence.[15]

By analogy then with human traits the deity is just or loving, for example, and establishes these qualities and related ways of acting as the defining criteria of moral rightness and goodness.[16] These criteria in turn underlie the more specific rules and qualities enunciated for the people, for example, do not steal or do not covet. It may even be said that the deity is not only just in a general sense but acts as humans are instructed to do:

> For the Lord your God is God of gods and Lord of lords, the great, the mighty, and the terrible God, who is not partial and takes no bribes. He executes justice for the fatherless and the widow, and loves the sojourner, giving him food and clothing. Deuteronomy 10:17–18[17]

In these sorts of stories, in Peter Berger's words, the human order reflects the "divine structure of the cosmos."[18] Morality on this model springs from the creative will of the deity. The model, I believe, underlies many mainstream versions of Judaism and Christianity.[19] A deity with certain characteristics establishes the criteria of morality. As we will see, the deity may create moral requirement in such a way that humans can apprehend its meaning and even grasp its validity without acknowledging God, but the theistic believer sees the divine being as the causal source of the moral order.[20]

2.4 Moral and legal order.   I have been talking about the creation of a moral order, but it is important to note that what is created may also be a legal system. Indeed we would expect this to be the case where the creation is modeled on a lawlike act of legislation. On the basis of a theoretical distinction between moral and legal systems, a distinction observers make, but one not necessarily made in the traditions themselves, we can say that the normative structure that a group explains through a story of creation may function as a legal as well as moral system; it may contain the sorts of rules, do the sort of jobs that a legal system does. For instance, it may provide some official apparatus for the judgment of cases and the administration of punishment.[21] Thus a moral system would contain basic moral norms that apply to primary areas of human experience such as personal security, sex and reproduction, economic relations, and political order. But these norms might also function as laws, for they would be accompanied by provisions for adjudication and enforcement. The normative social order, laid down by a god or gods, can be a single complex system that serves both as morality and law; I will call this, following Peter Berger, the "nomos" (from the Greek word for law).

A good example of a theologian who sees God creating a nomos is

Thomas Aquinas. On the view of Aquinas I adopt, "natural law" is not merely the human moral order created by God, it is also law; it has the marks or characteristics of law as enunciated by Aquinas, which include not only enactment by a sovereign, but conformity to what is morally right. To understand the natural *law,* one must understand it both as the moral order God establishes and as law in the technical sense. It is a "law" theory of morality because it refers to God's lawlike creation as its causal origin, and it is law proper because it has the characteristics of law, for example, it is enunciated by the sovereign who in this case is God.

"Natural law" in the Thomistic tradition is apprehended through human capacities independent of divine revelation, as we will see in the next section. But what of God's revealed nomos, how has it been understood both as morality and law? Rabbinic Judaism recognizes a dual revelation at Sinai, the biblical and the oral law; the latter is written down and interpreted in the Talmud and is understood as *halakhah* or Jewish law. Just exactly what the marks or characteristics of law are is a question on which contemporary theorists of law differ, and indeed interpreters of *halakhah* in the Judaic tradition have different views on exactly what the tradition has meant or should mean when *halakhah* is referred to as "law;" in particular, what is the relation of *halakhah* to *moral* right and wrong? One finds at least these three views: 1) To be valid, a law must be morally right; it is not enough for a law to come from a certain source, for example, a court or legislature; thus on this general theory of law what is legally valid as *halakhah* must also be morally right. Valid *halakhah* not only proceeds from the proper Rabbinic authorities but is morally correct;[22] 2) What makes laws valid is independent of their morality; it is enough if they proceed say, from the legislature; thus on this view of law a law could be valid as *halakhah*—it has the seal of Rabbinic authority—whether or not it is judged to be morally correct; some argue for example, on external moral grounds that the *halakhah* should be changed to allow the ordination of women;[23] and 3) Law contains within itself certain general principles, which are moral principles but also function as law; these principles simply exist as part of the legal system; they serve when precedents are not sufficient or when specific laws need to be changed. This view thus is a middle way between 1 and 2; laws can be valid simply because they issue from certain bodies, but one need not go outside the legal system to criticize laws from a moral point of view; the legal system contains principles which overlap with morality.[24] I believe this is the view Eliezer Berkovits expresses when he says in connection with changes in Talumdic law regarding the treatment of women:

> We might say that in all these cases the ultimate comprehensive concern of the Law in general was allowed to modify the form of the application of a specific law.[25]

In any case, despite diverging interpretations of natural law and *halakhah,* we can see that in both Judaic and Christian traditions God has been pictured as the source of morality and of law; God creates the nomos.

2.5 Types of norms.   There is another very significant thing we should note about the morally normative structures whose creation is explained in religious stories about a transhuman source: these structures may contain a variety of kinds of norms. Broadly speaking, norms can take the form of principles or rules of conduct, and virtues, traits of character.[26] Norms structure not only what we do but the kinds of persons we are. Believers are to act in loving and just ways, and are to be loving and just persons. We should not assume that the model of a legislativelike act of creation in Judaic and Christian traditions necessarily implies that only norms for conduct are prescribed; the deity of these traditions is often understood to create a way of life that encompasses both doing and being.

It might be thought in some cultures, however, that virtue is not subject to legal coercion and thus only norms for conduct do double duty as laws; virtues are part of the moral order that is outside the law. This may be an assumption of some systems, but I suspect that in many cultures where there are gods or spirits who reward and punish, character as well as conduct can be subject to law; perhaps human law will reach only to external conduct, but God, as it is said in some traditions, judges the heart. (I will say more about punishment in Chapter 2.)

In any case, virtues do not necessarily have the same role in every version of Judaism and Christianity. In some traditions, virtues are apparently seen as instrumental to conduct: be a truthful person in order to act truthfully. In other traditions, virtues are qualities that are ingredient in the realization of human fulfillment, true human good, and rules of conduct are merely instrumental. Sometimes rules and virtues are seen as independent yet complementary parts of morality. The relation of rules and virtues in a moral system depends on the vision of the moral life it embodies; various views of virtue have appeared in Judaic and Christian traditions.[27]

Some moral traditions include not only a level of duties and virtues that are required, but another level that is supererogatory, beyond the call of duty. What is supererogatory is still part of the system established by the deity, but it provides for a moral ideal that exceptional individuals choose and that is worthy of special praise.[28]

Norms can also be distinguished according to their scope or setting. Some norms for conduct and character have to do with roles in social institutions which pertain to sex and reproduction, the economy, or the political order, for example, the injunction to children to honor father and mother. In some cultures, certain norms are thought to apply to any member of the society, for example, the right not to be injured or killed, irrespective of social roles.[29] In some traditions, for example in many forms of Judaism and Christianity, norms may even be enunciated which are supposed to apply to anyone in any society, to human beings as such or even to all sentient beings, whatever their species.

Some sorts of norms may simply not appear in some traditions. And even where they are present, we should not expect to find all the norms of a tradition in a single authoritative text or ritual. It would take careful historical work to map the sorts of norms operative in a tradition at a particular place and time.

3. MODES OF LEARNING

3.1 *Learning the moral order.*

We have seen some religious ideas about the moral order and how it comes to be. But how is it apprehended? How is it handed down and appropriated by successive generations? Classic Judaic and Christian stories suggest the following motif: The creator of the moral order delivers it through an intermediary to a group of human beings who in turn pass it on to their descendants.[30] Moses receives the law on Sinai, gives it to Israel, and the people of Israel pass it on to successive generations. Let us call this process *revelation:* As a sovereign promulgates the law, the deity transmits the nomos to human beings. In contrast, Judaic and Christian traditions have often also recognized another type of learning process: The deity somehow implants the nomos in human beings so that it is apprehended independent of any specific divine communication. Let us call this model *inherent capacities.*

3.2 *Precept and example.*

We will begin with revelation; the deity is a sovereign and a teacher: "These are my statutes . . ." and "He has shown you what is good." The original teaching and successive teaching through the generations is often imaged as a process of instruction by precept. Through oral or written sources one learns the right sort of thing to do and the right sort of person to be. But it is important to note that both the original and the successive teaching is also done by example.[31] The deity, a primeval figure, or original progenitors *show* the way of life the group is to follow, the way that constitutes the group's ongoing life. This way of life is remembered, imitated, and taught through the ages; successive imitators become themselves models for imitation.

3.3 *The formation of the self.*

Whether through precept or example, then, one could learn patterns of conduct and character through revelation. But often the vision of a religious community will extend not merely to knowledge in an abstract sense, but to the sort of learning that influences how we choose and what we desire and feel. Life in the religious community—worship, for example, or other ritual practices—will develop in the believer not only knowledge in an abstract sense but dispositions to act, desire, and feel in the requisite ways. A relation to ultimate reality, maintained through the life of the community, can be seen as the active source of moral dispositions.[32]

3.4 Understanding or trust.   Thus the teaching may be by precept or example or both; it can extend beyond information to the formation of the self. Another important thing to look for is whether the recipients (the original ones or later generations) are supposed to *understand,* to recognize the rationale for the norms of the social order once taught, or whether they are expected to *trust* that the patterns they have been taught are right. On the one hand, the recipients might be said to understand why there is a rule against murder, for example: it is unjust or unloving. On the other hand, perhaps they simply believe the rule is right because they trust the creating agency. What seems to be suggested in many versions of Judaism and Christianity is that the deity is taken as a moral authority not merely in the sense that it functions as the supreme moral teacher who instructs humankind in what is right and wrong, but in the sense that its moral wisdom transcends that of human beings. Believers accept the deity as the wise formulator of the moral code.

3.5 Tradition and appropriation.   Whether human beings are supposed to understand or trust in the rightness of the rules and virtues they have been taught, there are two other important parts of the process. Just who hands down the moral order and applies it to current situations and just how is it to be appropriated—interpreted, extended, perhaps even revised—in the light of circumstances? The first question can be addressed by specifying certain figures and institutions within the group, for example, rabbis and religious courts or the Roman Catholic church as teaching authority and source of canon law. Or perhaps, as in some Protestant traditions, interpretation is assigned to individuals guided by the "Spirit", but even here the community has a role in shaping the moral understanding of each person. The second question can be addressed by working out rules of interpretation and distinctions between the authority of different sorts of inherited traditions. One can expect first to find a fundamental distinction between the directly communicated material itself and later extrapolations based on it. Christians have made distinctions between biblical "revelation" and human interpretations;[33] in Judaism, it is held that God handed down at Sinai not only the written law but also an oral part as well which is passed down through the centuries and becomes the basis of Jewish law.[34] In addition, one can expect to find distinctions between various interpretations of the revealed material, for example, the way in which various layers of the Talmudic tradition in Judaism have greater authority than others.[35]

In some traditions, the deity does not give once and for all moral instruction, but provides repeated guidance either to individuals or to authoritative figures. The neoorthodox Protestant idea that one is to hear the command of God in every new situation through the "Spirit" has affinities to the divination of spirits in other traditions. In these cases communication in the present takes place against the background of moral tradition, that is, previous instruction remembered and taught through the generations.[36]

3.6 Inherent human capacities.

I have been talking so far about a moral order that is revealed and taught from generation to generation. But there is another model of learning in some Judaic and Christian traditions: Even if a transhuman reality is said to be its ultimate cause, human beings grasp the moral order through their own capacities.[37] For example, Louis Jacobs, a contemporary Judaic thinker, argues that in all the major strands and strata of the Judaic tradition it is assumed or explicitly taught "that man is capable of discerning right from wrong by the natural light within him."[38] Sid Leiman has challenged Jacobs' historical claim, but the view Jacobs enunciates has appeared in Judaic and Christian sources in some periods.[39] Sometimes the "natural light" is said to lie in "reason," sometimes in "feeling." Sometimes the notion of "experience" is contrasted with revelation, but this is misleading for humans clearly experience the revelatory process.[40] Sometimes indeed the concept of revelation is extended to cover what is grasped through inherent capacities and given a special name, for example, "general revelation."[41] The notion of inherent capacities is intended to suggest that an awareness of the moral order (either basic criteria or specific norms or both) is somehow given to us simply as human beings. It is not simply that we have the capacity to be taught, but that we already grasp what is to be known.[42]

One more distinction; sometimes the appeal to inherent capacities means that one grasps independent of revelation what God wills and the fact that God wills it. It is as if by an inner voice one were hearing God on Sinai establishing the criteria of rightness and moral goodness and setting up a moral code. But often, especially in modern discussions of the natural light, not only is the moral order independent of revelation, but neither its content or its justification (its rationale, the beliefs that support it) make reference to God. Either it is claimed there are beliefs about human nature as such which justify moral convictions and requires no mention of a Creator, or as we will shortly see, there are first principles of moral knowledge which stand in no need of further justification (that is, support from other beliefs). Thus on this second view of inherent capacities, the natural light is not only grasped independently of revelation, its meaning (its content and rationale) stands alone without any need to refer to God.

3.7 *Moral reason.* An important historical version of the inherent capacities view is the idea that the moral order is implanted in or on the human mind. Like programmed moral computers, we just know (or are capable of knowing) the basic criteria of right and wrong. I have in mind here both neo-Aristotelian (for example, Thomistic) and neo-Kantian forms of Judaic and Christian tradition. (Some forms of these traditions interpret morality in terms of the ideas of the philosophers Aristotle and Kant; Aristotle was crucial for medieval thinkers such as Maimonides and Thomas Aquinas; Kant has been crucial especially for many modern Judaic and Christian thinkers.) The deity creates the Thomistic first principle of practical reason (good should be sought . . .) or the Kantian constitutive principle of moral rationality (choose as if you were making universal laws).[43] On these classical views of the demands of moral reason, the first principle is the defining criteria of rightness and moral goodness; justice, for example, is justified in terms of this most fundamental criterion or standard. I will have more to say about the Thomistic and the neo-Kantian standard as we proceed. With either of these programs, the individual performs moral operations on the basis of data about what is truly good for human (or other) beings. Humans can also know to a considerable extent what their good is—what really makes for happiness or fulfillment—independent of revelation.

On this view of moral reason, the basic criteria of rightness and moral goodness are fixed, not subject to change. On the traditional model of revealed teaching, the deity communicates criteria which mirror its own eternal nature; the criteria laid down are understood as unchangeable because they emanate from the deity. Now on the inherent capacities model the sense of an unchangeable standard or set of standards is transferred to the internal structure of the mind; the mind has its own unchanging laws that humans grasp simply by being human, that is, "naturally."

3.8 *Reason and tradition.* Where the communication of the moral order takes place through inherent human capacities, there are analogies to what happens when there is an external source of instruction. Others can help us, through precept or example, to develop our capacities for knowledge; the community can form habits of doing and being; although we come to know ultimately through our own capacities, we could have reason to rely on, to trust others, especially when we are young. And finally, there are also questions about how moral wisdom is passed down and applied: What if there are different views as to what our capacities teach? Whose is authoritative? Does what we know apply in all times and places or are some judgments valid only for particular cases? Issues such as these have been explored in traditions such as Roman Catholicism, where interpretations of the inherent capacities model play an important role.

3.9 *The two models combined.*

We have looked, then, at two notions of communication: one is external, the moral order is taught to individuals or groups; the other is internal, through human capacities. Some Judaic and Christian traditions seem to combine these models in a complex synthesis. There is moral knowledge through divine teaching and there is the moral insight that is possible through human capacities and the two are related in some way.[44] Moral knowledge is neither only a matter of "nurture" or of "nature," but a combination of the two. Sometimes, for example, it is said that human beings independently grasp the general criteria of morality through their own capacities; they know the basic qualities and ways of acting which define the meaning of moral requirement. But they learn specific norms only through revelation, and perhaps they take them on trust. Or perhaps humans are also credited with independently knowing specific norms as well, but human knowledge is incomplete or flawed in some way; human beings know the moral order in some inchoate way but divine instruction is necessary to draw it out.[45]

Where these sorts of syntheses appear in Judaic and Christian traditions, it seems that two major sorts of reasons have usually been offered to explain the necessity of revealed instruction. First, our inherent knowledge is finite and hence limited. In the idiom of Thomas Aquinas, the natural law we know through inherent human capacities, and the humanly enacted law based on it, are to a great extent sufficient for our temporal good but not for the end of eternal happiness; we do not know the facts necessary to relate ourselves correctly to God. Moreover, there is doubt and uncertainty about "contingent and particular matters" and hence a proliferation of different laws.[46] Saadya Gaon, a medieval Judaic thinker, apparently thought that some basic moral matters were clear to everyone, but that human beings without revelation would never agree about the specifics of law.[47]

Some thinkers also present "sin" as a second reason for the direct instruction of God. The idea is that although one can work out norms for oneself, the meaning of the norms is corrected, completed, or restored by divine instruction. For example, in some strands of the Christian tradition it is often assumed that one knows one ought to render aid to those in need. The tendency, however, to desire one's own good above that of others distorts or even corrupts one's knowledge; one will tend to limit what one thinks one should do to help others. But the teaching example of Jesus specifies that duty, makes clear the *lengths* to which one ought to go. The story of the Good Samaritan, it is said, teaches that one should render aid even if it is very costly; the acts and indeed the entire career of Jesus are thought to teach the sort of giving that is required; believers are to follow this example.

4. JUSTIFICATION

4.1 The legitimating rationale. A moral order, then, is made; a moral order is learned. But why is it correct, legitimate, justified? Sometimes we use the term "know" simply to mean grasp or apprehend; but sometimes it suggests that our beliefs are justified or correct, that they are warranted in light of certain reasons or evidence. I used the term "know" in the former sense in the section on learning, but now in this section our concern is with justification or legitimation. Why is a particular morality the correct one? However we come to *learn* the moral order, why is it legitimate? What reasons do we give to justify it? Why is it a moral order we should accept?

There is a rationale that is often attributed to believers: The moral order is "grounded" in ultimate reality; the requiredness, the legitimacy, of the moral order has its source in the fact that it derives from the "nature of things." Now this is very vague, and indeed believers and interpreters of religion have meant very different things by it.

4.2 Source of human good. One thing that this grounded-in-ultimate-reality rationale has been taken to mean is that the moral code is legitimate because it leads to true human good. And true human good, moreover, consists in some sort of relation to ultimate reality. (Human good, happiness, well-being, fulfilment, and flourishing are a family of concepts with different nuances.) The source of human good, in other words, is a relation to ultimate reality, and the "path" to this good is the moral code; the moral code is instrumentally necessary or an intrinsic part of human good; most often the moral code is seen as both instrumental and intrinsic, a necessary step to the fullness of human good and part of it as well.

An important variant of this idea, which Clifford Geertz seems to extend to all religions, is the idea that the good lies in conformity or adjustment to what is truly "real."[48] The idea that human good lies in a relation to ultimate reality is broader than this, however, for the relation need not be envisaged as conformity; it could consist, for example, in absorption, as in some mystical traditions. The conformity or adjustment model rests on an analogy to the requisites of natural growth. The analogy is between the flourishing of plant and animal life and the flourishing of the individual and society. Just as physical well-being can only be achieved in harmony with the structures of nature, with reality, so there are analogous regularities or structures on which social and individual well-being depend. To achieve true human good, then, one must conform to the ultimate structure of things, to the realities on which natural and social existence rest.

On one view, then, human good, conceived as a relation to ultimate reality, requires the moral code. In the vocabulary of moral theory, the right is defined in terms of the good; norms of conduct and character are justified because they contribute to human good. Thus the grounded-in ultimate-reality rationale in this sense boils down to assuming a particular conception of moral requirement—seek the good—and justifying the moral code as a step to God. But nothing has been said so far about why this conception of moral requirement (commonly called Thomistic) is justified; it is simply assumed.

4.3 *Justice as an independent criterion.* In some Western traditions another conception of moral requirement (commonly called Kantian) seems to be assumed. Rightness and moral goodness are not defined as what makes for the good, but as what can be accepted as a universal law, for example, some notion of justice.[49] In this view, justice or fairness as a central moral principle is not interpreted as a requirement of human good or fulfillment, but stands independently as a standard that regulates the way in which human beings strive to flourish.[50]

Where justice is interpreted as an independent principle as in some Protestant traditions, it is quite often said that it is only just or fair for human beings to uphold the set of rules and virtues established by ultimate reality; this is another often adduced sense of the grounded-in-ultimate-reality rationale. One seems to find the idea that the being that makes everything has the right to expect obedience; it would be as unjust for the stars and moon to rebel against their appointed courses, were they capable of doing so, as it is for humans to rail against God.[51] Simply because God created them or showed kindness to them, humans owe a debt of obedience.

And it is said not only that God has a right to obedience and imitation, but God commands and does *what* is right. The deity who is just lays down moral instructions that are just, and if we ought to do what is just, then we should conform to what the deity commands and exemplifies. Where a human figure is concerned—for instance, a parent—we could acknowledge a duty to obey, but that duty could conflict with our judgment that what in particular the parent asks is wrong; where God is concerned, however, the traditional believer holds that God never asks or does what is wrong.

4.4 *Underlying notions of rightness.* It is important to realize that where the moral code is seen as the path to human good, or rests on an independent criterion such as justice, a notion of moral requirement has been presupposed. Rightness and moral goodness are conceived as what makes for human good or what is just. These notions of rightness in one sense, therefore, could stand apart from their settings in particular webs of religious belief. For even if rightness is conceived as what makes for human good, human good might not be thought of as a relation to ultimate reality. Or if rightness is defined as justice, there could be just relations among humans whether or not there were just relations between humans and other beings in the universe. What is good or what is just could still be set *within* some other religious vision of things, for example, a modern humanist's like Camus, but the notion of good itself would not be conceived as a relation to ultimate reality and justice would not obtain between human beings and transhuman realities.

Some appeals to ultimate reality, then, really rest on underlying notions of right and wrong combined with specific beliefs about what is good or just which involve God. The basic notions themselves are not necessarily connected to beliefs about the nature of ultimate reality. These appeals, therefore, do not really *ground* the legitimacy of notions of moral requirement in ultimate reality; these appeals to ultimate reality *presuppose* basic defining criteria, such as, justice. The arguments do not refer to God to justify the conceptions of moral requirement; God appears only in the minor premises:

> Major Premise: Seek human good.
> Minor Premise: Human good lies in God and the way to God is through the moral code.
> Conclusion: Follow the moral code.
>
> Major Premise: Pay debts of justice.
> Minor Premise: Humans owe obedience as a debt of justice to God.
> Conclusion: Obey God.

And God's role in such arguments would still be the same even if the underlying conception of rightness and moral goodness did not take a specifically Kantian or Thomistic shape. The conception that is operative in some biblical traditions seems to involve a pluralistic appeal to both human good and principles such as justice or love; no theoretical choice as to which is prior or definitive has yet been imposed. But even in such traditions it is still the case that the appeal to God is mediated through an assumed conception of moral requirement: seek to flourish, and therefore follow God's precepts; do what is just, and therefore obey God.

4.5 *Ultimate grounding for a notion of rightness and moral goodness.* But there is another way that the moral order could be "grounded" in ultimate reality. Ultimate reality is not only the causal origin of specific norms of the moral order, it is somehow responsible for the establishment of the basic criteria. What we have looked at so far in this section is the idea that the deity's legislation is set within a framework of notions of moral requirement which in Judaic and Christian traditions are religiously interpreted (for example, a relation to deity as the final source of human good). But now we return to the idea of creation at a deeper level. The divine being not merely creates the norms of the moral code but establishes the very criteria of rightness and moral goodness. The creator does not merely say, for example, don't do X because X is unjust, but the creator establishes the "fact" that it is right to act justly and morally good to be a just person. In other words, notions of rightness and moral goodness are what they are because the transhuman source established them. Although the deity could change specific interhuman prescriptions, or order exceptions, the basic standards which constitute the meaning of the moral order reflect the nature of the deity and do not change.[52]

Thus the idea that a transhuman reality *creates* the moral order is a version of what is apparently a familiar theme in the history of religions: a given structure of moral requirement derives from and reflects ultimate reality. That rightness and moral goodness exist, and are what they are, is traced to the ultimate nature of things; the source of its meaning lies in the "really real."[53] The theme moreover apparently makes a twofold claim: rightness comes from and reflects the really real, and these facts are the ground or justification for accepting what rightness is. Thus when the creator of all the earth reveals itself and communicates to humans that love and justice are to be the basic principles of morality, the believer not only sees that God is the source of the moral order, but accepts God's criteria of rightness precisely because they are God's; the claim is that if rightness is derived from and mirrors the "ground of being," then rightness has been grounded, that is, justified.

It is easy to see how God's role could be appealed to when morality is revealed, but what about when it is learned through inherent capacities? On the first view of inherent capacities I discussed earlier one conceives what one grasps *as* what God has established and taught. Thus on this view of inherent capacities the created-by-God rationale can be directly invoked. But on the second view of inherent capacities one apprehends moral requirements whose content and justification are independent of any reference to God. And according to important historical views of moral reason, one grasps a self-justifying first principle; the first principle stands in no need of further justification; it is fixed and indubitable; one simply finds oneself bound by such a principle; one can't *think* otherwise.[54] Now of course one can still attribute such moral knowledge to God as its causal source (God implanted it), and one could even interpret it also as the natural *law*, that is, as God's law, but taken simply as morality, it does not seem to require the created-by-God justification. This is one interpretation of what Grotius, a 17th century thinker, may have meant when he is reported to have said that even if there were no God, the "natural law" would still be valid. It would not be valid as *law,* of course, if there were no Sovereign to establish it, but taken simply as moral requirement it contains its own justification, its own validity. Thus on such a view, what role can there be for the created-by-God justification?

As far as I can tell, thinkers such as Grotius, writing in the natural law tradition, hold that human reason is sufficient to ground the moral demand. Both the believer and the unbeliever grasp the content of moral requirement as the principle(s) of practical reason; both can find therein a *sufficient* ground or justification in the sense that for moral reasoning itself no higher or more ultimate appeal is necessary than the built-in constraints or directives of reason; the basic criterion or principle of rightness is given in the dictate of reason. In this sense, reason's specification of the meaning of rightness and moral goodness brings the quest for justification to an end. But nonetheless from the believer's perspective one knows the basic rules of a game but does not know why the rules are as they are. Only when the rules are explained as the created reflection of God is the "why these rules" question fully answered in a justificatory as well as a causal sense. Thus in one sense the chain of justification stops with the demand of reason; in another sense, however, one has not answered the justificatory question fully until one has referred to God.[55] Thus while the second inherent capacities model does not need to refer directly to God as a justification, it can make an indirect appeal. The inherently known rules are all you need to know to play the moral game, but you can also ask, Who established the rules and why these rules? At this point believers who endorse some form of the second inherent capacities view can invoke the created-by-God rationale.

Thus whether one grasps God's moral order through revelation or inherent capacities, one can refer to God's role not only as an explanation but also as a justification. If ultimate reality *is* the source of the existence of moral requirement, then to cite the source is to give a reason to accept it. If someone says why should we accept a certain criterion of rightness, and someone else says, because that is the criterion that flows from and mirrors ultimate reality, a legitimation has been proposed. Sometimes it is said that it is *right* that ultimate reality create the meaning of rightness, or that ultimate reality is *entitled* to do so; but in this version of the argument some basic (and still unexplained) notion of rightness or entitlement is being presupposed. The justification I want to identify is different; it focuses on the *givenness* of what ultimate reality establishes. The believer who cites a transhuman source may intend to provide a justification by drawing attention to an exclusive and inescapable function of ultimate reality.[56] The legitimacy of the criteria of rightness and moral goodness consists in their inevitability; this is how things are and must be; the meaning of right and wrong are not open to human choice; right and wrong are among the given conditions of human existence because they flow from and reflect ultimate reality.

5. CRITICAL DISCUSSION

5.1 Causal origins. We have looked at some familiar Judaic and Christian ideas about how moral structures come into being, how they are learned, and how they are justified. What kinds of objections can be raised against these ideas? What are the obstacles to belief? Some believers have traditionally held that the theistic framework provides not simply *a* satisfactory explanation and justification of morality but the only one that will really do; only if basic principles mirror God's eternal nature can the sense that the core of morality is unchanging be accounted for, and only if the ground of being is the source of morality can the justificatory question be answered in a decisive and final way. As we proceed, we will look at objections to the theistic account and to these claims for its necessity. Let us begin with the idea of causal source.

First, according to one sort of criticism, religious stories that attribute the moral order to ultimate reality are false because they are really unconscious obfuscations. Peter Berger in *The Sacred Canopy,* for example, argued that human beings can come to know that their moral structures are purely human constructions subject to change, and hence tenuous or precarious. But the possibility that codes could be changed subjects humans to anxiety; humans like security, especially in regard to the all-important nomos that defines, in a particular cultural setting, the very conditions of social existence. Thus human beings have had a tendency, Berger suggests, to suppress this anxiety by deceiving themselves about the origins of the nomos; they create stories about its transhuman origin; if the nomos is created by ultimate reality, then it will share in the permanence of the ultimate structures of things. Berger thinks that believers have simply projected their own criteria onto God; they enlarge, throw out, and reify their own moralities (like a movie projector projects an image). Over the course of history, people have suppressed their anxieties by attributing their norms to eternal reality.

Berger's account needs revision. First, a point of clarification. Note that merely attributing norms causally to ultimate reality would not mean they could not change; the moral order might not mirror the ultimate. Even if this were so, however, norms would not be vulnerable to *human* change; the laws of society would be as secure as the laws of nature. But Berger seems to have in mind traditions which image basic norms as the reflection of the *unchanging* nature of the ultimate itself. In forms of Judaism and Christianity, for example, the basic norms of the moral order mirror God's own nature, though God could change interhuman prescriptions (what is unjust for humans, for example, stealing, might not be for God, to whom everything "belongs").[57]

Second, Berger's view presents the religious imagination as engaged in a self-deceiving mystifying process designed to suppress the realization that human structures are precarious. Nearer the truth is the view that religious narratives or stories that picture a divine origin are explanatory and justificatory interpretations, parts of cultural theories that utilize metaphors and models to grasp the human condition, past, present, and future.[58] It is not that humans could realize their norms are not eternal but deceive themselves into thinking they are; rather people in many cultures including forms of Judaism and Christianity have believed that a basic principle or set of principles was unchanging and have explained this sense of permanence by tracing the moral demand to an unchanging transhuman reality.

Thus religious stories are based on the available information and the stock of concepts possessed in a particular culture. We can affirm a continuity between ourselves—we use the information and concepts available to us—and a Pacific people like the Tangu, even if we reject their account:

> It was my father who made the land as it is, who made men, who gave them a language so they could speak, who taught them to understand one another, who brought men and women together in villages . . .[59]

And this is not to say that religious stories are not multivalent in meaning. Complex facets of the life of a community may be portrayed in images and stories. The crucial contrast I want to make is between Berger's theory of religious "mystification" and a view of traditional stories which sees them as continuous with our own efforts to understand the origins of human life and moral bonds. Religious stories about the moral order are developed and adhered to because of a desire to understand and to relate ourselves to the ultimate parameters of existence, not by a need to quell anxiety through mystification. Whether the traditional picture of God the "Father" as the one who establishes the basic norms should be believed is the question; but its truth or falsity cannot be settled by simply asserting that the religious story falsely represents, that is, projects, human creations as divine. The contest is between two different explanatory theories; whether human morality is made in the image of God or God is made in the image of human morality requires a judgment based on the evidence.

But consider a second objection. Don't we know that all moralities are social creations, that is, they just *are* sets of normative beliefs held by the majority of a social group? A morality just is a kind of social consensus about character and conduct? And if moralities are social creations, how can they be *God's* creation?

The thesis that moralities are social creations in this sense can be accepted by those who believe that God creates morality, however. The people of Israel (or some other designation of those who are believers) accept God's criteria and moral code.[60] Even though God designs morality and causes it to come into being, when morality is delivered to humans (through revelation or inherent capacities) it exists as a social phenomenon. Thus belief in God as causal origin (God creates the nomos) and metaphysical prototype (God's nature is the pattern and morality exists in the mind of God) is not incompatible with the acknowledgement that even the model of God-derived morality is one that humans in particular times and places accept as an interpretation of their existence and one that exists at least on earth in a consensus of hearts and minds.[61]

The critic nonetheless may come forward with a third objection. Doesn't the idea that there are lots of moralities which have evolved in human history conflict with the concept of divine creation? The defender of the idea that God has established a definite morality and communicated it through revelation or inherent capacities can reply to this objection, however. The defender can say that God revealed the true morality only to one people who have the task of teaching it to others and that this plan is justifiable in light of divine wisdom; or it could be said that the inherent capacity to know the fundamental principle of morality is only imperfectly developed; human beings have misunderstood what the basic principle(s) of rightness is (are). Thus this defender tries to refute the descriptive claim that there are lots of moralities that diverge at the level of basic principles; the diversity is merely apparent, because the inherently grasped norm or set of norms has not been fully understood and applied.

Even if the critic could be persuaded of this view of inherent human capacities, whether to attribute their evolution and development to God as ultimate cause is another issue. The critic could say at this point that human morality simply emerges in a universe whose origins need no theistic explanation. The conviction that humans *must* acknowledge a basic norm or set of norms could be explained simply as the product of evolution in a Godless universe; humans have just come to be that way. Whether the believer's account, which traces the evolution of human capacities ultimately to God, is preferable would depend on the overall adequacy of the theistic worldview.

Finally, however, there are more traditional problems about belief in God as causal origin. If one is going to advance such an account, problems arise with the very notion that ultimate reality has a relation to moral categories. If the deity transcends ordinary characterization, including moral categories, then how can this deity be the source of the moral order? In what sense is the deity analogous—like but unlike—human agents who create things and have qualities such as love or justice? Issues about the nature of God have occupied thinkers for centuries. In addition, there is the problem of evidence. The classic problem of evidence for the existence of God, over and above worries about the creation model itself, has led many modern thinkers to reject the source motif, but others retain their belief.[62]

5.2 *Modes of learning.*

5.2 *Modes of learning.*   Traditional notions of revelation have been challenged on historical grounds. In the Sinai story, the "eternal Torah" as it is called in the Judaic tradition is created by God and then promulgated in a mountaintop revelation. But at least since the rise of historical criticism in the Enlightenment, questions have been raised about the believability of the revelatory event and the reliability of the biblical accounts. Are the biblical documents historically trustworthy? Do they report what happened? Do they have any relation at all to an actual historical occurrence? Are they complete fabrications or at least highly imaginary reconstructions?

Given these difficulties many people in the modern era would say that in all likelihood the Mosaic code is the product of a complex process of historical development; elements of it are similar to moral rules and laws in other ancient Near Eastern contexts, although parts may have originated in Israelitic legislation. In any case, what is attributed in Exodus or other biblical books to God's promulgation in fact originated in sociopolitical developments. The Sinai narrative therefore is reduced to the status of a false hypothesis.

In response to historical criticism, Seymour Siegel takes a position that many Judaic and Christian thinkers have adopted. He argues that the specific laws of the *halakhah* were not given by God to a prophet or through human writers; *halakhah* is the record of the human response to an "encounter" with God throughout the generations. Thus revelation is not the Bible or the Talmud, but the encounter; human beings have worked out a moral and a legal code in an effort to imitate the deity's justice and kindness.[63] The believer is bound to imitate God's justice and kindness; but in Siegel's view the body of halakhic prescriptions itself does not necessarily embody the will of God. This is not merely to say that because our beliefs about the historically transmitted instructions of God are uncertain or unreliable (human interpretations are fallible), we should therefore trust in our own judgment when it conflicts with a putative command of God; Siegel is not saying that since we can't be sure it is really God doing the commanding we should not trust in the rightness of the command but judge for ourselves. The view I attribute to Siegel (and to many other contemporary thinkers) is more radical: The biblical precepts supposedly given by God are in fact human attempts to apply justice and kindness to concrete cases in particular times and places. Thus moral and legal change are no longer a matter of adjusting the fabric of God's legislation, but the individual and the community become the legislators. The deity establishes and communicates the basic contours of the morality it would establish; God leaves the moral and legal details to human beings.

Revelation then becomes encounter reexperienced in each generation. Revelation is no longer a story about events that can be falsified by historical evidence (for example, how Israel's moral-legal code developed), but an encounter with God seen through the eyes of faith. God is now seen as the guiding force behind historical events (such as, the Exodus) or is revealed in inner experience. The Sinai story or other biblical accounts can now be seen as "symbols," "myths," or "narratives" which do not conflict with but add another layer of meaning to ordinary events.

Thus, as I read him, Siegel is an example of many modern Judaic and Christian theologians who come to the conclusion that the details of biblical instruction are not the "word of God," but fallible human constructions. Nonetheless many such theologians retain the view that through some sort of encounter, which is reported in scripture, but reexperienced in every generation, believers learn those basic qualities of the deity which define the moral order.

But if scripture and tradition are fallible, then what of the idea that one really learns the nature of God in encounters past and present? Are biblical or contemporary representations of the nature of God any more certain than the details of biblical law? Aren't believers thrown back on their own criteria just as they have to rely on their own judgment for specifics? For example, even assuming, as many Christian believers do, that Jesus spoke for or was God, how reliable are the earliest "witnesses," much less those who transmitted their memories? Did they not "experience" this figure through their own historically limited perspectives? But if this is so, then must we not give up the model of revelatory learning and admit that throughout history believers have relied on their own criteria of morality when they respond to the deity in an "encounter?"

The model of revelatory learning indeed has been abandoned— often in practice if not in theory—by many modern Judaic and Christian thinkers. Moral awareness comes from the human side. In this sense humans are their own moral lawgivers; they are auto-nomos, their own law.[64] Humans do not need revelation even to learn the basic criteria of rightness; humans are not only capable of working out moral and legal details but they can grasp basic moral criteria on their own; they are fully autonomous. Whereas in earlier centuries the inherent capacities version of the lawmaker model was synthesized with some function for revelation (for example, in Saadya or Thomas Aquinas), now revelation, even understood as encounter, is superfluous.[65]

Such a view of autonomy obviously needs a strong conception of inherent capacities. But here too difficulties arise, at least with certain classical views.

The inherent capacities model of how the nomos is learned, as we remember, can take the form of the theory that the moral order is implanted in our minds; we know in an immediate and clear way one or more basic principles or even that certain specific things are right and wrong. The first difficulty this view faces is that moral awareness does not seem to be this sort of thing; one just does not seem to know in such an immediate sense; even first principles do not seem so clear. Advocates of neo-Thomistic or neo-Kantian theories of moral reason have themselves not agreed on the meaning of the first principle or the exact way in which it is known.[66] And critics have denied that there are any "self-evident" or "a priori" principles of practical reason. If there are any principles of reason which guide the moral life, say the critics, they are merely "formal," that is, rules about consistent reasoning or reasoning from ends to means; they do not furnish substantive first principles.[67]

Critics claim, moreover, that we learn right and wrong through a complex process of social transmission and socialization; our views are so successfully instilled that we often seem to have an intuitive, immediate, and clear notion of what is right and wrong. But even conceptions of basic principles change, say the critics; both neo-Kantian and neo-Thomistic notions of an immutable built-in structure of moral reason take conceptions of moral requirement regnant in some times and places and elevate them into an unchanging starting point or foundation for morality by representing them as an inherent demand of reason.

Moreover, similar difficulties can also appear when one moves from the fundamental principle or criterion to the formulation of norms. The neo-Aristotelian Thomistic tradition is often interpreted as holding that the basic norm of morality is a constitutive element of reason; the idea that rightness and moral goodness consist in the fulfillment of basic ends or goods inscribed in human nature is a built-in feature of human reason; one really can't think otherwise; the basic principle of "practical" or moral reason simply *is* "do good [seek basic ends or goods] and avoid evil." But one has to look at one's nature to see what ends or goods are inscribed.

The controversy, of course, is going to be about what is really good for human (or other) beings. The Thomistic tradition is widely interpreted to have a characteristic theory of the good which is known "by nature." Humankind, along with everything else has an essence or nature designed by God; this essence or nature specifies an optimum state or good, that is, a telos or end, which it is the goal of each thing to realize, from the acorn that becomes an oak to human beings who not only strive to survive and to procreate but have the desire to achieve excellencies of mind (ultimately the knowledge of God) and character (the virtues of social existence such as justice).[68]

This teleology of natural kinds, as it is sometimes called, has been subject to much criticism.[69] (Teleology refers to a goal-directed system, from *telos*, end or goal, and *logos*, order or reason.) Briefly, as H.L.A. Hart remarks, we do not *necessarily* desire and value survival (although most people do), and beyond that human beings differ greatly as to the sorts of goods they seek as the fulfillment or actualization of their human nature. We simply do not have some optimum state, even one defined by certain general values or ends such as knowledge, love, or a relation to God.[70] There is no evidence to which one could appeal in order to establish one set of values rather than another.

Moreover, even if the notion of general values or goods survives, critics, often within the religious traditions, have raised questions about specific means. For example, the *magisterium*, the teaching authority of the Catholic Church, declares that the moral law forbids "artificial" contraception; if a couple has to suspend procreation for some good reason, only the *natural* period of infertility may be used (however determined). God supposedly not only communicates (through the knowledge of our nature) that sexual capacities are designed for procreation and love (these are the goods or ends they are intended to realize), but the deity also makes clear that we are not to interfere with the divine dominion, the rightful divine control over the generation of life; we are not given the authority to improve on nature in this area of experience. Critics have objected that even if it is clear from examining our nature that procreation and love are the ends of our sexual "faculties," we do not know on this basis that we should not extend natural infertility by chemical or mechanical means. We may know, say these critics, that we should both procreate (if possible) and love, but *how* we achieve these goals is not determined by our natural capacities any more than the fact that our hair tends to grow long determines how we should cut or wear it.[71] An appeal could be made here to revelation, but Catholics have been reluctant to use scripture as a basis for the ban on "artificial" birth control. Thus even where adherents of a tradition believe in various modes of divine communication, fierce debates can go on about *what* has been communicated.

Classical notions of a built-in principle of moral reason coupled with a natural knowledge of human good have therefore been subject to much criticism. Many modern philosophers claim that the basic criteria or principles of morality are not fixed as Kantians and Thomists thought but are open to human choice. There are no constraints in reason which determine the choice of criteria. Thus in this view humans do more than acknowledge the basic criteria and form moral and legal precepts accordingly; humans themselves establish the criterion or criteria.[72]

The modern theologian, then, not only has to face the problem of historical criticism, but must respond to attacks on the idea of a fixed starting-point inherent in moral reason. Emil Fackenheim, for example, embraces the view that reason does not establish the criteria. The believer chooses God as the criterion. The believer chooses on the basis of values or reasons. Made in the image of God, humans value, say, love and justice, and choose the loving and just deity as the criterion of rightness and moral goodness.[73] For Fackenheim autonomy consists not in moral approval of God's commands, but in choosing God as the criterion of moral judgment.[74] Thus in one stroke Fackenheim adopts a "post-Kantian" view of moral reason and also secures for the God who is encountered an "essential" role; autonomy is not the possession of moral knowledge entirely independent of revelation, but the act of choosing the criterion itself; thus God is not extraneous to one's concept of the moral demand but for the believer the very criterion itself. Note that Fackenheim is not an "existentialist" or "emotivist" who believes that values (and hence the choice of moral criteria) are an entirely arbitrary matter of taste or preference; made in the image of God the believer's values reflect the deity's essential nature. Nor need he suggest that the acceptance of criteria is something performed by the individual completely apart from tradition and community; the individual stands in a tradition (or traditions) of criteria and specific judgments which are conveyed and interpreted by communities.

Thus as Siegel modifies the traditional view of revelation, so Fackenheim revises an inherited notion of moral reason. The success of modern efforts (Judaic or Christian) to formulate a synthesis of revelation and reason will depend on both of these moves.[75]

5.3 Justification. Geertz argues that religions characteristically try to ground moral norms in the nature of reality; there is a widespread tendency to seek a "metaphysical grounding for values." As we saw in the earlier section on justification, this statement could signify at least two sorts of justificatory strategies: (1) an appeal to ultimate reality or a relation to it which rests on some assumed notion of rightness; (2) an appeal to ultimate reality as the origin of morality and moral goodness. Let us look again at each of these moves.

Consider again the idea that human moral structures are linked to ultimate reality through underlying moral notions; for example, ultimate reality is the source of human good or the relation to God is based on justice. When ultimate reality is conceived in one of these ways, a "worldview", a people's "picture of the way things in sheer actuality are, their concept of nature, of self, of society . . . their most comprehensive idea of order," in Geertz's terminology, already has moral import. Thus the fact that religions synthesize the way things are and the way life ought to be, so that "human actions are tuned to cosmic conditions," and there is a "congruence" between the "structure of reality" and the "approved style of life," does not necessarily signify an attempt to justify moral norms in terms of some *morally neutral* state of affairs. The fusion or synthesis to which Geertz often draws our attention, the way in which a religious tradition "grounds the most specific requirements of human action in the most general contexts of human existence," is often actually a function of the way in which values (notions of human good), factual beliefs, and notions of rightness and moral goodness work together to link the framework of reality to moral structures.[76] Often, as I have noted, a norm such as justice is assumed as a defining criterion of moral requirement. How such a principle is interpreted and how it is related to factual beliefs will shape an ethos. For example, the Roman Catholic tradition is usually assumed to construe justice as a part of human good; thinkers in this tradition operate with that underlying notion of rightness. But not only this general assumption, but how justice is interpreted and related to factual beliefs, will shape the tradition's teaching.

Consider for example the abortion question. In the Roman Catholic tradition, God as the creator is thought to have a right over the lives of creatures. God loans or entrusts life to us. As the ultimate sovereign, the deity can delegate as much control to us as it desires. The Church teaches that God never delegates the right to take life directly under any circumstances (although some modern Catholics argue the contrary), so one should not, for example, perform abortions even to save the life of the mother.[77] What this argument assumes is the moral judgment that it is *just* for God to have this right. This moral assumption, moreover, is integrated with a set of factual beliefs. Who lives or dies is explicable at one level in scientific terms, but ultimately we are in the hands of God; the destiny of human beings and hence their final good is not limited to the human sphere.

One might argue, therefore, that if one delves far enough, one would find that not only views of the good but differences in factual beliefs and interpretations of principles such as justice could account for many cultural divergences. Thus moral principles—interpreted in various ways—seem to be woven into complex fabrics of meaning which link ultimate reality and human action. Being and doing are "grounded" in ultimate reality, linked to religious entities or relations, by means of valuational, factual, and moral assumptions.

There is, however, another type of justificatory appeal, as we know, which would involve a different kind of reference to ultimate reality. It is one thing to justify patterns of conduct and character by reference to some underlying notion of rightness and moral goodness along with related beliefs about facts and values. It is another enterprise entirely to ask why that notion of rightness should be binding in the first place. One wants to know whether there is any warrant for notions of rightness (and the way one interprets them), or whether our basic norms are a matter of individual or cultural preference. Now Geertz seemed to hold that moral views are really arbitrary but that religious traditions hold the contrary and present ultimate reality as their warrant.[78] I argued above that religious traditions often do something else, namely, they relate conduct and character to ultimate reality by means of a complex fusion of facts, values, and assumed moral norms. But sometimes, especially when traditions are subject to intense intellectual scrutiny, the question about a warrant is asked and then answered in terms of ultimate reality itself. In mainstream Western traditions, as we saw, God is the creator of everything that is, so

God is said to establish the standards of morality; for example, justice (some interpretation thereof) and other principles or qualities constitute rightness, because the ultimate source gives it this meaning. And if the moral order is established by God, then its justification is supposedly the fact that it is derived from and reflects the ultimate nature of things. Referring the moral order to God ends the chain of justification, answers the question *why* in a decisive and final way. Any merely human justification, so some believers have said, is challengable. Even if I stake my justification on some supposedly inherent demand of reason or human nature, one can always ask why *should* things be made that way? But if I say that God established such-and-such as the defining criteria of rightness and moral goodness, then there is nothing more to be said. One simply must accept what the "ground of being" establishes. Thus in this sense only the grounded-in-ultimate-reality rationale is finally satisfactory.

What objections then can be made to the created-by-ultimate-reality justification? We should note that the traditions often assume that humans accept the criteria of rightness not just because God is the ultimate cause and prototype; the criteria are not accepted simply as given or inevitable, but are ones to which humans assent. As Jacob Neusner puts it,

> Judaism perceives the commandments as expressions of one's acceptance of the yoke of the kingdom of heaven and submission to God's will. That acceptance cannot be coerced, but requires thoughtful and complete affirmation.[79]

Thus where the meaning of moral requirement is communicated through revelation, believers trace its content back to God; and when asked but why should one think that this is the correct (valid, legitimate, justified) content, the answer will be not only because God set it up that way and because it reflects the immutable nature of God, but because God is a being who is necessarily loving and just. The believer accepts God as the creator of morality because of God's qualities.

Even where the believer holds that independent of revelation moral reason determines a fixed standard(s) of rightness and moral goodness the question nonetheless can be asked, as I noted earlier, Why this standard? And the believer answers by saying that this standard reflects the very nature of God. Moreover, the believer also knows that God is all-powerful and all-knowing. There is a built-in correlation between the believer's moral reason and God's nature, but the believer accepts God as the legitimate creator of human morality because of all the deities' qualities; all these qualities comprise the complex set of reasons according to which the believer acknowledges God (a being with a certain nature) as the *legitimate* source of the criteria of morality.

A similar set of reasons obtain but in a different way also for the believer who does not hold that there are fixed criteria of moral reason. Fackenheim's believer has values on the basis of which God is chosen as the criterion of rightness. The believer values God's love, for example, but also God's wisdom and power.[80] The believer enacts God's traditional role; the believer (presumably with others in the religious community) establishes the criteria and the reasons the believer has correspond to the role of God's reason or nature on the Kantian or Thomistic model. The believer's choice is guided by reasons, just as God's choice is guided by the divine reason or nature. Fackenheim could have said, more in line with traditional affirmations of God's role, that the believer accepts God as the one who establishes the basic criteria of moral judgment. But this way of putting his view amounts to much the same as saying that the believer chooses God or God's will *as* the criterion. The believer, on the basis of his or her own values, chooses to define moral requirement or to allow it to be defined in terms of God's nature. The believer accepts a God-established morality.

The believer thus accepts God as the creator of the moral order. But insofar as the believer has reasons for accepting God, then the chain of justification does not really end with an appeal to the fact that God is ultimate cause and metaphysical model. It is the deity's qualities overall which ground the believer's acceptance, but these qualities legitimate God's role for the believer precisely because such qualities are valued by the believer. It is the believer's reasons in this sense which are finally determinative. It would seem that acceptance of God is *dependent* on the believer's own concerns.

The believer has no cause to be perturbed. That the believer has reasons for accepting God is assumed by mainstream versions of the traditions. It is only opposed by those who think that to grant humans even this modest capacity is an affront to the utter dependence of the creature on the creator. The mainstream believer, moreover, has the last word about dependence, for God creates the creature as one who has the capacity to have reasons; the creature, on the basis of God-given capacities, believes it is justified to accept God as the creator of moral requirement. In the end, the movement of creator to creature is to be completed by the creature's movement to the creator as we will see in Chapters 2 and 3; the believer's response begins the journey that makes the circle complete:

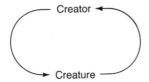

Of course, the mainsteam believer who accepts God as the creator of the moral order on the basis of God's qualities may share the appreciation of these qualities with those who do not believe in God. Both the believer and unbeliever can approve of, say, love and justice. Thus the mainstream believer can freely admit to standing on the same ground with the unbeliever. If the believer became an unbeliever, he or she presumably would still recognize or choose love and justice as the basic criteria of moral requirement. As Robert Adams puts it, ". . . a person is *theonomous* to the extent that . . . he regards his moral principles as given him by God, and adheres to them partly out of love or loyalty to God; but he also prizes them for there own sakes, so that they are the principles he *would* give himself if he were giving himself a moral law."[81]

If the believer and unbeliever share common ground, then they both could be asked, why love and justice? Why do you value these so much? Neither the unbeliever or the believer need think that values are arbitrary as some "existentialists" or "emotivists" have claimed. Even if we give up the view that there are self-justifying first principles, we need not fall over to the view that we simply construct our standards of morality on the basis of arbitrary values, values for which no further reasons can be given.[82] As recent theorists of knowledge called "holists" argue, we can perhaps give reasons based on other parts of our "web of belief."[83] For example, James Gustafson argues that we can justify our values by what we know about the human and the nonhuman world. In regard specifically to human life, we can know something of the "requisites" of society, such as, some form of care for the young. Beyond the requisites we can learn from literature, the social sciences, and other sources about human well-being; there may not be an "essential" set of ends for us to discover, but neither are values arbitrary preferences. We can give reasons, if Gustafson is right, for our view of human good.[84]

These are deep waters but I hope the outline of the debate is clear. What is at stake is how and why we accept one morality rather than another.

5.4 *Rights, patriarchy, and obedience.*   If one believes that scripture and tradition do not provide a direct and certain access to God, and if one loses confidence in the notion that there is a first principle of morality inherent in human capacities, then one might feel somewhat adrift. But if the holists are right, we can make do. All of our beliefs depend for their justification on other beliefs. We always assume some beliefs even when changing others. Thus we will stand on part of our raft, to use a famous metaphor, even while repairing another part. We will rely on some assumptions about what is and what ought to be even while changing others.

Indeed over and above objections noted so far, some modern thinkers, in particular feminist theologians, have proposed that the entire idea of a lawlike notion of creation is inadequate and ought to be jettisoned. Relying not merely on their own approval of such qualities as love or justice, but on specific values and moral convictions, these thinkers argue that the fundamental relation between God and morality must be reconceived.

Let us look first at one objection that does not try to overturn the entire model, but merely to correct it. If God is Sovereign or Lord, then God has dominion over human life and the conclusion has been drawn in some traditions that women do not have the right to procure abortions; God has not delegated this dominion to human beings. Contemporary feminists, however, argue that *this* image of the creator's dominion mirrors a pattern of male domination; if the notion of divine sovereignty over life is to be retained, then some notion of it must be found which allows women (or men if there were analogous contexts) a right over their bodies. Thus, parallel to constitutional limits on political authority, the rights of women (and men) would be integrated with the rights of the Governor. God is just, but what justice means even for God must be revised.

A much stronger objection, however, is brought by other theologians.[85] In a patriarchal cultural tradition, a male-dominant authority relation has been taken as the model which explains and justifies moral requirement in general: God as Sovereign or Lord (and related images of God as father, master, husband). These images of authority are patriarchal because males occupy superior roles (supposedly by right). If the human roles were not seen originally as morally legitimate, of course, they would not have been used to image the divine-human relation. But once we see moral objections to patriarchal human roles and relations, then we see that such a model of God's relation to morality is also flawed: God has been imaged as a male lawgiver. Such an image is not only flawed in itself but this picture of the religious relationship reinforces patriarchal human relations; the patriarchal deity wills a patriarchal code.

Moreover, not only are the images used to model the divine–human relation attacked as morally inadequate for example, a patriarchal conception of authority relations, but images of authority even if not wrongly conceived would be morally limiting. The lawmaker model skews morality in the direction of relations of authority and obedience; God is a *beneficent* sovereign to be sure, but the human duty is principally obedience. The dependence of the creature on the Creator is imaged in such a way that the person is "under orders." While the model allows some measure of autonomy (depending on the version) the response of obedience is retained. In this sense, the human retains the position of subject or child in relation to God, and the corresponding moral metaphors are used to image the divine–human relation. Thus moral relations that do not involve authority are not—at least not characteristically or widely or predominantly—employed where the lawmaker model is retained. This objection is similar to claims about moral autonomy, but it is different. The point is not that humans on their own know what is right or wrong, and thus are in a position to judge morally any supposed command of God's, or that humans choose God as the criterion on the basis of their own values; the point is that the model of submission to God's will is morally inadequate.

The modest form of this objection says that moral conceptions *other* than obedience and authority should also be used to image the divine–human relation. In its stronger form, this objection says that even if authority relations are justified in some areas of human social life they are entirely inappropriate in the depiction of the relation of God and human beings. Only mutual self-determination in communion with other persons and God will do. What is morally crucial is self–determination in community, not relations of obedience. Ideal human relations are imaged something like the anarchist community on Ursula Le Guin's planet Anarres in *The Dispossessed*. Moral norms should not be depicted as the criteria or judgments of a lawgiver, but as the "co-creation" of agents who together fashion forms of community.[86] If a creator were acknowledged, then it would perhaps be a model for imitation, as the revolutionary hero Odo (a woman) is on Anarres.[87] Thus the objection argues that human moral development is truncated if obedience to a lawgiver is taken as the paradigmatic moral relation.[88] It is truncated not merely if humans are not allowed to accept God or judge commands for themselves, but if humans are under orders.

6. CONCLUSION

We have looked at some ways in which the origin, learning, and justification of moral codes can be religiously interpreted. And we have also looked at some of the obstacles to believing in traditional accounts which link origin, learning, and justification to an ultimate agency. In particular, I have noted reasons for not accepting the claim that only the theistic model can satisfactorily explain and justify moral requirements.

But however we interpret the nature of our basic moral views, it is certainly the case that without patterns of value and factual belief, as well as interpretations of moral norms, moralities would not be what they are. Particular combinations of valuational, factual, and moral judgment shape moralities in distinctive ways. In this sense, it is correct to say that a moral system and a sacred canopy can be inextricably interwoven. However, if the believer and unbeliever share some assumptions—their allegiance to qualities such as justice and love—then the chasm between them is not so deep as it might appear. To be sure, the believer says that humans are created in the image of God and the unbeliever says that God is created in the image of humans; to the unbeliever, the story believers accept is false and the notion of a deity with a certain nature who establishes the moral law is seen as an extrapolation of human traits, a fictive construction; to the believer, the norms humans endorse are imperfect copies of the nature of God. This is a conflict between whole ways of seeing the human condition and to adjudicate it one has to consider evidence of various sorts. Believers and unbelievers may share in basic normative assumptions although they diverge in other ways; their webs of belief may overlap. And as contemporary feminists note, our substantive moral beliefs are likely to be as important, if not more important, than the picture we have of their foundations.

NOTES

1. Wendy O'Flaherty, *The Origins of Evil in Hindu Mythology* (Berkeley: University of California Press, 1976), pp. 23–27.

2. Ibid., p. 26.

3. See *Evil and the God of Love*, rev. ed. (San Francisco: Harper and Row, 1978).

4. For an interpretation of Genesis see Susan Niditch, *Chaos to Cosmos* (Chico, CA: Scholars Press, 1985); Niditch traces the movement from chaos to ideal creation and from ideal creation to reality. On the Genesis stories and other cosmogonies in ancient Israel, see Douglas Knight, "Cosmogony and Order in the Hebrew Tradition," in Robin Lovin and Frank Reynolds, eds., *Cosmogony and Ethical Order: New Studies in Comparative Religious Ethics:* (Chicago: University of Chicago Press, 1985), pp. 133–157. I use the RSV here for convenience, but see Phyllis Trible, *God and the Rhetoric of Sexuality* (Philadelphia: Fortress Press, 1978) who argues that "man" in 2.16 is the sexually undifferentiated "earth creature," later separated into male and female (pp. 80–82, 86–7, 95–8).

5. Burridge, "Levels of Being," in *Religion and Morality*, ed. Gene Outka and John P. Reeder, Jr. (Garden City, NY: Doubleday, 1973), p. 102.

6. See Paul Ramsey, "A Christian Approach to the Question of Sexual Relations Outside Marriage," *Journal of Religion, XLV*(April 1965), 114. However, see Trible, *God and the Rhetoric of Sexuality* for a critique of the view that the gender roles assigned in Genesis are the divine will for life after Eden.

7. Alison Black argues that in general Confucian models of creation do not resemble Western notions of a deliberate act of making but instead convey the idea that natural and social orders are the outward "expression" of the underlying principle or structure of the cosmos. See Black's *Man and Nature in the Philosophical Thought of Wang Fu-Chih* (Seattle: University of Washington Press 1987). On this reading, the question, How does the moral order come to be?, is answered very differently than in the Western traditions examined here, and we would have a good example of how important it is to distinguish the source question from particular cultural answers. There may be certain Western neo-Platonic notions of emanation which resemble the Confucian model. On neo-Platonic traditions see John P. Kenney, "Theism and Divine Production in Ancient Realistic Theology," in *God and Creation* ed. David Barrell and Bernard McGinn (Notre Dame University Press, forthcoming). For other treatments of Confucian traditions, see Lee Yearley, "A Confucian Crisis: Mencius' Two Cosmogonies and Their Ethics," in Lovin and Reynolds, eds., *Cosmogony and Ethical Order*, pp. 310–327; and Tu Wei-Ming, "The 'Moral Universal' from the Perspective of East Asian Thought," *Philosophy East and West, 31*(July 1981), 259–272.

8. To be contrasted both with the models of making and expression perhaps are stories which do not trace the moral order to a transhuman reality but nonetheless locate it in a religious scheme of meaning; the question, whence the moral order, can be answered with-

out reference to a transhuman source. In a Buddhist scripture, for example, the *Aggañña Suttānta,* respect for private property and its contrary, stealing, come into being as part of a picture of the destruction and reconstruction of the world. No more precise explanation is given; morality and immorality arise in a transition from "ethereal spirituality," in Stanley Tambiah's phrase, to the world as we know it. In traditions such as this, the moral order does not seem to be traced to a transhuman source, but a story about origins is placed within a religious worldview. See Tambiah, *World Conqueror and World Renouncer* (Cambridge: Cambridge University Press, 1976).

9. The six commandments in Exodus 20:12–17 are preceded by four injunctions that establish basic aspects of Israel's relation to the deity. They are sometimes referred to as "religious," in contrast to the succeeding six which are called "moral." This contrast is misleading, however, because in some interpretations of the religion of ancient Israel, the relation to the deity is understood to have a moral basis. For discussion of the ten commandments, see Walter Harrelson, *The Ten Commandments and Human Rights* (Philadelphia: Fortress Press, 1980); and Arthur Dyck, *On Human Care* (Nashville, TN: Abington, 1977), chap. 5.

10. I assume only the most basic elements of a theory of moral discourse: In various cultures or traditions there are general criteria of moral rightness and goodness, of moral requirement or morality, as I shall say. See Frederick Carney, "Theological Ethics," in *The Encyclopedia of Bioethics,* in Warren T. Reich, ed. (New York: The Free Press, 1978), pp. 429–437, for a discussion of the relation of judgments about acts and judgments about character. For discussions of the relation of general standards or criteria to specific rules and judgments, see Neil Cooper, *The Diversity of Moral Thinking* (Oxford: Clarendon Press, 1981); and David Wong, *Moral Relativity* (Berkeley: University of California Press, 1984). Some would object to the notion of general defining criteria or standards because it suggests that specific judgments are deductively generated from a foundational principle; my view is that one does find deductive reasoning of this sort in moral systems, but one also finds that the content of general norms is inductively changed on the basis of specific judgments.

11. On models and their relation to metaphors, see Sallie McFague, *Metaphorical Theology: Models of God in Religious Language* (Philadelphia: Fortress, 1982). The essays in *Cosmogony and Ethical Order,* ed. Lovin and Reynolds, deal with a variety of notions of the origins of the moral order. See also Arthur Adkins—"Laws Versus Claims in Early Greek Religious Ethics," *History of Religions,* 20(February 1982), 222, who warns against assuming that "divine law" has as much importance in other traditions as it does in Judaism and Christianity. Note again that all the categories—source, sanction, and salvation—are broader than the Judaic and Christian patterns I discuss. The notion of source need not be couched in the metaphor of making much less the legislative model; nor need the moral order reflect the nature of ultimate reality; the sanctioning reality need not be imaged as a judge or necessarily conform in itself to the morality it supports; salvation refers to a transmoral mode of being which does not have to be positively connected in one way or another to the moral order.

12. A group of gods or quasi-divine ancestors could be involved instead of a single figure. Compare Lee Yearley on the "sages" cosmogony in the Confucian thinker Mencius ("A Confucian Crisis," Lovin and Reynolds, eds. *Cosmogony and Ethical Order*).

13. Comparisons with Hindu tradition could be instructive. In a famous Hindu text, *The Laws of Manu,* the inconceivable "Self-Existent" is said to take the form of a being called Purusha or Brahman, and the basic classes of society emerge from parts of its body. See ed. and trans. George Buehler, *The Laws of Manu* (Oxford: Clarendon University Press, 1886). Is this a different model of making or creation, or is it more like Black's notion of an "expression" of an underlying structure? For a discussion of multiple resources for interpreting the Hindu tradition, see David Miller, "Sources of Hindu Ethical Studies: A Critical Review," *Journal of Religious Ethics,* 9(Fall 1981), 186–198.

14. In some religious traditions a reference to a creator who stands outside creation may be absent but, nonetheless, some being or force within the cosmos is causally responsible for the generation of norms in human experience. See Yearley, "A Confucian Crisis." I have spoken only of a transhuman creator, although the deity is usually pictured in Western traditions as transcendent of the cosmos as well.

15. See Carney, "Theological Ethics."

16. I am indebted here to Philip L. Quinn, "Divine Command Ethics: A Causal View," in *Divine Command Morality: Historical and Contemporary Readings*, ed. Janie Marie Idziak (New York and Toronto: The Edwin Mellen Press, 1979), pp. 305–325. See also Reeder, "A Response to Graber's Divine Command Theory of Ethics," *Journal of Religious Ethics*, *3*(1975), 157–163. On the mainstream model, the believer accepts a moral parallel to what H.L.A. Hart calls a "rule of recognition" (*The Concept of Law* [Oxford: Clarendon Press, 1981]): God's will establishes what is right and morally good. This rule can be expressed performatively or causally as Quinn puts it: God's command makes things obligatory. Or one could say, as I usually do here, that God is to be the one who establishes the meaning or defining criteria of rightness and moral goodness. In Neil Cooper's terminology (*The Diversity of Moral Thinking*), God is to make the criteria-laying-down judgments. This view accounts for the common conviction that, say, love or justice are the defining criteria, in contrast to the view that the defining criterion simply is "willed or commanded by God." For a statement of the latter sort of view, with the proviso that it would only be accepted were God loving, see Robert M. Adams, "A Modified Divine Command Theory of Ethical Wrongness," in *Religion and Morality*, ed. Outka and Reeder, Jr., pp. 318–347; See the new form of Adams' theory in "Divine Command Metaethics Modified Again," *Journal of Religious Ethics*, 7(Spring 1979), 66–79 and "Moral Arguments for Theistic Belief," in *Rationality and Religious Belief*, ed. C.F. Delaney (Notre Dame: University of Notre Dame Press, 1979), 116–140. For criticism of the legal analogy, see John L. Hammond, "Divine Command Theories and Human Analogies," *Journal of Religious Ethics, 14*(Spring 1986), 216–223. Compare, R.S. Swinburne, *The Coherence of Theism* (Oxford: Oxford Press, 1977). For a helpful collection of essays, see also *Divine Commands and Morality*, ed. Paul Helm (Oxford: Oxford University Press, 1981).

17. See Jacob Neusner, *The Way of Torah: An Introduction to Judaism*, (Belmont, CA: Wadsworth, 1979), pp. 66–67; cf. p. 85.

18. Berger, *The Sacred Canopy* (Garden City, NY: Doubleday, 1969), pp. 33–38. In some traditions, perhaps it is better to think of there being one world order in which, in Patrick Miller's words about ancient Ugaritic texts, "the world of the gods and the world of man were a sort of mutual reflection, each being the pattern for the other." *The Divine Warrior in Early Israel* (Cambridge: Harvard University Press, 1973), p. 23.

19. See Keith Ward who insists that God creates the moral law as an image of "his own necessary being and perfection"—*The Divine Image* (London: SPCK, 1976), p. 109–110; Ward, in my view, expresses the mainstream model which is also captured in Adams' correlation of morality and the will of a loving deity. Note that this model differs from both what is called "theological rationalism" *and* "theological voluntarism." Some thinkers, Thomas Aquinas, for example, are said to have held that moral requirement does not get its meaning from an act of divine will or command at all; morality is that which reflects the divine reason or nature independent of the divine will. William of Ockham and other "voluntarists", in contrast, are supposed to have held that it is only the creator's will or command which creates right and wrong; whatever the other features of the deity, it is only the fact of being commanded by the all-powerful and all-knowing creator which establishes moral requirement. Even if God is by nature just, for example, and one knows that nothing unjust would ever be commanded, it is only the command of the omnipotent and omniscient creator that makes things morally required. I see both of these positions as departures from the mainstream model. On the interpretation of Aquinas and Ockham that makes most sense to me, both hold that human morality is established by the command of the deity *in accordance with its nature*.

Why should a theologian argue for voluntarism or rationalism? The voluntarist theologian, who holds that will or command per se creates rightness, wants to express the utter dependence of morality on God; there is nothing which limits God's decision, for morality itself comes into existence and has the meaning it has because of the divine decree. The rationalist theologian in contrast does not think that the voluntarist account catches the sense in which moral requirement is what it is because it reflects the nature of a specific sort of creator. To affirm this, the rationalist will say that moral requirement exists prior to and independent of the divine will. On the face of it, theological voluntarism and rationalism are incompatible. But the concerns that lie behind them are not. The mainstream view expresses the concerns of both rationalists and voluntarists; morality is both a reflection of God's immutable essence and dependent on the creator's enactment. For a view close to mine which argues that Aquinas and Ockham are much more alike than traditional interpretations have allowed, see Linwood Urban, "William of Ockham's Theological Ethics," *Franciscan Studies, 33*(1973), 310–350. See also for a thorough but more traditional interpretation, W. K. Frankena, "The Ethics of Right Reason," *The Monist, 66*(January 1983), 1–8.

20. Thus the term *voluntarist* should be reserved for those who held that rightness is established simply by the will or command of the omnipotent and omniscient creator irrespective of whatever other qualities this entity has or what is commanded, for example, Quinn's theory in "A Causal View." This theory is similar to a form of legal positivism in philosophy of law. See A. P. D'Entreves, *Natural Law*, 2nd. ed. (London: Hutchinson, 1972), p. 69 ff. Sid Leiman suggests that there are sources in Judaic tradition which enunciate the voluntarist alternative, for example, Mishnah Berakhoth 5:3 and Babylonian Talmud, Berakhoth 33b. See "Critique of Louis Jacobs," in *Contemporary Jewish Ethics*, ed. Menachem Kellner (New York: Sanhedrin Press, 1978), p. 59. See Quinn's *Divine Commands and Moral Requirements* (Oxford: Clarendon Press, 1978) for a discussion of a variety of divine command theories.

21. For a notion of law, see David Little and Sumner B. Twiss, *Comparative Religious Ethics* (San Francisco: Harper and Row, 1978).

22. This is what H.L.A. Hart calls the "natural law" or Thomistic view of law. See Aquinas on the defining characteristics of law. *Summa Theologiae*, ed. and trans. Thomas Gilby, O.P., Vol. 28, (London: Blackfriars, 1963), 1a2ae. 90, pp. 5–17. Aharon Lichtenstein says that "Halakhah constitutes—or at least contains—an ethical system" but does not explicitly adopt the "natural law" theory of law. See Lichtenstein's "Does Jewish Tradition Recognize an Ethic Independent of Halakhah?," in *Contemporary Jewish Ethics*, ed. Menachem Kellner (New York: Sanhedrin Press, 1978), p. 106. To hold that *halakhah* is both a moral and legal system one would have to hold only that it *in fact* satisfies the criteria both of moral and legal validity, whatever these are; but I think Lichtenstein might hold that the system is moral in a stronger sense: It is law, but law whose validity depends on its moral rightness. Of course, in a classic Judaic framework it seems assumed that if a prescription has in fact been correctly derived from revealed sources, then it *will* be morally right, for God will not legally require anything morally wrong.

23. See Hart, *The Concept of Law;* and Seymour Siegel, "Ethics and the Halakhah," in *Conservative Judaism and Jewish Law*, ed. Seymour Siegel (New York: Rabbinical Assembly, 1977), pp. 124–132.

24. See Ronald Dworkin, *Taking Rights Seriously*, 2nd ed. (Cambridge: Harvard University Press, 1978); *Law's Empire* (Cambridge: Harvard Press, 1986); Marvin Fox, "The Philosophical Foundations of Jewish Ethics: Some Initial Reflections," Second Annual Rabbi Louis Feinberg Memorial Lecture in Judaic Studies, Judaic Studies Program, University of Cincinnati.

25. "The Status of Women Within Judaism," in *Contemporary Jewish Ethics*, ed. Kellner, p. 365. Compare Rachel Adler, "The Jew Who Wan't There: Halacha and the Jewish Woman," in *Contemporary Jewish Ethics*, ed. Kellner pp. 348–354.

26. On the notion of virtue, see Stanley Hauerwas, *A Community of Character* (Notre Dame, IN: University of Notre Dame Press, 1981); and Alasdair MacIntyre, *After Virtue*, 2nd ed. (Notre Dame, IN: Notre Dame University Press, 1984).

27. Much has been written of late about an "ethics of virtue" in contrast to an ethics of principles or rules. It is important to note that advocates of an ethic of virtue can mean at least two things: 1) In a certain tradition (or traditions), the moral life is construed not only as principles or rules but as a matter of virtue; this is a claim that we should not misdescribe moral traditions by emphasizing only conduct. (2) A certain tradition—for example, some version of Judaic or Christian ethics—should be developed in such a way that moral virtues and related rules are seen as instrumental to or ingredients in human good or fulfillment; this claim is more than a matter of emphasis, it argues for a neo-Aristotelian or neo-Thomistic ethic in opposition to a neo-Kantian approach that does not derive rightness from convictions about happiness or human good. For an examination of various sorts of virtue ethics, see Gregory E. Pence, "Recent Work on Virtures," *American Philosophical Quarterly, 21*(October 1984), 281–297. In Chapter 2, I will discuss another sense in which an ethic of virtue has been contrasted with an ethic of duty, namely, the notion that moral goodness involves *not* being governed by a notion of what one *ought* morally to desire and do.

28. For an excellent analysis of meanings of supererogation, see Millard Schumaker, *Supererogation: An Analysis and Bibliography*, (Edmonton, Alberta: St. Stephen's College, 1977). For a discussion of Judaic tradition, see Aaron Lichtenstein, "Does Jewish Tradition Recognize an Ethic Independent of Halakha?," in *Contemporary Jewish Ethics*, ed. Kellner, pp. 102–123.

29. For a contemporary treatment, see Alan Donagan, *The Theory of Morality*, (Chicago: University of Chicago Press, 1977) on institutional and non-institutional moral rules. It would be interesting to study this passage from the Hindu epic the *Mahābhārata:* Bhisma said: "I shall discourse on the duties that are eternal. The suppression of wrath, truthfulness of speech, justice, forgiveness, begetting children upon one's own wedded wife, purity of conduct, avoidance of quarrel, simplicity, and maintenance of dependents—these nine duties belong to all the four orders (equally)." Quoted in *The Hindu Tradition*, ed. Ainslee Embree (New York: Vintage, 1972), p. 81; the *Mahābhārata*, XII: 60.

30. On the concept of tradition, see Edward Shils, *Tradition* (Chicago: University of Chicago Press, 1981). See also W. C. Smith, *The Meaning and End of Religion* (New York: New American Library, 1964), chap. 6, "The Cumulative Tradition."

31. See John Stratton Hawley, ed., *Saints and Virtues* (Berkeley: University of California Press, 1987).

32. See the essays on liturgy and ethics in *The Journal of Religious Ethics*, 7(Fall 1979). Kay Warren notes that rituals in the culture of Mayan Trixanos Indians do not set out rules but instead "summarize key forms of social connectedness between individuals and present striking images through which Trixanos should orient themselves to others." See "Creation Narratives and the Moral Order: Implications of Multiple Models in Highland Guatemala," in *Cosmogony and Ethical Order*, ed. Lovin and Reynolds, pp. 251–276.

33. See Robert Lingat, *The Classical Law of India*, trans. J. Duncan M. Derrett (Berkeley: University of California Press, 1973), for a discussion of the distinction in Hindu thought between *śruti*, words heard by primeval figures from gods or other manifestations of ultimate reality, and *smrti*, what is remembered (that is, traditions based on *śruti* but of lesser authority).

34. See Neusner, *Way of Torah*, p. 66.

35. See the Introduction in David Feldman, *Marital Relations, Birth Control, and Abortion in Jewish Law* (New York: Schocken Books, 1974).

36. See Karl Barth, *Church Dogmatics*, 11/2 (Edinburgh: T. and T. Clark, 1957), chap. 7. Compare William Werpehowski, "Command and History in the Ethics of Karl Barth," *Journal of Religious Ethics*, 9(Fall 1981), 298–320.

37. On the inherent knowledge of morality in certain Chinese traditions, see Lee Yearley, "Mencius on Human Nature: The Forms of His Religious Thought," *Journal of the American Academy of Religion* XLIII(June 1975), 188–190. But Yearley also claims that aspects of Mencius' thought imply a transhuman reference.

38. "The Relationship between Religion and Ethics in Jewish Thought," in *Religion and Morality*, ed. Outka and Reeder, Jr., p. 159; reprinted in *Contemporary Jewish Ethics*, ed. Kellner, pp. 41–57.

39. "Critique of Louis Jacobs," in *Contemporary Jewish Ethics*, ed. Kellner, p. 58–60.

40. See for example, James Gustafson, *Ethics from a Theocentric Perspective*, vol. 1 (Chicago: University of Chicago Press, 1981) chapt 3.

41. There is considerable debate in Judaic tradition in regard to the so-called Noachide laws, or commandments supposedly given to the sons of Noah—that is, to everyone prior to the revelation at Sinai and to all non-Jews subsequent to that. David M. Feldman gives the list as follows: "(1) The establishment of courts of justice; the prohibition (2) of blasphemy; (3) of idolatry; (4) of incest; (5) of bloodshed; (6) of robbery; (7) of eating 'flesh torn from a living animal' " (cruelty, according to Feldman's note). See Feldman's *Marital Relations, Birth Control, and Abortion in Jewish Law* (New York: Schocken Books, 1974), p. 56. According to David Novak in *The Image of the Non-Jew in Judaism: An Historical and Constructive Study of the Noahide Laws* (New York and Toronto: Edwin Mellen Press, 1983), some figures in the tradition take these "laws" as rationally known and others insist they are revealed. Novak believes that for Maimonides they are both known through reason and revealed; their true significance is known in what is revealed to all human beings, and one

has a "share in the world to come" only when one obeys the laws as the command of God (pp. 278–279; 301–304). But by "revealed" Noachide laws, Novak means not a pre-Mosaic Sinailike revelation but God speaking in the "spirit"; Novak quotes Maimonides as saying: ". . . but anyone in the world whose spirit moves him and understands by his own intellect to stand apart before the Lord to minister to Him and serve Him, to know the Lord and to walk straight as God made him . . . such a person is sanctified with the greatest sanctity and the Lord will be his portion and his inheritance forever and ever, and he will merit what he deserves in the world-to-come . . ." (p. 303). For the view that Maimonides did not teach "natural law," see Marvin Fox, "Maimonides and Aquinas on Natural Law," in *Dine Israel, III*(1972), 5–36; for the view that Maimonides could have, see Michael Levine, "The Role of Reason in the Ethics of Maimonides," *Journal of Religious Ethics, 14*(Fall 1986), 279–295. Compare Steven S. Schwarzschild, "Do Noachites Have to Believe in Revelation?" *Jewish Quarterly Review, 52*(April 1962), 297–308, and cont. in *53*(July 1962), 30–65.

42. In the Thomistic tradition, "natural" signifies what is known independent of revelation and the ends the divine designer has provided.

43. See *Foundations of the Metaphysics of Morals,* trans. Lewis White Beck (New York: Library of Liberal Arts, 1959), for the ways Kant expressed the fundamental principle. Aquinas apparently taught there were other "primary precepts" of the natural law. See John Langan, "Beatitude and Moral Law in St. Thomas," *Journal of Religious Ethics, 5*(1977), 189–90. According to Langan, contrary to the common interpretation I assume, Aquinas does not derive the precepts of the natural law directly from "good is to be done" and knowledge of goods to which humans are inclined (cf. 186–7, 193–4). Compare W. K. Frankena in "Right Reason," pp. 19–20.

44. I present the idea of revelation, following many examples from Judaic and Christian tradition, as a matter of teaching or instruction. In Lee Yearley's terminology this motif would fall under the "saviour" model if human beings are dependent on an external agent to impart knowledge which transcends their abilities to understand altogether. If those instructed no longer need the teacher once taught, then it would fall under the "teacher" model. The notion of inherent knowledge coupled with the idea that some external help is needed would also fall under the "teacher" category. See his "Teachers and Saviours," *Journal of Religion, 65*(April 1985), 225–243.

45. It is even sometimes said that God must implant or "infuse" capacities above and beyond those we have "by nature." As Frankena points out, some figures in the right reason tradition have held that special divine help ("infused" virtue) is needed to get "reason" working right ("Right Reason," pp. 10, 14); Frankena thinks that Aquinas held that "a considerable rightness of reason (and moral virtue) can be attained naturally . . . but that complete rightness of reason [complete moral virtue, plus theological virtue] cannot."

46. Thomas Aquinas, *Summa Theologiae*, trans. Thomas Gilby, O.P., 1a2ae. 91, 4: pp. 29–33. Thomas gives two other reasons: Only God can judge "interior acts" and only God could forbid all evils without doing more harm than good.

47. Saadya Gaon, *Book of Doctrines and Beliefs*, in *Three Jewish Philosophers*, ed. and trans. Alexander Altmann (New York: Atheneum, 1972), pp. 103–105; see notes 1 and 2, p. 105. For a discussion of the difficulty in interpreting Saadya and a critical evaluation, see Marvin Fox, "On the Rational Commandments in Saadia's Philosophy: A Reexamination," in *Modern Jewish Ethics*, ed. Marvin Fox (Ohio State University Press, 1975), pp. 174–187.

48. Clifford Geertz, "Ethos, World View, and the Analysis of Sacred Symbols," in *The Interpretation of Cultures* (New York: Basic Books, 1973), pp. 126–141.

49. In my view, this is a crucial distinction often expressed in the contrast between teleological and deontological theories of ethics. Utilitarianism is not a teleological theory on this view because it does not define the right as part of human good. It defines the right as the maximization of good, counting each as one (it is consequentialist in this sense), but this requirement is not an ingredient in human good, it is a requirement which regulates the pursuit of good. Rawls, for example, is correct to see utilitarianism as a rival to his own principles of justice: Perfectionism or Aristotelianism, however, should be seen as entirely different, for it would not merely presuppose a different theory of human good but would derive a notion of justice from it. See *A Theory of Justice* (Cambridge: Harvard University Press, 1971). Compare other versions of the teleological–deontological distinction, for example, W. K. Frankena, *Ethics*, 2nd ed. (Englewood Cliffs, NJ: Prentice-Hall, Inc., 1973); Paul W. Tay-

lor, *Principles of Ethics: An Introduction* (Belmont, CA: Dickenson Publishing, 1975).

50. It is commonly said that in the Thomistic tradition justice is part of true human good. For a recent statement of this view, see John Finnis, *Natural Law and Natural Rights* (Oxford: Clarendon Press, 1980). For the view that a concept of moral requirement not derived from human good or well-being is really the "ghost" of a divine law conception of ethics, see G.E.M. Anscombe, "Modern Moral Philosophy," in Anscombe, *Ethics, Religion, and Politics* (Minneapolis: University of Minnesota Press, 1981); MacIntyre, *After Virtue*, 2nd ed.; and Richard Taylor, *Ethics, Faith, and Reason* (Englewood Cliffs, NJ:Prentice-Hall, Inc., 1985).

51. Sometimes gratitude is appealed to as an independent category or as a species of justice. See Paul F. Camenisch, "Gift and Gratitude in Ethics," *The Journal of Religious Ethics*, 9(Spring 1981), 1–34.

52. See Giles Milhaven, "Moral Absolutes and Thomas Aquinas," in *Absolutes in Moral Theology?*, ed. Charles Curran (Washington, DC: Corpus, 1968), pp. 154–185; and Urban, "William of Ockham."

53. The thesis that in many societies the moral order is conceived to be "rooted" or "grounded" (not only in a causal but also a justificatory sense) in an unchanging sacred reality is enunciated by many anthropologists and historians of religion; it informs the introduction and the illuminating set of essays in *Cosmogony and Ethical Order*, ed. Lovin and Reynolds.

54. A number of philosophers think that their version of Kantianism expresses the demand of reason and conveys what either the Golden Rule or love of neighbor really signify. Rabbi Hillel, a Pharisee whose teaching was crucial for the development of Rabbinic Judaism, is reported to have said, "What is hateful to yourself, do not to your fellow. That is the whole Torah. All the rest is commentary. Now go forth and learn!" Jesus, of course, is depicted as having made love of neighbor the basic principle on which the law rests (Matthew 22:37–40). In contemporary philosophy, R. M. Hare argues that universalizability (treat like cases alike)—plus a rational consideration of what one would really want to be accepted as a rule that applies to yourself as well as others—is the basis of morality. See Hare's *Freedom and Reason* (New York: Oxford University Press, 1965). In this Hare would seem to follow Hillel. Alan Donagan, however, sees universalizability as a formal test but urges love of neighbor as the basic standard. See Donagan's *The Theory of Morality* (Chicago: University of Chicago Press, 1977).

55. Compare Frankena, however, who says that Thomas "would not go along" with Grotius; "Right Reason," p. 17.

56. Berger may have this sort of justification in mind in *The Sacred Canopy*, when he stresses the idea that humans allay their anxieties by believing the moral order will not change. Geertz seems to suggest the argument in his essays, although he stresses the idea of human good as conformity to the real. p. 130.

57. See Milhaven, "Moral Absolutes." In mainstream versions of Judaism and Christianity God will not change the basic criteria, for they reflect the divine essence. Critics of theological voluntarism were not accusing its defenders of supposing that God was in fact free to will anything other than what reflected the divine essence; their concern was that a moral theory which suggests that moral requirement is created solely by the fiat of the divine sovereign, without specifying what the character of the sovereign is to be, leaves open the logical possibility that the sovereign might command anything at all or change its mind.

58. In *The Sacred Canopy*, as I read it, Berger said only that religions *tend* to convert human constructions into transhuman realities and thus guarantee them permanence (pp. 89–90, 24–5, 27, 32–3, 35–7). This "projection" not only suppresses anxiety, but suppresses the knowledge that the norms are purely human constructions, subject to change. Berger wanted to allow nonetheless that some religions do not so mystify the nature of the nomos and hence "alienate" human beings from their own nomos-creating capacities (p. 83ff, 89–90, 95). I agree with Van A. Harvey, however, that the "logic" of Berger's position seems to drive him to the conclusion that religions as such mystify and alienate. If those traditions which supposedly demystify particular social orders (by showing that they do not reflect eternal reality) root their own moral standards in the nature and will of the transcendent, do they not also "project" the merely human onto the divine? The problem with Berger's theory in *The Sacred Canopy* is that the supposedly merely sociological perspective includes a

truth claim; insofar as many religions or perhaps even religions as such are inherently falsi-
fying, that is, they falsely attribute a transhuman reality and origin to what is metaphysically
and causally merely human, it is hard to see how such a "perspective" can be compatible in
any sense with the belief that a religious account is true. On *The Sacred Canopy* and later
works where Berger tries in other ways to make a sociological and a theological perspective
compatible, see Harvey, "Some Problematical Aspects of Peter Berger's Theory of Religion,"
Journal of the American Academy of Religion, 40 (March 1973), 75–93, and "Religious Faith and
the Sociology of Knowledge: The Unburdening of Peter Berger," *Religious Studies Review 5*
(January 1979), 1–10; see also the review essay on Berger by Marie Augusta Neal, *Religious
Studies Review 5* (January 1979), 10–15. Lee Yearley comments on the sort of functionalist
theory which explains why people "really" develop and adhere to religious legitimations in
"Toward a Typology of Religious Thought: A Chinese Example," *Journal of Religion, 55* (October 1975), 440–441.

59. Kenelm Burridge, "Levels of Being," in *Religion and Morality*, ed. Outka and
Reeder, Jr., p. 94. I do not agree with Ricoeur that the explanation of origins (etiology) is
not a proper function of myths. See Ricoeur's *The Symbolism of Evil*, trans. Emerson Bu-
chanan (New York; Evanston; and London: Harper and Row, 1967), p. 164. One thing that
some narrative myths do is to explain where things came from (or where they are going).
This is not to deny of course that these same myths may also have other functions—for example, as he puts it, they open up dimensions of experience (pp. 165–166); myths of evil,
in his view, are not historical accounts but disclosures of the nature of human freedom (pp.
235–6, 251–252). As I see it, some myths not only characterize the human situation, they
explain it. Myths may stand midway between "primordial symbols" and "speculation" (see p.
237), but that is no reason to suggest that etiological explanation is just a way in which other
things are said. When Ricoeur himself wishes to appropriate the insight of myths, he is not
so much discarding their misleading etiological husks to discover the relevant kernel of
truth, as he is taking insights from the myths and combining them with another explanatory
framework to create a new web of belief. Modern cultures have their explanatory narratives,
in other words (the Big Bang, and so forth).

60. Thus it is God who sets the standards, but morality is still a social "creation" in
David Wong's sense. Wong contrasts the notion of moralities as social creations with any
view which holds that there is an "irreducible moral reality" external to the systems adopted
by individuals and groups or that the standards of morality are dictated by the nature of
things. But even these views are compatible with Wong's theory of moralities as social creations. If it is believed, for example, that justice exists as a cosmic force or entity, justice is
still socially accepted as a standard for a moral system, and if the nature of things requires
certain moral standards, those are still accepted as part of what Wong calls an adequate
moral system. Thus the thesis that humans accept standards and clusters of rules and virtues, and that moralities are social creations in this sense, is independent of beliefs about
why certain standards are mandated or what their metaphysical status is. Wong and others
of course could offer arguments against the self-understandings of traditions which refer to
God or the nature of things, but the self-understandings themselves are not contrary to the
notion of moralities as social creations.

61. See James M. Gustafson, *Treasures in Earthen Vessels: The Church as a Human Community* (New York: Harper and Brothers, 1961).

62. I am not convinced by those who argue that some religious beliefs can be rational
or justified independent of other beliefs; theistic belief seems to rest in some sense on other
beliefs about our experience. Compare James M. Gustafson, *Ethics from a Theocentric Perspective*, Vol. 1 (Chicago: University of Chicago Press, 1981). On evidentialism and defenses of
the view that some religious beliefs can be properly "basic" see *Faith and Rationality: Reason
and Belief in God*, ed. Alvin Plantinga and Nicholas Wolterstorff (Notre Dame, IN: Notre
Dame University Press, 1983), and *Rationality, Religious Belief, and Moral Commitment: New Essays in the Philosophy of Religion*, ed. Robert Audi and William J. Wainwright (Ithaca and London: Cornell University Press, 1986). In particular, I do not see why a demand for evidence
in regard to religious beliefs need be part of a foundationalist as opposed to a coherentist
epistemology. William Alston argued that it need not in "Plantinga's Epistemology of Religious Belief," in *Alvin Plantinga*, ed. James Tomberlin and Peter Van Inwagen (Dordrecht:
D. Reidel, 1985), but Plantinga notes this move and argues against it in "Coherentism and

the Evidentialist Objection to Belief in God," in Audi and Wainwright, eds. *Rationality, Religious Belief, and Moral Commitment*, pp. 109–138. Plantinga argues against J. L. Mackie's assumption in *The Miracle of Theism* (Oxford: Clarendon Press, 1982) that theism is or is like a scientific hypothesis relative to some body of evidence. "Is Theism Really a Miracle," *Faith and Philosophy, 3* (April 1986), 132–133. See Philip L. Quinn's criticism of Plantinga, "In Search of the Foundations of Theism," *Faith and Philosophy, 2* (October 1985), 469–486; Plantinga replied in "The Foundations of Theism: A Reply," *Faith and Philosophy, 3* (July 1986), 298–313.

63. Seymour Siegel "The Meaning of Jewish Law in Conservative Judaism: An Overview and Summary," and "Ethics and the Halakhah," in *Conservative Judaism and Jewish Law*, ed. Seymour Siegel (New York: Rabbinical Assembly, 1977), pp. xiii–xxvi, 124–132. Siegel may mean that those who encounter the deity acknowledge an obligation of gratitude and/or in the encounter justice and kindness are accepted as basic criteria; the deity could either teach something that was not grasped before or draw out inchoate knowledge. On the relation of historical criticism to religious belief, see Van A. Harvey's *The Historian and the Believer: The Morality of Historical Knowledge and Christian Belief* (New York: Macmillan, 1966); for counter arguments, see William J. Abraham, *Divine Revelation and the Limits of Historical Criticism* (Oxford University Press, 1982) for a typology of views, see Avery Dulles, *Models of Revelation* (Garden City, N.Y.: Doubleday, 1983); also John Hick *Philosophy of Religion, 3E*, chapt. 5.

64. On "moral autonomy," compare James Rachels, "God and Human Attitudes," *Religious Studies, 7*(1971), 325–337; Philip L. Quinn, "Religious Obedience and Moral Autonomy," *Religious Studies, 11*(1975), 265–281; Gene Outka, "Religious and Moral Duty," in *Religion and Morality*, ed. Outka and Reeder, Jr., pp. 204–254; Robert M. Adams, "Autonomy and Theological Ethics," *Religious Studies 15* (1979), 191–194; Ronald Green, "Abraham, Isaac and the Jewish Tradition," *Journal of Religious Ethics, 10*(Spring 1982), 1–21; Emil Fackenheim, "The Revealed Morality of Judaism and Modern Thought," and Norbert Samuelson, "Revealed Morality and Modern Thought," in *Contemporary Jewish Ethics*, ed. Kellner, pp. 61–83, 84–99. See Jeffrey Stout, *The Flight from Authority* (Notre Dame: Notre Dame Press, 1981) pp. 234 ff. who sees Enlightenment appeals to moral autonomy as response to 16C. and 17C. conflicts of religious authorities.

65. In regard to God's supposed command to Abraham to kill his son Isaac, Kant believed that the "human duty" not to kill Isaac was "certain in and of itself" in contrast to the uncertain command of God. See *Religion Within the Limits of Reason Alone*, trans. T. M. Greene and H. Hudson (New York: Harper, 1960), p. 175, and *Der Streit der Facultäten* (Hamburg: Verlag von Felix Meiner, 1959). Kant also apparently taught a second view: not only are beliefs about God's commands uncertain, but even if one knew that they came from God, one would still have to judge each of them for oneself. One could not trust they were right. The basic principle of morality is, roughly, choose so that your "maxim" (course of action) could be a universal "law." It is only when specific courses of action pass this test that they become morally obligatory. Thus we can only impose obligation on ourselves. Even if we knew that a command came from God (by some means other than what has been commanded itself), that command does not become obligatory until we submit it to and it passes the bar of approval of the first principle. A natural objection arises: why couldn't the believer accept the maxim "Follow God's (genuine) instructions," and thus trust in what God commands? Presumably given God's nature whatever God commands passes the test of the first principle. The Kantian would have to have some other reason for insisting that the individual judge each and every specific command. For a modern version of Kant's argument, see Rachels, "God and Human Attitudes," and for criticisms see Quinn, "Religious Obedience and Moral Autonomy," and Adams, "Autonomy and Theological Ethics." See also Fackenheim, "The Revealed Morality of Judaism" and Outka, "Religious and Moral Duty."

66. On Thomas' first principle, compare Germain Grisez, "The First Principle of Practical Reason," *Natural Law Forum (Notre Dame Journal of Jurisprudence), 10*(1965), 168–196, reprinted in *Aquinas*, ed. Anthony Kenny (Garden City, NY: Doubleday, 1969), pp. 340–382; and Vernon J. Bourke, "The Synderesis Rule and Right Reason," in *The Monist, 66*(January 1983), 71–82.

67. For criticisms of Alan Gewirth's neo-Kantian attempt to derive human rights from the rational principle of consistency and basic facts about human nature in *Reason and*

Morality (Chicago: University of Chicago Press, 1978), see Alastair MacIntyre, *After Virtue;* David Wong, *Moral Relativity;* Ronald Green, "Alan Gewirth, *Reason and Morality*," *Religious Studies Review,* 5 (July 1979), 187–190. See J.L. Mackie, *Ethics: Inventing Right and Wrong* (London: Penguin, 1977), chapter 4, for the thesis that notions of "universalizability" covertly convey substantive moral commitments. For a collection of essays on Gewirth and his response to critics, see Edward Regis, Jr., ed. *Gewirth's Ethical Rationalism* (Chicago and London: University of Chicago Press, 1984). Some critics have argued (and some religious thinkers would insist) that one statement of the Kant's "categorical imperative," roughly, never treat persons merely as means but also as ends, really rests on theological premises, for example, one is to "respect persons" because they are made in the image of God, and one owes it to God to respect what is made in God's image. See Gene Outka, "Respect for Persons," in James F. Childress, and John MacQuarrie, eds. *The Westminster Dictionary of Christian Ethics* (Philadelphia: Westminister Press, 1986). Compare David S. Shapiro, "The Doctrine of the Image of God and *Imitatio Dei,*" in Kellner, *Contemporary Jewish Ethics,* pp. 127–151.

68. See Hart, *Concept of Law,* pp. 183–189. According to Frederique Apffel Marglin, the Hindu concept of *dharma* signifies the order of the cosmos; everything has a proper place and a proper activity. See Marglin's "Power, Poverty, and Pollution: Aspects of the Caste System Reconsidered," *Contributions to Indian Sociology,* 11(1977), 246–247. Marglin quotes J. A. van Buitenen ("Dharma and Moksa," *Philosophy East and West 7,* 36): "It is the *dharma* of the sun to shine . . . , of the rivers to flow, of the cow to yield milk, of the *brahmin* to officiate, of the *kṣatriya* to rule, of the *vaiśya* to farm." It would be interesting to compare *dharma* and "natural law" in the Thomistic tradition where the law of the deity encompasses both what we would call the natural and the social order, and prescribes particular activities based on the essential nature of different sorts of things and their inherent goals.

69. See Hart, *Concept of Law.*

70. Compare Giles Milhaven, "Toward an Epistemology of Ethics," in *Norm and Context in Christian Ethics,* ed. Gene Outka and Paul Ramsey (New York: Scribner's, 1968), pp. 225 ff.

71. An example of Milhaven's in "Epistemology."

72. There may be a profound historical and metaphorical connection between quasi-legislative divine-creation theories, Kant's attempt to make human reason the legislator instead of God, and existentialist views of individual commitment as the source of morality. See Iris Murdoch, *The Sovereignty of Good* (New York: Schocken Books, 1971); and Frederick Olafson, *Principles and Persons: An Ethical Interpretation of Existentialism* (Baltimore and London: Johns Hopkins Press, 1967).

73. Compare Adams "A Modified Theory."

74. "The Revealed Morality of Judaism and Modern Thought," *Contemporary Jewish Ethics,* ed. Kellner. Compare Patterson Brown, "Religious Morality" and "Religious Morality: A Reply to Flew and Campbell," in Janine Marie Idziak, ed., *Divine Command Morality: Historical and Contemporary Readings* (New York and Toronto: Edwin Mellen, 1979), pp. 244–253; pp. 254–258. In "Patterson Brown on God's Will as the Criterion of Morality," Idziak, *Divine Command Morality,* pp. 259–268, I argued that most theologians see God as the ideal exemplar of *moral* standards, and do not adopt God's will as the criterion of rightness and goodness. I have changed my mind on these matters; I would now say that although mainstream thinkers often do seem to present God as the ideal embodiment of moral standards, they also see God as the one who establishes such standards through revelation or "natural law"; I still think it is less common to find that they accept God or God's will *as* the criterion, as Brown, Adams in "A Modified Theory," or Fackenheim would put it.

75. See for example, Thomas W. Ogletree, *The Use of the Bible in Christian Ethics* (Philadelphia: Fortress Press, 1983).

76. See Lovin and Reynolds, *Cosmogony and Ethical Order.*

77. For a clear example of this thinking applied to euthanasia, see Joseph V. Sullivan, "The Immorality of Euthanasia," in *Beneficent Euthanasia,* ed. Marvin Kohl (Buffalo, NY: Prometheus Books, 1975), pp. 12–33.

78. Geertz, "Ethos World View, and the Analysis of Sacred Symbols," pp. 130–131. Geertz seems to hold the view that moral convictions are matters of preference or taste. In

"Ethos," p. 131, he remarks that "In itself, either side, the normative or the metaphysical, is arbitrary, but taken together they form a gestalt with a particular kind of inevitability" which is socially useful. (Berger also seems to endorse this position—for example, p. 7, *Sacred Canopy*.) My view is that Geertz' skepticism may be unfounded; it clearly reflects in any case the period in which many philosophers, existentialists and others, held that there was no way to extract "ought" from "is": there was no way to reason from the way things are to the way they ought to be; moral principles are expressions of arbitrary emotions or preferences. See the discussion ahead in the text. For criticism of this view, see Gilbert Harman, *The Nature of Morality* (New York: Oxford, 1976); for a view of the history of "emotivism" or "subjectivism" see Alasdair MacIntyre, *After Virtue*.

79. See Jacob Neusner, *Way of Torah*, 2nd ed. (Belmont, CA: Wadsworth, 1979) pp. 64–65. Compare Eliezer Schweid, "The Authority Principle in Biblical Morality," *Journal of Religious Ethics*, 8 (Fall 1980), 180–203; see also other articles on Jewish law and ethics in this issue; also see Paul W. Gooch, "Authority and Justification in Theological Ethics; A Study in I Corinthians 7," *Journal of Religious Ethics, 11* (1983), 62–74.

80. See Adams, "A Modified Theory."

81. Adams, "Autonomy and Theological Ethics"; p. 194. Compare Adams, "Divine Command Metaethics Modified Again," *Journal of Religious Ethics*, 7 (Spring 1979), 66–79. Kai Nielsen in *Ethics Without God* (Buffalo: Prometheus Press, 1973) argues that since believers say that what God wills is morally good (or right), they are assuming that goodness means something else than willed by God; whether they mean that the concept of God includes goodness or that some particular being is characterized as good, they assume independent criteria of goodness; if morally good really meant willed by God, then to say God wills what is morally good would be to say, God wills what God wills. If believers respond by saying that rightness gets its meaning from God (the mainstream model), then Nielsen could restate his point: if the believer accepts God's meaning because of God's qualities, then the qualities are the believer's reasons and here the believer stands on the same ground as the unbeliever. On my view the mainstream model and Nielsen are not opposed on this point. For a discussion of what the believer could mean by saying God is good or does what is right, see Glenn Graber, "A Critical Bibliography of Recent Discussions of Religious Ethics by Philosophers," *Journal of Religious Ethics 2* (Fall 1974), 53–80, and Adams, "A Modified Theory." On Nielsen, compare Jeffrey Stout in *Ethics After Babel: The Languages of Morals and Their Discontents* (Boston: Beacon Press, forthcoming). For a discussion of the view that God is chosen as the omniscient "ideal observer", see David Ray Griffin, "The Holy, Necessary Goodness, and Morality," *Journal of Religious Ethics 8* (Fall 1980), 340–343.

82. According to some theorists, one "validates" rules and virtues by appealing to a basic principle or principles (along with factual premises); one "vindicates" the basic principles themselves. Little and Twiss for example—in *Comparative Religious Ethics*, p. 111 ff.—include under the category of vindication a variety of considerations ranging from the fact that oneself or others accept a principle to various beliefs about the nature of things. Vindicatory reasons are merely "suggestive," rather than "logically compelling." Some philosophers, for example Alan Gewirth in *Reason and Morality*, would not accept this characterization of the attempt to ground basic principles in human agency and the requirements of reason. For discussions of Little and Twiss' theory of moral reasoning, see Edmund Santurri, "The Comparative Study of Religious Ethics," *Religious Studies Review*, 6(October 1980), 296–301; and Jeffrey Stout, "Weber's Progeny, Once Removed," *Religious Studies Review*, 6(October 1980), 289–295.

83. See Richard Rorty, *The Consequences of Pragmatism* (Minneapolis: University of Minnesota, 1982). On religious ethics in particular, see Jeffrey Stout, *Flight from Authority* (Notre Dame: University of Notre Dame Press, 1981). Stout applies his views about moral beliefs to Little and Twiss, *Comparative Religious Ethics;* Green, *Religious Reason;* and Frankena, "Is Morality Logically Dependent on Religion?," in *Religion and Morality*, ed. Outka and Reeder, Jr., pp. 295–317. See also Stout's essay "Metaethics and the Death of Meaning: Adams and the Case of the Tantalizing Closing"—*Journal of Religious Ethics*, 6(Spring 1978), 1–18—which deals with Adam's "A Modified Divine Command Theory." Adams responded in "Divine Command Metaethics Modified Again," pp. 66–79. See Scott Davis, "Ethical Properties and Divine Commands," *Journal of Religious Ethics 11* (Fall 1983), 280–300. On Stout, see Edmund Santurri, "The Flight to Pragmatism," *Religious Studies Review 9* (October

1983), 330–339.

84. Gustafson, *Ethics from a Theocentric Perspective*, Vols. 1 and 2, passim.

85. See Mary Daly, *Beyond God the Father* (Boston: Beacon Press, 1973); McFague, *Metaphorical Theology*, chap. 5; and *Models of God: Theology for an Ecological Nuclear Age* (Phila.: Fortress Press, 1987). Rosemary Ruether, *Sexism and God-Talk* (Boston: Beacon Press, 1983); Dorothee Soelle, *Beyond Mere Obedience* (New York: Pilgrim Press, 1982). Trible in *God and the Rhetoric of Sexuality* shows that images drawn from women's experience are also used to characterize the deity in biblical sources.

86. See Beverly Harrison, *Our Right to Choose: Toward a New Ethic of Abortion* (Boston: Beacon Press, 1983), p. 112. Harrison argues that an awareness of the historically constructed character of moral meaning need not imply "subjectivism."

87. Note that this critique seems to cut only against the legislative model of divine creation. Perhaps some other model of creation which still traces morality to a transcendent being could be devised. Some feminist thinkers, however, have argued that any notion of creation posits an unwarranted gap between the "ground of being" and human reality; these thinkers propose that the human and transhuman are related in an organic whole. For another sort of criticism of traditional notions of the lordship or sovereignty of God based on an awareness of human responsibility in the nuclear age, see Gordon D. Kaufman, *Theology for a Nuclear Age* (Manchester: Manchester University Press; and Philadelphia: Westminster Press, 1985).

88. Compare Patrick Nowell-Smith, "Duty and God's Will," *Christian Ethics and Contemporary Philosophy*, ed. Ian T. Ramsey (New York: MacMillan, 1966), pp. 95–132.

II

Sanction

1. MORAL EVIL AND THE CONCEPT OF SANCTION

1.1 The origin of evil. As we have seen, religious stories often account for the source of a moral order. Religious traditions also often offer explanations of why human beings *violate* moral norms, why there is moral evil in the world. For example, as I noted in Chapter 1, some Western traditions seem to use the Genesis story to explain the human tendency to evil (as opposed to, or in addition to, being about humankind's entrance into the moral condition); the story is said to show how Adam and Eve go from moral goodness to moral evil. Out of greed or a prideful desire to escape the dependent position in which God had placed them, Adam and Eve as the ancestors of humankind turn from their morally perfect and happy state and violate their relation with God. As a consequence their condition is changed; in addition to being exposed to suffering and death, humankind will now tend to do what is evil. As the original human beings break their relation to God, subsequent generations break the ties that relate them to their neighbor. It is often said, however, that the Genesis story does not teach "original sin," the idea of inherited and inescapable evil, which figures significantly in some Christian traditions.[1] Nonetheless the story can be taken to signify a transition from moral innocence to a world where moral evil is potentially present and even likely; Adam's and Eve's disobedience is the paradigm of evil to come.[2]

Where the story is read as an account of the origin of evil, it may also be said that the norms subsequently laid down by the deity will take the dark side of human nature into account; the moral order created by the deity is designed, in part at least, to contain disobedience and selfishness.[3] But in addition Judaic and Christian traditions develop ideas about what happens when moral evil does break out. How is moral evil to be dealt with and what is the prognosis for human beings? Given that God has instituted a moral order, and that humans violate it, what happens at the human and the transhuman levels?[4]

1.2 *The concept of sanction.* I want to use the concept of sanction to cover several sorts of strategies for dealing with moral evil. But one has to be careful about the term *sanction,* for the concept can be given a number of meanings. According to John Ladd, the basic meaning of sanction is a "punishment due the violator of a law and administered by the authority originating the law";[5] in addition, many traditions add the idea of rewards for good conduct. This sense of sanction presupposes a legal system, but there is another broader meaning: any inducement to conform to a rule of conduct, which includes the sort of pressure we associate with morality itself. It is important to note that moral pressure is not entirely "internal," that is, proceeding from the conscience of the individual, but includes the "external" judgments of members of the community. Moral pressure we can understand, then, as the individual's own conviction and its correlative social reinforcement.[6] The crucial point is that legal sanctions originate in legal authority and consist in various harms or benefits, while moral ones comes from the individual and members of the social group and consist in appeals to a sense of right and wrong or a desire for social approval.[7]

The first element in the notion of sanction—rewards and punishments and other pressures—is portrayed in some religious traditions as a function of ultimate reality as well as the human community. The deity in many versions of Judaism and Christianity functions not only as a lawmaker but as a moral and legal judge, a superhuman agent who observes every action and thought. The deity, over and above any legal pressure applied by the community, is suppposed to be the ultimate force that rewards and punishes.[8]

I want to introduce a second element in the concept of sanction, the notion of restitution or redress. Just as legal sanctions, in addition to moral pressures, motivate conformity to basic social requirements, so we need moral and legal mechanisms to restore to the victims of wrongdoing what they have lost or to provide some sort of compensation. In many traditions this aspect of the notion of sanction is also entrusted to a transhuman agency. The biblical figure of Job seems to have expected the deity to restore, in a way that exceeded the power of the human community, what the poor have lost to the rapacious rich.

The third element I want to put into the concept of sanction is the overcoming of moral imperfection. In human society, we are conscious of instances in which we have not conformed to moral demands; many thinkers have noted a deep-seated tendency to seek our own good, which often conflicts with norms that require us to act on behalf of others as well as ourselves. Societies develop various mechanisms of forgiveness or reconciliation for the wrongdoer and, in addition, in some traditions one finds ideas about how antisocial tendencies—moral impurities—can be cleansed or removed from individuals or the society as a whole. The overcoming of moral imperfection, then, has two aspects: the alleviation of the guilt of offenders and the possibility of moral improvement or even perfection. This too, as we will see, is said to be accomplished not only by human beings but through some ultimate agent.

The purpose then of a system of rewards and punishments, a means of righting wrongs, and methods for overcoming moral evil is to close the gap between what the moral-legal order requires and how people actually behave. And as the mechanisms of law remedy the limitations of morality, for example, by adding enforcement, so the religious reality remedies the defects of human sanctions.[9] In addition to whatever human institutions can do, the religious reality acts to bring, as Geertz puts it, what *is* into conformity with what *ought* to be.[10] As Rudolf Otto would say, the Holy is the *guarantor* of morality;[11] in various ways, it brings moral striving to fruition.

2. REWARDS AND PUNISHMENTS

2.1 God as judge. In addition to the coercive measures or positive inducements offered by the political structures of a society, there is apparently a belief in many parts of the world that some being or force will give good experiences to those who are morally good and bad experiences to those who are morally bad. The idea is found, at least according to standard interpreters, in sources as diverse as biblical notions of divine judgment and the concept of *karma* in certain Asian traditions.[12] Again, I will not try to offer an historical interpretation, but let me refer to some passages from the book of *Job* which suggest ideas of rewards and punishments that have figured prominently in Judaic and Christian traditions.[13]

Job is an individual who seems to have obeyed God's commandments: He is happy in every respect. God has rewarded his virtue. But suddenly he is attacked by a series of misfortunes—illness, the death of children, loss of riches. Job believes he is innocent and is forced to doubt the justice of God. But several other figures (Eliphaz, Bildad, Zophar, and Elihu) try to convince him that the traditional doctrine—our main interest here—is true. Eliphaz remarks:

> Consider, what innocent ever perished,
> Or where have the righteous been destroyed?
> I have observed that they who plow evil
> And sow trouble reap the same. Job 4:7–8

Elihu also affirms God's perfect justice:

> So, you sensible men hear me,
> Far be it from God to do evil,
> From Shaddai [one of the names of the deity] to do
> wrong.
> Nay he pays a man for his work,
> Brings home a man's conduct to him.
> Surely God would not do evil,
> Nor Shaddai pervert justice. . . .
> He pays no respect to princes,
> Nor favors rich over poor. Job 34:10–12, 19a;
> compare 8:3–4

The prosperity of the wicked is only momentary:

> I have seen the fool strike root,
> Then his abode suddenly accursed,
> His children abandoned helpless,
> Crushed in the gate, defenseless.
> His harvest the hungry consume,
> Snatching it among the thorns,
> While the thirsty pant for their wealth. Job 5:3–5; compare
> 15:2–35; 20:5[14]

The punishment is delivered in illness, natural disaster, or harm at the hands of other humans, with death as the culmination:

> God puts me in custody of the vicious,
> Tosses me into the hand of the wicked. Job 16:11
> He [the person to be punished] is snatched from his
> comfortable tent
> And marched before the King of Terrors [the god of the
> dead] Job 18:14[15]

God operates therefore not only as a judge, ascertaining guilt or innocence and settling sentences, but also puts the sentences into effect; just rewards and punishments are as certain as the regularities of nature. God moreover is all-seeing:[16]

> For his eyes are on man's conduct,
> He sees his every step.
> There is no darkness, no shadow
> Where evil doers can hide.
>
> For he sets no man a date
> To come before God in judgment.
> He shatters the mighty without inquiry.
> Because he knows their deeds . . . Job 34:21–25

2.2 *Retributive justice.*   Now what idea are we dealing with? According to many interpreters, we seem to be dealing with the notion of retributive justice: Moral goodness should be rewarded and moral evil punished. Political authority, or by extension some transhuman agency, brings negative or positive experiences to individuals according to whether they have violated or upheld the moral order: According to the goodness (badness) of one's conduct and character, one has moral worth or merit (disvalue or demerit), which is sometimes thought of as something that admits of degrees or units and can be scored and recorded; according to merit or demerit, one is rewarded or punished. The model, in my terminology, is that of law, the legal-political administration of rewards and punishments. A mechanism of legal order has been added to the moral system.

Now it is important to distinguish retributive justice from another notion it may resemble in some contexts, the idea of distributive justice according to the criterion of merit. Distributive justice has to do with the allocation, the assignment, of the benefits and burdens of social existence. Should all members of a society have the same opportunities or the same income or wealth? If there are going to be inequalities, what is the standard according to which things are distributed? It has sometimes been suggested that the social pie (or elements thereof) should be distributed according to specific sorts of merit. One is said in a capitalistic competitive system to earn or deserve one's wealth, or to take another example, as Gene Outka notes, a criterion for the distribution of health care could be the merit of the recipients, in particular their own efforts to prevent disease.[17] But distributive justice, even where the criterion is merit, is not the same as retributive justice, administered by human or divine agencies. The reward one gets for moral goodness signifies an element of well-being or happiness over and above what one earns or deserves in the system of goods and services.

2.3 *Reasons for retributive justice.*   Now if we are dealing with the notion of retributive justice, what does it accomplish? What is its rationale?[18] It is often assumed that retributive justice is necessary for intrinsic moral reasons; it is simply right that evil be punished and virtue rewarded. Even if the wrong cannot be righted, the wrongdoer must be "brought to justice," the debt paid, some harm inflicted to balance the evil done. And the righteous deserve a special increment of happiness or well-being. It may also be argued that rewards and punishments serve to deter moral wrongdoing: Negative and positive inducements furnish extrinsic motivations that stop or at least reduce evil.[19] It may also be thought that punishments serve a rehabilitative or disciplinary function; they do not merely deter, they effect a change in the wrongdoer's character. Sometimes one finds the idea that suffering is not inflicted because of past wrongdoing, but as a kind of training to ward off future evil.

2.4   Dramas of retribution: Who, how, what, where, when, to whom.   How exactly is retribution accomplished? In *Job,* the deity is (or is supposed to be) the administrating agent; the deity strikes through natural or human causes;[20] various forms of suffering ensue; the retribution takes place in earthly life, although not immediately (sometimes it takes a while to start, like a faulty electric motor!); it falls on individuals and households. In forms of Judaism and Christianity which developed out of biblical materials such as *Job,* the earthly context for retribution is often retained but the scene of the drama is extended to the afterlife or the end of history. The medieval Judaic thinker Saadya Gaon expressed these thoughts about this life and the "Future World":

> Our Lord (be He exalted and glorified) has informed us that acts of obedience to God, if repeatedly performed by men, are termed merits, and acts of disobedience, if repeatedly performed, are called demerits; moreover, that He preserves the record of every deed of every one of his servants . . . God in His wisdom has decided that He should requite His servants in this world only for that class of deeds (good or evil) which are in the minority in order that there may remain for the Future World the class of deeds which are in the majority. . . . since He is the God of Justice, it follows that He must have prepared for both [wrong-doer and wronged] a second place where He will judge between them in equity, and mete out reward to the one according to the pain he suffered at the hands of the wrong-doer, and bring punishment upon the other according to the pleasure which . . . he derived from his wrongdoings and evil acts.[21]

Thus for Saadya when those who are good on the whole suffer in this world, they are getting what they deserve for the minority of their deeds which were bad. When those who are on the whole bad flourish in this world, they are getting what they deserve for the minority of their deeds which were good. Rewards and punishments for the majority of one's deeds must wait until the next world.

It is interesting to note that even more weight is assigned to the afterlife in other versions of the traditions. Sometimes it is said that earthly suffering is not deserved, even for a minority of deeds, and indeed this was Job's complaint; he did not deserve to suffer at all. Job did not think that the afterlife was a place where rewards and punishments occur, but in some traditions rewards and punishments are entirely delayed until then; even if the righteous and the wicked do not get anything of what they deserve on earth, accounts will be settled in the afterlife.

Of course, if God permits the righteous to suffer and the wicked to flourish now, there must be some reason for the delay. Some believers have suggested, for example, that natural and moral evil are a price which has to be paid if humans are to grow into the sorts of beings who can enjoy eternal fellowship with God; our very nature as finite creatures designed for an eternal destiny means that we may be exposed to natural evil, and if we are free to respond to God, we are free to do evil to one another.[22]

But others, like Father Paneloux in Camus' novel *The Plague,* have not been able to find a reason. Like Job, Father Paneloux first believed that, "The just man need have no fear." Only the guilty, those who deserve punishment, die in the plague (which symbolizes not only natural but moral evil, such as the Nazis). Eventually he changes his mind, for those who are entirely innocent suffer, and he claims that the death of a child "passes our human understanding." Dr. Rieux, the unbeliever, may also believe that the good should be rewarded and the evil punished (he certainly believes that no one should suffer as the victims of the plague do), but for him there is no afterlife and no deity who has reasons for the delay or who will settle accounts; the universe does not conform to the moral demand.[23]

The believer, however, holds fast. There are reasons for the delay, even if they pass human understanding, and in the end all will be well. If there has been undeserved suffering at the hands of nature, for example, Camus' child with the plague, then that suffering will be made good in the final relation with God. If there has been suffering at the hands of the wicked, for example, the victims of the Nazis, then that suffering will be redressed. As I will now try to show, the traditions have often stressed, independent of rewards and punishments, the notion of divine redress or restitution.

3. RESTITUTION

3.1 *Wrong redressed.* There is an idea perhaps suggested in *Job* which also surfaces in other texts and traditions: The wrong humans do to one another will be undone, the harm redressed. In the passage just quoted, Saadya takes the pain one has wrongly suffered as the measure for one's reward; this seems to blend the idea of compensation into the idea of reward. But the two notions are distinct; it is one thing to be rewarded for good conduct, another to be compensated for suffering wrongly undergone. Thus the individuals who engage in a dialogue with Job seem to believe that the deity not only uses a system of rewards and punishments, but acts to right wrongdoing. If the rich and powerful take advantage of the poor, then God takes what the oppressor has and returns it to the oppressed. Not only are the wicked doomed to suffer, but violations of the moral order will be redressed:

> His [the wicked's] children must redress the poor,
> His hands give back his wealth. Job 20:10

> The riches he gorged he vomits
> God expels them from his gut. Job 20:15

> Though he heap silver like dust,
> And lay up stacks of raiment,
> What he stored the righteous will wear,
> The innocent will divide the silver. Job 27:16–17

Eliphaz makes clear that God protects those liable to be oppressed because they are weak. God

> ... exalts the lowly on high,
> Lifts the forlorn to safety.
> He thwarts the plots of the crafty,
> So their hands attain no gain. Job 5:11–12

> Thus he saves the simple from the sword,
> The poor from the clutch of the strong,
> So that the humble have hope,
> And evil's mouth is stopped. Job 5:15–16

Elihu also says that God will not only not keep the wicked alive, he will give "justice to the oppressed" (Job 36:6). What the worldview of the comforters and Elihu affirms, therefore, is that despite Job's conclusion to the contrary,

> Earth is [not] given to the control of the wicked. Job 9:24a

3.2 *Wrong at the hands of human beings.*   Now what is the basic idea here? Suffering at the hands of wicked people could be regarded as punishment, and Job, as we know, complains that the wrong person is getting punished. But in the book of *Job* another idea seems to appear (or at least it appears in traditions built on *Job*): Some suffering at the hands of wicked people is not punishment at all. If the system of punishment goes awry, then the deity, or whatever force is allocating rewards and punishments, is accused of retributive injustice, but where the suffering is not seen as punishment at all, then the problem is different. Some people are denying others what they are due, what they are owed, according to the principles that structure the social fabric—basic prohibitions against injury, for example, or principles of distributive justice that govern the allocation of benefits and burdens.[24] The blame falls in the first instance on the human perpetrators: They are responsible for what they commit. If the deity is also blamed, then the complaint is that this being *allows* the wrong in the first place or does not *redress* it when it occurs.[25] If God allows the wicked to hurt others, then not only must the wicked be punished, but the innocent must be recompensed. Job does not merely protest that the wicked are allowed to go on being wicked but that God does not care:

> The wicked remove landmarks;
> They seize flock and shepherd.
> Orphans' asses they drive away;
> They take the widow's ox for a pledge.
> They push the needy from the path;
> The poor of the earth are driven into hiding ...
> Naked they go without clothing,
> Hungry, they carry the sheaves.
> Between the millstones they press oil,
> The presses they tread, but thirst.
> From the city the dying groan,
> The throats of the wounded cry;
> Yet God thinks nothing amiss. Job 24:2–4, 10–12

3.3 *Restoration or compensation.* In sum, then, suffering can be seen as a violation of the moral order, not because it is a wrongful punishment, but because it violates norms against injury or distributive justice or in some other way deprives the individual of his or her due. Aside from the proper allocation of rewards and punishments, a moral system protects and promotes our well-being through various norms; the particular moralities in which we live specify what is due or owed. When people are wronged relative to what they are owed according to a moral system, then the question of restitution or redress arises; restoration regains the status quo ante; compensation aims to provide something of equivalent value if what is lost cannot be replaced.

And in the religious traditions, these themes can be independent of what is taught about rewards and punishments. Some thinkers, for example, have not held that rewards and punishments were required at least for intrinsic moral reasons; goodness is its own reward (this is different from saying, as some Protestants have, that no one deserves God's favor;

that just means no one is good enough—at least on their own—to merit a reward). Whatever is believed about rewards and punishments, we can expect to find some account of how the oppressed can and will be delivered.

3.4 Dramas of restitution. Thus where there is suffering at the hands of morally evil people, and it is not seen as punishment, societies often develop methods of restoration or compensation. There are usually moral and legal rules (with penalties for noncompliance) to the effect that if X does A to Y, then X should make restoration or compensation to Y by doing B. The human community can make some headway at restoration or compensation, but its efforts sometimes fail or are incommensurate; a murder victim cannot be brought back to life, and is any amount of money compensation? The belief of Job's comforters is that the deity will intervene to crush human evil and restore what is right. Ultimate reality or its instrumentalities will right moral wrongs.[26]

It seems that in the book of *Job,* if there was to be compensation or restoration, it had to be in this life. In Sheol, the afterlife, just as there were no rewards and punishments, so there is no opportunity for righting wrongs. But in many strands of the traditions, just as rewards and punishments are postponed, so the process of restoration and compensation can be located in some other mode of existence. Nonetheless that God acts to free the oppressed and to aid the poor now, within history, has been an important theme for many Jews and Christians.[27] Here is how Cornel West puts it:

> The African slaves' search for identity could find historical purpose in the exodus of Israel out of slavery and personal meaning in the bold identification of Jesus Christ with the lowly and downtrodden. Christianity also is first and foremost a theodicy, a triumphant account of good over evil. The intellectual life of the African slaves in the United States—like that of all oppressed peoples—consisted primarily of reckoning with the dominant form of evil in their lives. The Christian emphasis on against-the-evidence hope for triumph over evil struck deep among many of them.
> By trying to understand the plight of black people in the light of the Bible, black theologians claim to preserve the biblical truth that God sides with the oppressed and acts on their behalf.[28]

4. GUILT AND MORAL PERFECTION

4.1 Guilt and goodness. Traditions based on biblical sources such as *Job,* then, often provide for rewards and punishments and for the redress of violations. They may also have mechanisms for overcoming the evil of the past and eliminating future evil; they may hope for a time when rewards and punishments and redress will not be necessary. Two related ideas are suggested, it seems to me, in more than one tradition.

First, the notion that moral guilt can be erased and second, that moral growth or even perfection can be achieved.

We are familiar with ideas about the removal of guilt and the growth of goodness in Western traditions. In *Job*, for example, one also seems to find, in addition to enforcement and restoration, a notion of how the guilt of the individual can be erased. Elihu presents his belief in the possibility of a guardian angel who would not only intervene before the divine Judge on Job's behalf but would provide a "ransom," some sort of payment or restitution:

> One may be chastened on a bed of pain . . .
> His soul draws near the Pit,
> His life to waters of Death.
> Unless he have by him an angel,
> A spokesman, one out of the thousand,
> To tell of the man's uprightness,
> To have pity on him and say,
> "Spare him from going down to the Pit,
> I have found him a ransom."
> His flesh becomes plump as a boy's,
> He returns to the days of his youth.
> He prays to God and he accepts him,
> He sees his face with joy.
> He announces to men his salvation,
> He sings before men and says,
> "I sinned and perverted the right,
> Yet, he did not fully requite me.
> He saved my soul from the pit
> And my life sees the light." Job 33:19, 22–28

Elihu's vision, however, is not of a permanent state of affairs:

> All these things God does,
> Twice or thrice over with a man,
> To turn back his soul from the Pit,
> To light him with light of life. Job 33:29–30

What is absent in the book of *Job*, so far as I can tell, is the notion that humans can and will improve, that a time will come when there would be no more wrongdoing, when there would be no need for a ransom. In some other parts of the religion of ancient Israel and later in Judaism and Christianity, the hope is expressed for a Kingdom of God, a time of moral perfection.[29]

4.2 Legal guilt. Let's look at these ideas more closely to see what some interpretations might mean.

First of all there is the removal of guilt in a legal sense. To be guilty is to have the *status* of a wrongdoer, someone who deserves punishment; having guilt can be linked, as we have seen, to the notion of demerit, a bad moral-legal score; one is an offender legally speaking for one's offense is linked to punishment. Now one may erase guilt and demerit in various ways. One way is to pay the penalty, to expiate the crime. Another way is to have someone else pay the penalty either directly by standing in for the guilty party or indirectly by making some form of payment. In *A Tale of Two Cities,* Sidney Carton is beheaded in place of someone else; the guardian angel in *Job* pays a "ransom." Still another way is to have merit transferred to one's account or to be pardoned, to have the sentence waived. In either case the demerit, and hence the deserved punishment, is canceled.

4.3 Moral guilt.   Moral guilt is more complicated. There is first of all something parallel to legal guilt and how it is removed. In a sense, if I do something wrong, I did it, and nothing can change that. But there is the notion of forgiveness, which has a long and important history in Western traditions. Under certain conditions, for example, our repentance, people decide not to see us as offenders, to overlook our wrongdoing, to put it aside in their relationship to us, in ways of feeling and acting toward us. And it even may be that it makes sense to speak of us forgiving ourselves. In these notions of forgiveness there is a parallel on the moral level to the legal remissions I just sketched.[30] The moral *status* of the parties prior to the wrongdoing is regained. But there is also moral guilt in a psychological sense. Even if I forgive myself as others do, I may still *feel* guilty, as the expression goes; how can I be healed, stop my self-torture? If the victims and the wrongdoers have been reconciled, then both parties can perhaps "forget" as well as forgive. They don't literally forget, of course, for remembering can be a way of being morally stronger. But as the victims try to heal, so the wrongdoers try to get rid of debilitating forms of guilt.

4.4 Justice and mercy.   In Judaic and Christian traditions God is said to pardon and forgive. God through certain modes of "atonement" is prepared to erase legal guilt and to forgive.

Sometimes it is said that one is guilty, but one may receive mercy; the *sentence* itself stands, but God suspends or reduces the penalty.[31] God is not only prepared to forego resentment and to reestablish the moral status quo ante, the deity as legal sovereign will mercifully remit the punishment people deserve. But how can God be both just and merciful? If justice requires that one get the punishment one deserves, then isn't God unjust if the guilty go unpunished? Philip Quinn suggests that this classical problem can be handled in two ways. One could say that to be just is to give people what they deserve, and that if people repent or meet other conditions then they deserve mercy. God

> ... mercifully spares all and only those sinners who repent. Because their merited punishment deserves to be remitted, he gives them what they deserve and so acts justly in exercising his mercy towards them. He punishes all and only those sinners who do not repent.[32]

One could say alternatively, and this is more in the mainstream according to Quinn, that even if everyone deserves punishment, and no one *deserves* mercy even if they repent, God's remission of some and not of others would still be just:

> ... if God is perfectly just, he exercises mercy towards all and only those sinners who are such that he has reasons for remitting their deserved punishments, and he does not exercise mercy towards those sinners who are such that he has no reason for remitting their deserved punishment, but punishes them instead. If God acted in this way, he would not act unfairly.[33]

Thus God treats the sinners graciously, better than deserved, but grace is not unfair or unjust for there are *reasons* for God's selection of those to have mercy on, reasons such as their repentance.[34]

Thus in these two ways justice is "reconciled" with mercy. Deep convictions about the nature of justice are behind these solutions; both in effect propose that justice is something more than the strict allocation of rewards and punishments.[35] Either mercy is deserved and thus part of justice, or justice encompasses more than merely what is deserved. It does seem less traditional to say that mercy is deserved, but what of the idea that justice is broader than desert? This strategy seems to set up a conflict between two kinds of justice—desert and reasons for having mercy.

Indeed an even more traditional way of putting the problem is in terms of a conflict between two different sorts of moral considerations: What justice demands (by way of punishment) is one thing, mercy another. On this account, the issue is whether mercy may or should *override* justice; even if God has reasons for having mercy on some and not others, these are not reasons that make the decision just, but reasons (perhaps not understandable for humans) for mercy *supplanting* justice.

4.5 *Moral growth and moral perfection.* Restoring the status quo ante through the removal of legal and moral guilt is the first step to moral goodness. But it obviously does not reach the roots of evil in the individual or the group. What prospects are there for moral improvement? Can the individual or group become disposed to do what is right instead of what is wrong? What is envisaged in many traditions is a process of moral growth. Sometimes this is pictured as happening to individuals, sometimes there is hope for a general process of growth or even a time of perfection for the group as a whole or even for all humankind. Moral perfection can be taken as final destiny or, as we will see in Chapter 3, as a stage prior to a transmoral goal.

What would it mean not merely to become better persons but to reach moral perfection? In the most basic sense, of course, moral perfection might mean simply conforming completely to a pattern of principles and virtues; the desire to conform to what is morally required is strong enough to overcome any contrary desires. But in the religious traditions moral perfection often has two other senses that take one beyond the traditional moral paradigm, even perfectly adhered to: first, the idea that morally perfect individuals would act differently and have qualities of character that were different but better than what is ordinarily required; second, the idea that the morally perfect person does not even need to be motivated by moral requirement anymore.

The first additional sense of moral perfection—norms for conduct and character that are different but better than what are ordinarily required—is sometimes imaged in Western traditions, for example, in terms of a contrast between "justice" and "love." "Justice" signifies a mode of moral relations where each person can claim from others his or her due (based on self-interest, or perhaps the requirements of reason, or even on a common good of community). "Justice" in this sense does not refer merely to distributive, restitutive, or retributive justice, but signifies a mode of moral relations which encompasses all areas of the moral life. Each person can make claims on others based on a commonly acknowledged system of duties and, in some traditions, rights. An ethic of "justice" often borrows the vocabulary of justice in the narrower sense and speaks of what is owed or due. "Love," in contrast, signifies a way of relating that expresses a concern or love for others which renders claims, duties, what is owed or due, and rights unnecessary. The settlers on Ursula LeGuin's utopian planet Anarres in her novel *The Dispossessed,* for example, live according to an ethic of mutual concern. They are concerned for their neighbor, as well as for themselves, and they trust their neighbor to be concerned for them. While there are limits on what they can sacrifice for others (given scarce resources), they give generously because they believe that their well-being is safe in the hands of their neighbor.[36] They do not have to employ a system of duties or rights.

The world of "justice" then is a world of duties or rights in which sometimes hostile individuals make claims on one another; the world of mutual love is a world where personal security and sexual-familial, economic, and political relations rest on shared concern. The world of "justice" is also often said to require certain sorts of institutions, such as, monogamous marriage, private property, and a coercive state and legal apparatus. While it is conceivable that the use of violence would not be necessary to ensure what people are due, in the world as we know it the structure of duties or rights is to be protected by the arm of the state. But legal-political enforcement could drop away in the new community of "love."[37] In a community of love, such as Anarres, new forms of sexual relations, new modes of relating to various goods on which well-being depends, and new devices for organizing cooperation and decision making are created. Some visions of moral perfection also see aspects of the human condition such as sexuality itself disappearing, and hence any need for moral regulation, much less conventional structures of marriage. But as I will note in Chapter 3, the transformation of the biological condition is often part of a transmoral state.

Note that "love" in this sense does not neglect justice in the sense of fairness or call for the complete sacrifice of one's own good.[38] On Anarres people seek their own personal good, as well the good of others, and this is legitimate; they are genuinely concerned for others, but their action on behalf of others is limited because of scarcity and a justified concern for themselves. Thus what Chaim Reines says is at the heart of Rabbinic ethics is true of the ethic of Anarres, for it combines both love and respect; love your neighbor *as yourself* signifies that concern for self as well as for others is approved; one loves one's neighbor fairly, that is, with equal respect for the needs of each, and one recognizes one's own needs as legitimate.[39] While one's help is restricted by a legitimate awareness of the needs of the self, one still relates to others without relying on notions of what is due, owed, or claimed between individuals; in this sense, the ethic is a morality of "love" over against "justice", but respect for all, including the self, is assumed. There is even room for acts of supererogation where one chooses to give unrestrictedly, ignoring the legitimate limits of aid to others, but the structure of the ethic includes the good of all, including the self.[40]

What has happened is that love of neighbor is now envisaged as operating directly without a structure of specific duties or rights; in this sense Anarres would be characterized as a morality of love in contrast to a morality of "justice"; "love" includes the flourishing of self and others; "love" transcends and fulfills "justice" because it accomplishes the goals of "justice" without the conflicts between self and others which an ethic of rights or duties preserves.[41]

Where a morality of "love" is sought, the transition from a morality of justice is often said to be accomplished by a change in the individual's relation to God; as the believer comes to trust that his or her basic well-being is secure in the deity, then the individual can transcend a morality that guards the good of each from the deprivations of others; individuals do not have to rely on a morality of rightful claims, for their good rests in God; they are free to love others.[42] This transition begins imperfectly— trust in God is not complete—but in a glorious future it reaches perfection.

In some Christian traditions, however, a further step is taken. In anticipation of the Kingdom to come where even scarcity is overcome and one would not need to put limits on love for others, believers begin even in this world to practice unrestricted benevolence. Not all Christians by any means have held that this was their task on earth, and it seems to be rejected in major strands of Judaic tradition at least for life in this world.[43] Even as a way of life on earth, it would seem to require a principle of distribution *among* neighbors (what do I give to whom?). And some recipients are going to have to *keep* their gifts and not give them back. Concerning the famous passage in a legal commentary which concerns two men on a journey, one of whom has water sufficient for himself, but not enough to share with the other, Louis Jacobs remarks that if the one with the water ought to hand it over to the neighbor, then the neighbor would also be expected to hand it back.[44] Thus a principle according to which some could accept the sacrifice of others would have to be adopted in order to stop an infinite regress of self-giving.[45]

But the important point is that those who have tried to practice unrestricted benevolence on earth have had special reasons for doing so; as we will see ahead, they have conceived of the drama of God's victory over evil and their own role in a special way. And in addition one must realize that this ethic, even though it calls for earthly self-sacrifice, does not reject the concern for the self as illegitimate; it believes the good of the self is eternally secure and preserves therefore the good of the self as well as the good of the neighbor.[46] The issue is not whether concern for others should or should not lead to total disregard for the self, but whether to disregard the earthly well-being of the self.

The second additional sense of moral perfection has to do not with moving from "justice" to "love", but with how our moral striving is related to the rest of our makeup. If we are morally perfect, it is often assumed, our desire to conform to morality is always *dominant*. We have a dominant desire to conform to a morally required pattern of conduct and character, whether that be couched as "love" or "justice." The settlers on LeGuin's Anarres love, that is, they desire the well-being of their neighbor as well as their own; but they also seem to desire to love because that is the morally best way of life; they are motivated by a desire to embody the moral ideal.

But moral perfection could also mean that we do not need to have a *desire* to conform to moral requirement. Our character and conduct would embody the moral demand without our desiring to embody it because it is morally required; this is what is sometimes called "spontaneous goodness."[47] When there is no remaining opposition between desiring the moral ideal and other desires, the desire to conform to the ideal can drop away.[48] The job of moral requirement, as we remember, was to establish bonds of social unity in our hierarchy of desires, but if the tension with other desires is removed, then we would not need to think of ourselves as moved by the desire to embody the ideal. In this second sense, then, we would be morally perfect when we no longer have to think of ourselves as constrained by moral motivation. We desire the substance of a moral paradigm, without desiring it because it is the moral paradigm. We know the moral ideal, but we do not need the desire to seek it as such.[49]

Gershom Scholem, for example, notes that in classic Judaic conceptions of the Messianic age the "understanding and the fulfillment of the Torah (the revealed will of the deity for the fabric of human life) will . . . be infinitely richer than they are now (under the present conditions of history)." But he also identifies another conception:

> The greater the assumption of changes in nature of revolutions in man's moral character—which latter were determined by the extinction of the destructive power of the evil inclination in the Messianic age—the greater did the modification also have to become which under such circumstances affected the operation of the law. A positive commandment or prohibition could scarcely be the same when it no longer has for its object the separation of good and evil to which man was called, but rather arose from the Messianic spontaneity of human freedom purely flowing forth. Since by its nature this freedom realizes only the good, it has no real need for all those "fences" and restrictions with which the *Halakhah* [the moral-legal order] was surrounded in order to secure it from the temptations of evil.[50]

Scholem *may* intend to suggest not only the end of "fences" (additional regulations) around the core of the law, but of moral and legal motivation; people would no longer need to be motivated to do the sorts of things they ought do or be the sorts of persons they ought to be because they are required to, but they would desire the *substance* of *halakhah* spontaneously.[51]

Now to talk of perfect moral goodness either as dominant desire to conform to the moral ideal or as spontaneous goodness is not necessarily to picture a state that stands apart from the rest of our desires as such. Some Western thinkers, particularly those in the tradition of the philosopher Kant, do see moral goodness as something generically different from something imposed on, our natural inclinations or desires.[52] But other thinkers and communities have thought of moral goodness as patterns of conduct and character that are in accord with our deepest desires or inclinations; we can be led astray, however, because we do not grasp our true good; a lesser or false good diverts us and we will experience a conflict of desires; moral duty will appear as a demand, as a motivational constraint, just as on the Kantian model. On this view, however, moral goodness corresponds to a desire to reach our deepest fulfillment, a desire to flourish in a distinctively human way. This, shall we say, is an Aristotelian model of moral goodness, although I don't think it is limited to Western traditions.[53]

Moral perfection, then, assumes that we remain moral beings—our thoughts, desires, and emotions must be socially ordered—but we somehow have overcome obstacles to moral goodness.[54] Moral perfection can take several forms. The standard paradigm of ordinary requirement and a dominant desire to conform to moral requirement can be modified by changing our conception of the ideal and how it is motivated. Here is a diagram of the possibilities:

1. Ordinary requirement ("justice"), and dominant motive to conform to moral requirment
2. Ordinary requirement ("justice"), and spontaneous goodness
3. Extraordinary requirement ("love"), and dominant motive to conform to moral requirement
4. Extraordinary requirement ("love"), and spontaneous goodness

As I use the expression, moral perfection can refer to any of these four states. The settlers on Le Guin's Anarres seem to reach level 3, but some Judaic and Christian visionaries have hoped for level 4.

4.6 *Dramas of the victory of good over evil.* What role can some representation of ultimate reality play in the removal of guilt and the achievement of moral growth or perfection? First, as we have seen, the deity may be pictured as a legal sovereign who has the authority to remit punishment or remove legal guilt. Second, if an ultimate agency is seen in personal terms, then it would make sense to talk, say, of a deity's forgiveness; where there are moral relations to a deity, one can violate them and need forgiveness.[55] In Judaic and Christian traditions it is often said that one owes obedience to the deity and the deity requires conformity to the moral order between humans; since a violation of an interhuman duty is also a violation of one's duty to God, one needs forgiveness from the deity. And the deity, in contrast to the imperfect forgiveness of humans, offers the hope of complete reconciliation.[56] On the condition of repentance, God will forgive the guilt of the past.[57] In addition, the deity could have some effect on the burdens of psychological guilt; the relation to the deity could be interpreted as a kind of therapy. The deity's love, it is commonly said, is sufficiently powerful to aid those tortured by guilt.

And there are a variety of ways in which the deity could engender or help to engender moral goodness; trust in God enables love to grow or, as some Christian traditions claim, God engenders goodness through the "Spirit" or "grace." "Justice" is possible for sinful beings but through the experience of divine love the believer comes to trust God and can reach the level of "love." Thus the hoped for transformation can encompass both the *what* and the *how*. It can encompass a new level of conduct and character and a transformation of motivation such that the desire for goodness is dominant or the sense of moral demand or requirement drops away.

My historical assumption, then, is that some Judaic and Christian traditions have seen the new mode of being as a state of moral perfection (fully achieved in history, at the end of history, or after death).[58] Some have focused instead on a transmoral goal as we will see in Chapter 3. Mainstream traditions, I believe, have often combined the two: an eschatological vision can project a time of moral perfection *followed by* a transmoral state or simply mingle the two in a complex set of symbols.[59] More on these possibilities in Chapter 3, but for now let us concentrate on hopes for some form of moral perfection.

The religious communities have seen themselves in various sorts of relation to such a hope. Some have believed that their task was not to achieve the new world—the deity would have to do that—but to realize it partially or anticipate it in their own communal relationships and hence to witness to others. To realize the Kingdom, for example, would be to renounce violence now; to anticipate it would be to continue to have private property, although this will not be a feature of the Kingdom, and to adopt a strenuous ethic of sharing which expresses the believer's commitment to the good of all.

To renounce violence, however, is not necessarily to withdraw from social structures into a segregated community. For example, John Yoder, a contemporary Mennonite theologian, emphatically rejects the notion that as a representative of the "radical Reformation" he advocates a "withdrawal" from society or a "sectarian" form of Christianity.[60] For Yoder, the Christian community is in the world, though not of it; it becomes "an instrument for serving and saving the larger culture"; only occasionally is there a "radical opposition."[61] To refuse to accept political structures that require the use of violence (coercion and injury) is not to withdraw from the world but to live in terms of a nonviolent ethic and to try to transform the world accordingly: "Even before the broken world can be made whole by the Second Coming, the witnesses to the first coming are enabled to go on proleptically in the redemption of creation . . . The believing community as an empirical social entity is a power for change."[62]

It seems clear that Yoder does not expect gradual progress until there is no need for the coercive state; it is finally God who will bring the Second Coming. In the interim: "The alternative community discharges a modeling mission. The church is called to be now what the world is called to be ultimately."[63] Although "to renounce violence is [not] to renounce power" itself—the church can play a limited role in social struggles—what is renounced is coercion and injury by the state, the power of the *Sword*.[64] Thus the "church can be a foretaste of the peace for which the world was made . . . Although immersed in this world, the church by her way of being represents the promise of another world, which is not somewhere else but is to come here."[65] The believing community can make a difference in the world but its task is not to work for gradual progress; rather it is to embody so far as possible the new moral order in itself, to realize it in the partial way that is possible before the final consummation.

Others have thought that the believing community has to participate in the "fallen" moral order, such as, the use of political force, while at the same time preserving the moral ideal in some way. This statement from Irenaeus, for example, illustrates the view of God's will that Yoder opposes:

> For since man, by departing from God, reached such a pitch of fury as even to look upon his brother as his enemy, and engaged without fear in every kind of restless conduct, and murder, and avarice; God imposed upon mankind the fear of man, as they did not acknowledge the fear of God, in order that, being subjected to the authority of men, and kept under restraint by their laws, they might attain to some degree of justice, and exercise mutual forbearance through dread of the sword suspended full in their view, as the apostle says: "For he beareth not the sword in vain; for he is the minister of God, the avenger for the wrath upon him who does evil." . . . Earthly rule, therefore, has been appointed by God for the benefit of nations, and not by the devil, who is never at rest at all, nay, who does not love to see even nations conducting themselves after a quiet manner, so that under the fear of human rule, men may not eat each other up like fishes; but that, by means of the establishment of laws, they may keep down an excess of wickedness among the nations.[66]

Various forms of integration and adjustment between "justice" and "love," therefore, have been worked out. In some Christian traditions, for example, one finds the life of "love" allocated to special groups of believers, or to personal relations especially within the believing community. It can also be interpreted as an ideal toward which one moves. The believer may hope for real progress before the final consummation; the full Kingdom comes only at the end of history but real progress can be made now. Some believers at least should participate in the use of force so long as necessary, while struggling for social change so that revolution and war will no longer be needed. Even if believers use the Sword now, at some point within history violence also can be put aside; the ultimate transformation is still in God's hands but history can move closer to the moral ideal.[67] One of the principal authors of contemporary Roman Catholic "liberation theology," Gustavo Gutierrez, illustrates this pattern, although he may hold that the final destiny of humankind is transmoral (see Chapter 3).[68] And one also finds the hope for this-worldly progess in the writings of certain contemporary feminist theologians, although here violence is often ruled out as a method of social change.[69]

Still others have thought that the new world remains only a transcendent possibility, and that the task for human beings is to fashion the world of "justice," the world of institutions such as private property and marriage and the coercive state, in accordance with the will of the deity.[70] Jacob Neusner puts the point of view of the Mishnah, the earliest stratum of the Talmudic tradition, as follows:

> It is, finally, a statement of affirmation of this world, of the realm of society, state, and commerce, and at the same time a vigorous denial that how things are is how things should be or will be. For the Mishnaic system speaks of the building of a state, government, and civil and criminal system, of the conduct of transactions of property, commerce, trade, of forming the economic unit of a family through transfer of women and property and the ending of such a family-economic unit, and similar matters, touching all manner of dull details of ordinary and everyday life.[71]

The world can be improved (things are not as they should be), but it is not going to be replaced by a radically new order. This is not merely the recognition that some aspects of the human condition are not going away—sexuality, needs for food, clothing, and shelter—but a vision of an ongoing need for moral and legal requirement and for claims, duties, or rights, and specific concepts such as property. The Mishnaic impulse as Neusner depicts it has, I believe, profound resonances in Christian traditions. For Reinhold Niebuhr, for example, believers have a responsibility for the structures that preserve peace, equality, and liberty among self-interested individuals and groups.[72] Hope for the Kingdom of God stimulates greater efforts for "justice" but it exists only as an ideal "beyond history."[73] Because one loves one's neighbor one works for "justice", but it is a mistake to look for progress in history leading to Anarres.

5. CRITICAL DISCUSSION

5.1 The guarantor of morality. There are then a variety of ideas in Judaic and Christian traditions about retribution, restoration/compensation, and guilt/regeneration. Challenges abound. Can the suffering of the Holocaust be accepted as divine punishment or, as Richard Rubenstein believes, is it decisive *evidence* against the hypothesis that God rewards and punishes, or even exists? Is the notion that the root of moral evil is rebellion or self-assertion against the Sovereign a reflection of male experience, whereas women oppressed by patriarchy tend not to affirm the self sufficiently?[74]

Bracketing the question whether divine rewards and punishments and a patriarchal-legal conception of evil should be rejected, there is a traditional theme we should consider.

In Chapter 1 I discussed the idea that ultimate reality was the source of the moral order and observed that many believers hold that this is the only adequate explanation and justification of the moral demand. There is an analogous claim about the idea of sanction. The basic idea is that it is necessary to believe in God (or some similar conception of ultimate reality) as the "guarantor" of the moral order. Hermann Cohen, a nineteenth-century Judaic thinker, put it this way:

> ... the God of Judaism is the God of morality. That means that His significance lies wholly in His disclosure as well as His guarantee of ethics. He is the Author and the Guarantor of the moral universe.[75]

> ... when I live in accordance with moral concepts, I am no animal, but a member of the moral universe. It is, however, only the idea of God which gives me the confidence that morality will become reality on earth. And because I cannot live without this confidence, I cannot live without God.[76]

I want to treat two ways in which this general theme has been developed. First, there is the claim that without a consciousness of one's relation to God, the machinery of morality just will not work; belief in God is necessary in order to provide or strengthen the *motivations* that make morality function. If we are to have our morality, then, we must believe in God (or some similar force). Second, it is argued that morality demands complete realization, achievement in ideal form; we cannot undertake the moral enterprise—we cannot form moral *intentions*—unless we can hope for the perfect allocation of rewards and punishment, the righting of all wrongs, and the complete removal of guilt and the achievement of moral perfection. And if human experience does not provide the possibility of this outcome, then to retain moral intentions we must be able to hope for, that is, believe in the possibility of, some transhuman realization.[77]

Let us take up these two types of claims in turn.

5.2 *Making morality work.* The first sort of argument—an argument about reasons and motivations—can concern rewards and punishments, redress, or forgiveness and goodness.

First, beyond the power of governments, human beings need to *fear* the retribution of the gods; otherwise, it is said, they will not adhere sufficiently (assuming this could be specified) to what is right; their desire to do what is right for its own sake is weak. In addition, they need *positive inducements*. Religion must provide, in other words, the necessary sticks and carrots, extrinsic motivations for conforming to morality.

Second, people need to believe that others will do rightly by them, or that some transhuman agency will step in to fill the breach, to restore or compensate. Without an assurance that wrongs will be righted, the strength of one's motivation to do what is right would be weakened. Even assuming that one should do what is right for its own sake, that rightness should be a sufficient reason or motivation regardless of whether others do rightly towards oneself, it is still the case that one's determination will flag if one is not assured that right will be done in return.

Or the necessity for divine restoration or compensation might be put another way. On some views of the moral demand, the moral order leads in one way or the other to well-being or happiness. If I act morally because I believe that morality is a social practice for mutual well-being, then I must count on others acting morally as well. And at least two variants of this idea are important in the traditions. First, there is the neo–Aristotelian view of morality where the right is defined in terms of the good: Moral relations are a path to and intrinsic in human well-being; but because of evil people, those who are virtuous may be prevented from enjoying the full fruits of human community which are constitutive of well-being. Second, there is the view of morality which sees human beings entering into a contract or compact: They agree to abide by the moral rules in order to further their interests; the actions of evil people, however, injure us directly or create situations where to do our duty means we cut ourselves off from the benefits morality is supposed to provide. Ronald Green illustrates the problem as follows:

> Imagine a small, democratic nation engaged in a war against a cruel and aggressive tyranny. All the citizens of the defending nation know that if they lose the war they will not only sacrifice their normal freedoms, but for at least a time will be exposed to systematic programs of torture and extermination. Based on the past behavior of this tyrannical neighbor-state, it is estimated that up to 20 per cent of the defending nation's population may lose their lives in the persecutions to follow. Imagine further that successful defense of the nation rests, finally, on the retention of a vital bridgehead, which depends, in turn, upon the willingness of a handful of soldiers placed there by the random play of events to fight to the death if necessary. Now, assuming the defensive efforts of this nation to be morally just, the question "Why should I be moral?" in this context becomes "Why should I, if I become one of the defenders at that bridgehead, do my duty?"[78]

On either version of the idea that morality is supposed to provide well-being or happiness, the difficulty is that at the merely human level, individual fulfillment is not always the outcome of moral striving. If the individual who does his or her duty suffers as a result, then for this individual moral goodness has not culminated in well-being; but the restoration provided by a transhuman force in another mode of existence provides this result. What the transhuman force and location do is to insure that the rationale, and hence the motivational structure, for morality is intact. Whereas the first interpretation of the redress motif identified a problem with the *strength* of motivation and found a religious answer, this interpretation holds that without belief in the possibility of a transhuman force that can and will insure well-being, the motivation for moral striving is *incomplete,* for its benefits are often denied to particular individuals.

Third, and this argument is often presented apart from the two just mentioned, one cannot really begin to attain moral goodness without a proper relation to God. In contrast to a thinker like Kant who held that belief in God was not necessary in order to have the psychic wherewithal to begin at least to live rightly, Donald Evans claims, for example, that we must reach a stance of "basic trust" towards ultimate reality in order to achieve an openness to others in which we and they can find fulfillment; what is right and morally good is what leads to true human fulfillment and without basic trust human beings are not able to escape the defensive self-seeking that walls-off neighbors and prevents self-giving; without such trust we would fail to find those relations that are truly fulfilling. Our stance toward others, therefore, is a function of our stance towards ultimate reality:

> This trust-readiness towards particulars is an expression of an assurance that our human life has significance in a cosmos which is fundamentally for us rather than against us.[79]

Evans means, I believe, that the person who trusts in the enduring benevolence of ultimate reality does not tend to hoard, to protect, to guard feverishly against the deprivations of others; rather, knowing that one's ultimate good is secure, the individual with basic trust can allow those responses of mutual giving and receiving in which fulfillment consists; thus in traditional theological language, receiving life as a gift of a loving God, one is enabled to love others; having been loved oneself, feeling secure in that love, one is not defensively preoccupied with oneself and *can* allow oneself to love others.[80]

Thus while Evans (and other writers) might admit that other moralities are possible without basic trust, the morality that is humankind's true possibility, its genuine vocation, compared with which all else is a shallow and sorry substitute, is the morality of love and love requires trust.[81] Even if love under the conditions of sin must utilize the apparatus of justice, one cannot begin to love without trust. And although some individuals may have basic trust without explicit faith, the attitude implies belief in the benevolent ultimate. Growth in moral goodness is impossible without the relation to God.

5.3 Carrots and sticks, assurance, and trust.

What would the critic say in response to these arguments? First, in regard to the necessity of punishments and rewards, it is an empirical contention that societies or individuals need these motivations over and above those intrinsic to the moral demand itself, and even if they do, many societies seem to work with merely *human* carrots and sticks.[82]

Second, in regard to the idea that a belief in divine restitution is necessary lest one's motivation to do what is right is too *weak*, this argument is also open to empirical refutation; legal systems, although imperfect, do exist in part to redress wrongs, and even if our motivation is strengthened by this sort of assurance, there is no clear evidence that we need divine restoration as well to keep morality going.

But how would a critic respond to the argument that God must insure well-being if morality is to have its basic motivation *complete*? First, the critic could attack either version of the idea that morality is the path to well-being or happiness. For example, Robert Adams argues against the contractarian view by observing that it is not clear whether it really is in everyone's interest ordinarily to abide by the moral rules. Perhaps it is not in one's interest to keep the moral rules if one can cover-up wrongdoing or perhaps one is strong enough not to fear others or need their help; the critic asks, in other words, whether this ethical theory adequately accounts for moral duty. Second, as Adams also notes the critic could argue that our desire for happiness may not conflict with our duty even in bridge-head situations, for we might define our happiness as sticking by out duty no matter what it costs us; the critic thus would challenge the assumption that the full meaning of well-being must extend beyond moral virtue itself; it is not the case that happiness must be more than moral goodness.[83]

But even granting some view of morality which makes happiness or well-being its telos, does the argument work? Could humans live with an awareness that the motivational structure of morality is not always complete on the merely human scene? Given the great benefits that ordinarily adhere to morality, would that not be sufficient motivation for at least a general conformity to morality? Perhaps humans can live with the potential of conflict between ordinary situations where they expect to participate in the goods of moral community and the situation where to fulfill their duty would be to cut them off from the good (without the hope of a transhuman fulfillment). The issue is not settled, but it seems to me that humans could believe that the motivational structure of morality works most of the time for most people, and this is sufficient for ordinary life; in extraordinary situations, individuals could either opt out or decide to hang on despite the consequences for themselves.[84]

And as for the trust argument, Evans is certainly right to say that how one sees the social and natural environment will set the presuppositions and limits of one's morality; taking nature as, at best, a provider of scarce resources and seeing other human animals as greedy competitors will set the stage for a morality of claims and counterclaims, while being able to count on the benevolence of the universe might well allow one's loving-kindness to flower. But the critic would insist that it is the experience of benevolence from outside oneself that matters; it is not necessary that one trust in *ultimate* reality. Camus, for example, could conceivably come to believe in the possibility of LeGuin's Anarres, a society where being able *to trust other humans* allows love to grow, without changing any of his beliefs about the implacable indifference of the universe.

5.4 *The argument for complete realization.* The arguments about carrots and sticks, assurance, and trust were designed to show that morality could not function, or at least could not function adequately, without God. But as I noted there is another claim to the effect that morality demands complete conformity with the moral ideal, and that to believe that what morality demands is possible, one must believe in the possibility at least of another mode of existence and transhuman assistance. The arguments we have just looked at concerned beliefs and related reasons and motivations that were supposedly necessary for the moral life; this new argument tries to show that certain beliefs are necessary to form moral *intentions*. (I have in mind here Kant's arguments for belief in God, grace, and immortality, but I am not saying that what follows is what he claimed.) By intention I mean setting it as one's purpose to achieve a state of affairs, in Kantian language making that state one's end; to act one must intend to achieve a state of affairs. The issue then is whether I can intend and act to achieve a state of affairs believing it to be impossible; to intend the ideal realization of the moral demand and to strive to attain it, so some have argued, I must believe that it is possible, and to believe that the ideal realization of the moral demand is possible, I must also believe in the possibility at least of an agency which will help to bring about the ideal state and a location where it could take place.[85]

The argument goes, roughly speaking, like this: (1) Morality demands that rewards and punishments be correctly apportioned, that the victims of oppression receive restitution, and that we each be able to achieve complete guiltlessness and moral goodness. (2) But it is apparent that human capacities and opportunities are insufficient; often the guilty go unpunished, the oppressed are not compensated, and we are not able to hope for moral goodness. (3) Thus if morality demands that we aim at an ideal state of retribution, restitution, and goodness, then we can see that our effort is doomed to futility; it is hopeless to try to achieve what morality demands; the individual cannot realistically hope for a just reward, final redress, or complete guiltlessness and goodness. (4) Now if it is true that the human scene does not provide for the possibility of the states of affairs that morality demands and, therefore, our effort to seek these states is futile, then one cannot intend to attain them. If one believes it is futile to attempt something, then one cannot form the intention to strive for it; and if one cannot intend it, one cannot strive for it. If the moral demand is futile, then, one cannot aim at it; moral striving would have to be abandoned. (5) Thus either moral striving is futile and we must abandon it, or we must believe that the fulfillment of the moral enterprise is possible in some way that exceeds human capacities and opportunities. To form moral intentions and to continue to strive morally we must be able at least to *hope* for the completion of the moral enterprise, we must believe that fullfillment is possible. And to believe that, we must believe in the possibility of something that exceeds human resources; since the fulfillment of the moral demand does not seem possible either through human powers or within the scope of human life, we must believe in the possibility of some force that exceeds human capacities and some mode of existence beyond the human scene.

In sum, if we are not to abandon moral striving, we must believe in the possibility of God and the afterlife (or some other set of analogous forces and states) in order to guarantee the possibility of moral fulfillment: correct retribution, complete restitution, and perfect goodness.[86] Most believers in mainstream Judaic and Christian traditions of course have believed such a state and such a force really exist, but the argument under consideration is only for their possibility: if the ideal realization of the moral demand is to be possible, then something like God and immortality must be possible. The argument then concludes: (6) Because of the very nature of the moral demand, we are justified in believing in the possibility of a transhuman force and location, by means of which the moral demand can be fully realized.

5.5 *Must moral striving aim at ideal fulfillment?* The first line of criticism against this formulation of the problem and the alternatives is straightforward; while some moralities may demand the complete fulfillment of moral goals, this is not necessarily built into every morality. We might be committed to aiming only at as complete a fulfillment as possible within human limitations. For example, if we are committed to restitution, our moral system might demand only that we strive for the best system of restoration and compensation we can achieve in our time and place.[87]

5.6 *Futility and the absurd.* But suppose our morality did require complete fulfillment. Some religious thinkers would say that we would either have to admit that moral striving is futile, or believe that what it demands is possible of realization.[88] The reason futility is unacceptable is that you cannot intend and strive for something you believe is futile; if you believed that moral striving were futile, you would have to abandon it. This claim seems to rest on the assumption that if one believes it is futile to attempt something, then one cannot strive for it; one cannot actually intend and strive to do something one believes is impossible.

But this is an assumption that some modern thinkers would not accept. If I seek perfect justice but I believe that it is impossible to attain, I need not give up intending to achieve it. Although in a psychological sense this intention would be difficult for most people, there is nothing impossible in the nature of the intention itself; I can intend and strive for what I believe to be impossible. I simply fly in the face of reality, I mount plans, believing them to be impossible of fulfillment. My intention may be "irrational" in the sense that I am not adjusting to reality, but I am not irrational in the sense that I do not understand the situation or cannot calculate the costs. It is precisely this sort of clear-headed intention to achieve the impossible which Camus may have sometimes meant when he spoke of the *absurd,* the "lucid" confrontation between what we intend to achieve and what we can hope for (believe is possible) in a godless universe.[89]

5.7 Futility and wish-fulfillment.

Thus even if we think that striving for ideal fulfillment is futile, we are not required to abandon it. But suppose we believed the contrary: if it is futile we must abandon it. Would we be justified in believing that what morality demands *is* possible of fulfillment? Would we be justified in believing in the possibility of a transhuman solution in order not to abandon morality? Would this be wish-fulfillment? Would we not be adjusting our view of reality so that we can keep intending to achieve a goal we are unwilling to give up?[90]

One line of argument, associated with Kant, goes as follows.[91] When we desire things, for example, a new yacht, and convince ourselves we can attain them, despite serious evidence to the contrary, this is wish-fulfillment; we rearrange our view of reality so that we believe our wishes and intentions can be fulfilled. But this is an ordinary desire; even if it is hard for us to get rid of it, we could. But the demand of morality is not like an ordinary desire; it is required by our very being, we cannot escape it. We must *acknowledge* the moral demand (even if we do not always act upon it), for it is required by our nature. We must acknowledge that we should intend to fulfill the moral demand. In contrast to cases where ordinary desires are involved, therefore, we are justified in believing that the moral demand is possible of attainment despite evidence to the contrary; since our nature *requires* the moral demand we must believe it can be attained.

I do not see, however, why the difference between ordinary desires and the moral demand makes any difference in the *status* of our beliefs about the possibility of attainment. All the preceding argument seems to show is that we need not engage in one sort of wish-fulfillment because we can give up ordinary desires, but that we must engage in another sort *if* we are to intend and strive for what our nature requires. Even though our nature requires that we should intend to fulfill the moral demand, whether we do intend it or not is another matter. If we believed that striving for the demand was futile, then we could not intend it (on the assumption that a futile goal cannot be intended); in order to intend and strive for the moral goal and thus to do what our nature says we should, we would have to adjust our beliefs just as in the yacht case.

To make the argument work for a generic difference between wish-fulfillment and belief in a transhuman force and occasion, one would have to assume that if we ought to achieve the moral goal, we must be able to—

in this sense *ought* would have to imply *can*.[92] We would have to believe that in order for something to be what we morally ought to accomplish (and hence intend and strive for) it must be accomplishable. Thus since perfect moral goodness, for example, *is* what we ought to seek (and we cannot reject that belief), then we must believe it is possible. But why should we assume that doability (in this sense at least) is a necessary condition of something being what we ought morally to do? Camus' Sisyphus could believe that there are moral reasons for trying to roll the rock to the top of the hill and making it stay there; Sisyphus can believe he ought to intend and strive for this goal. But Sisyphus could also believe that the attempt will always be frustrated; the rock keeps rolling down.

Of course, the phrase wish-fulfillment has negative connotations. We think of people who are unwilling to alter their picture of reality, lest they give up a cherished set of desires and intentions. But if the moral demand were a requirement of our nature, or even if we see it as merely much more important than any other intentions we adopt, we might think of ourselves as justified in believing that it is possible of attainment, even if there is evidence to the contrary. One sort of consideration would outweigh the other and we could distinguish this sort of adjustment of our beliefs from those sorts of cases of wish-fulfillment which have negative connotations. The consequences of not believing are much more serious than in ordinary cases; if we do not adjust our beliefs, we are left in the position of abandoning something vastly more important than new yachts. Whatever theory of morality we hold (required by our nature or whatever), human experience would be at cross-purposes with itself if we could not believe that the moral demand is possible of attainment and hence continue to intend it. Thus while it is true that we are adjusting our beliefs in the same way in the yacht case and in the case of moral demand, the difference in the two might incline us to think of the former as unjustified (hence deserving of the negative connotations of "wish-fulfillment") but the latter as legitimate.

In sum, if one did continue to believe that the moral demand was for complete fulfillment, and that a futile intention has to be abandoned, then one might choose to adjust one's beliefs so as to be able to affirm, to hope for, the possibility of attainment. One's adjustment would be like cases of wish-fulfillment, but the nature or importance of moral striving might lead one to distinguish the ordinary cases from the moral context where one is faced with the option of abandoning the moral demand or adjusting beliefs.

To get to this point, however, as I have noted, one would have to grant that ideal realization is demanded and that a futile intention must be abandoned. Doctor Rieux in *The Plague* illustrates a modern figure who apparently does not aim at ideal realization, but has confidence that limited struggles are not entirely in vain. He believes that his "victories will never be lasting"; for Rieux the plague is a "never ending defeat." In the plague people die, and plagues recur. Thus if Rieux's intention were to win a complete and lasting victory over suffering, his struggle would be futile (he would be like the mythological figure Sisyphus about whom Camus wrote who rolls the rock up the hill only to have it come down again and again). But if his intention is to ameliorate the effects of the plague, to retard it, to fight it to a stalemate on a particular occasion, then his struggle is not in vain; as R. M. Hare would say, he believes he can carry through *some* moral intentions.[93] Dr. Rieux

> . . . knew the tale he had to tell could not be one of final victory. It could only be the record of what had to be done, and what assuredly would have to be done again in the never ending fight against terror and its relentless onslaughts, despite their personal afflictions, by all who, while unable to be saints but refusing to bow down to pestilences, strive their utmost to be healers.
>
> And indeed, as he listened to the cries of joy rising from the town, Rieux remembered that such joy is always imperiled. He knew what those jubilant crowds did not know but could have learned from books: that the plague bacillus never dies or disappears for good; that it can lie dormant for years and years in furniture and linen chests; that it bides its time in bedrooms, cellars, trunks, and bookshelves; that perhaps the day would come when, for the bane and the enlightening of men, it would rouse up its rats again and send them forth to die in a happy city.[94]

5.8 Radical revisions.   The discussion so far about ideal realization, of course, has assumed that what is at stake is the belief in a force and occasion that guarantees at least the possibility if not the reality of the fulfillment of the moral demand. But some theologians have recently challenged the idea that any guarantee should be desired, and the traditional "anthropocentric" conception of the moral demand has also come under scrutiny.

For example, Sharon Welch argues that the "belief that history has already been saved in the definitive eschatological action of God in Jesus Christ . . . masks . . . the continued existence of social structures of sinful exploitation and domination." Says Welch:

> In contrast to the guaranteed victory over evil promised in Christian triumphalism, the claims of liberation theologians have a historical, concrete basis: the experience of redemption in base Christian communities, in the women's movement, in the black church. "Transcendence" is distinctly historical: it consists in the power to overcome given historical conditions.[95]

Welch means, I believe, that the belief that God has begun and will complete the victory of good over evil, that God has provided for the eventual ideal realization of the moral demand, displaces attention from concrete oppression by hiding from view (masking) the awareness that the entire responsibility for overcoming evil really lies in human hands. Like

Dr. Rieux, Welch sees a continual struggle against evil, without any guarantee that a definitive victory can or will be achieved.

While Welch dispenses with the traditional confidence that God will achieve the victory of good over evil, James Gustafson challenges the view that the deity wants to achieve a state of happiness and perfect goodness for the individual if not in this life then in some other. According to Gustafson, scientific evidence does not support the belief in an afterlife where these goals could be accomplished. Whatever God is and whatever God's purpose is, the deity does not provide for the eternal destiny of individual persons. Nor does the evidence allow for the idea that the perfectability of the human species itself is one of God's purposes, for in all likelihood the race is doomed to extinction along with the solar system. The deity's purpose, says Gustafson, is for the good of the cosmos, but that state of affairs does not seem to include individual or species survival. Since Gustafson values and assents to God's purpose, he rejects what he calls an "anthropocentric" morality which focuses on the happiness and goodness of humans.[96]

Thus whereas earlier thinkers might postulate God and immortality (or somesuch) in order to aim at ideal realization, or settle like Dr. Rieux for limited achievements, Gustafson alters his view of what morality demands. He no longer holds that morality aims solely or even mainly at the happiness or moral goodness of the human individual. Gustafson is confident that the deity will bring about the good of the entire cosmos. But the deity's purpose for the good of the whole does not necessarily include the good of particular human individuals or even guarantee that today's suffering is necessary for tomorrow's good (Gustafson's deity is not a utilitarian). Gustafson's view then is both a moral and a theological revision. Morality no longer demands happiness and moral goodness for the individual, and God does not guarantee the possibility of these goals. But interestingly enough Gustafson retains the traditional Western notion that God does guarantee the possibility and indeed the reality of what morality demands, the good of the cosmos, for that is the deity's goal, and the deity will bring that purpose to fruition.

6. CONCLUSION

I have tried to show that at least certain versions of the making-morality-work and intending-the-ideal theses are not convincing. While carrots and sticks, assured restitution, and trust in God might make morality work better, it seems disputable whether God is necessary, even to have a morality of "love." The argument about intention takes another tack; belief in the possibility of the transhuman is necessary if we are not to abandon moral intentions. I have tried to sketch, however, the sorts of assumptions the argument rests on (morality demands complete fulfillment, a futile intention must be abandoned, believing in order to conform to the demand of our nature is not wish-fulfillment), and I have tried briefly to indicate objections to each in turn.

Whether the objections to the two major sorts of arguments seem convincing or not, it is certainly the case that religious systems have provided a variety of beliefs about rewards and punishments, restoration/compensation, and guilt/moral goodness. Many religious systems have "guaranteed" that humans could hope not merely for partial moral accomplishments but for a glorious consummation. Thus whether or not the moral demand *requires* such a guarantee, Judaic and Christian traditions (among others) have provided it. Some theologians such as Welch do not want to retain this guarantee; but even when a theologian such as Gustafson radically challenges the inherited view of the moral demand, his new version of the tradition retains the belief that God is the "guarantor" of morality.

NOTES

1. For a discussion of this interpretation, see John Hick, *Evil and the God of Love*, rev. ed. (San Francisco: Harper and Row, 1978), pp. 59 ff, 201 ff. See his critique, chap. 12, p. 243 and passim. Compare Clyde Holbrook, "Jonathan Edwards Addresses Some 'Modern Critics' of Original Sin," *Journal of Religion*, *63* (July 1983), 211–230. Compare also Richard R. LaCroix, "The Paradox of Eden," *International Journal for Philosophy of Religion*, *15* (1984), 171; and Allen H. Podet, "La Croix's Paradox: An Analysis," *International Journal for Philosophy of Religion*, *18* (1985), 69–72; also Peter Slater, "Tillich on the Fall and the Temptation of Goodness," *The Journal of Religion*, *65* (April 1985), 196–207.

2. In order to hold on to the idea that we are not guilty unless we sin freely and also to affirm that sin is universal, Kant tried to reinterpret traditional Christian notions of original sin. See Ronald Green, "The Limits of the Ethical in Kierkegaard's 'Concept of Anxiety,' and Kant's 'Religion Within the Limits of Reason Alone' " in *International Kierkegaard Commentary Vol. 8: The Concept of Anxiety*, ed. Robert Perkins (Macon: Mercer University Press, 1985), pp. 63–87. Gordon E. Michaelson, Jr., "The Inscrutability of Moral Evil in Kant." *The Thomist*, *Vol. 51* (April 1987) 246–269 and Philip L. Quinn, "Original Sin, Radical Evil and Moral Identity," *Faith and Philosophy*, *1*(April 1984), 188–202. Kant suggested the idea of a free and inexplicable adoption of the evil maxim that on occasion duty will not rule over inclination (either duty will be subordinated to inclination or the two would have equal force; Quinn, "Original Sin," p. 196); this adoption is not in time and space but somehow accounts for the possibility and the actuality of evil done in ordinary experience. But what exactly does it mean to make a decision or adopt a maxim out of time? And why would everyone adopt the evil maxim? See Quinn, "Original Sin," pp. 196–197. A contemporary thinker would most likely hold on to the idea that one is not responsible unless free, and might account for universality as an overwhelming probability given psychological and social circumstances; the evil meta-maxim would be explained as a disposition to do less than one's duty on occasion.

3. On the idea that the revealed Torah takes sin into account, see Ronald M. Green, *Religious Reason: The Rational and Moral Basis of Religious Belief* (New York: Oxford University Press, 1978), pp. 154–155. On the problem of moral failure and how religious traditions deal with it, see Green and Charles Reynolds, "Focus Introduction," *Journal of Religious Ethics*, *14*(Spring 1986). 144, 146, 149–150.

4. In Wendy O'Flaherty's interpretation of several Hindu myths, the inhabitants of the original time live without classes or property; in the words of the texts, they are "happy and equal . . . all their needs are supplied by magic wishing trees"; there is "no injury or quarrels or hate or famine" . . . since "of their own accord, and by means of dharma, all creatures protected one another. . . ." There is no need for government, for the coercive mechanisms of law—O'Flaherty, *The Origins of Evil in Hindu Mythology* (Berkeley: University of California Press, 1976), pp. 23–27. But either greed or the power of time which leads to greed overpowers the inhabitants; the trees disappear, there is conflict and injury, and it is necessary that there be a "king" or "rod of chastisement." Now according to O'Flaherty the inhabitants of the original time are in a premoral state, but become human and do evil, with no intervening period of moral goodness. But note that the Hindu stories admit of an interpretation similar to the transition from moral goodness to moral evil that some Western thinkers see in the Genesis account. In the original time, creatures protect one another of their own accord, by means of *dharma* (duty); what is not needed before the time of greed and conflict is law, the coercive sanction of government (kingship). Thus the Hindu myths, or some of them at least, could be read as about a transition from moral perfection to a time when evil has to be controlled by government and law.

5. John Ladd, *The Structure of a Moral Code* (Cambridge: Harvard University Press, 1957), p. 52.

6. Compare H. L. A. Hart, *The Concept of Law* (Oxford: Clarendon Press, 1981); and Ladd, *Moral Code,* pp. 54–55.

7. In her novel *The Dispossessed* (New York: Avon Books, 1974), Ursula Le Guin depicts a utopian society without law, where no one has authority to coerce but where social pressure becomes almost as stifling, as inimical to personal autonomy, as the power of a state.

8. In the tradition of Weber, rewards and punishments are seen as an "ethicization" of suffering: suffering is the problem; to say it is deserved is a solution. See Gananath Obeyesekere, "Rebirth Eschatology and Its Transformations: A Contribution to the Sociology of Early Buddhism," in *Karma and Rebirth in Classical Indian Traditions,* ed. Wendy O'Flaherty (Berkeley, Los Angeles, and London: University of California Press, 1980), pp. 137–164; or Clifford Geertz, "Religion as a Cultural System," in *The Interpretation of Cultures* (New York: Basic Books, 1973), pp. 87–125. From a Kantian perspective, fulfillment of the moral is the question doctrines such as the judgment of God or *karma* answer. Suffering is sometimes explained nonmorally, but I assume that the imperfection of the moral order itself is a difficulty which some religious systems address. In this, I follow Green in *Religious Reason.* Unfortunately I was not able to treat Green's *Religion and Moral Reason: A New Method for Comparative Study* (NY: Oxford Univ. Press, 1987).

9. See Hart, *The Concept of Law.*

10. Geertz, "Religion as a Cultural System," in *Interpretation of Cultures,* p. 106.

11. Rudolf Otto, *The Idea of the Holy* (New York: Oxford University Press, 1958).

12. Gananath Obeyesekere in "Rebirth Eschatology" tries to show how the idea of *karma* is a result of an earlier rebirth eschatology becoming "ethicized." Compare his "Theodicy, Sin, and Salvation in a Sociology of Buddhism," in *Dialectic of Practical Religion,* ed. E. R. Leach (Cambridge: Cambridge University Press, 1968), pp. 7–40. In a cultural system with a nonethicized rebirth eschatology, "ethics" or morality consists of norms and socially authorized rewards and punishments, and religion consists in beliefs about remedies for suffering beyond this life. When a rebirth eschatology is ethicized, an afterlife, rebirth, or series of rebirths become the sphere for rewards and punishments; the "secular" apparatus of norm violation and retribution is extended or projected onto the postdeath structure, in contrast to systems where a favorable or unfavorable afterlife or rebirth has nothing to do with moral goodness. Obeyesekere's basic contrast between rebirth schemes that are not seen as rewards and punishments for moral conduct and those that are is illuminating (I bypass the question whether his evolutionary hypothesis is correct). But I think he overstates his case. It is possible to have a system of moral norms which is *religiously* interpreted without extending rewards and punishments to the afterlife. For example, Job believed that God commanded the basic precepts of social existence; whatever "secular rationale"—to use Obeyesekere's term—might or might not have been present, obedience to these norms was

part of the obedience owed to the deity; in this sense, to violate a "moral tenet" was also to violate a "religious tenet." And to be sure this deity did reward and punish; the deity added a layer of rewards and punishments to what the society provided. But the sphere of retribution was limited to this world; Sheol was the destiny of good and evil alike. Thus unless Obeyesekere defines religion as necessarily having to do with the afterlife or rebirth, the norms and sanctions that structure social existence can be religiously interpreted without rewards and punishments extending beyond this life.

13. See Green, *Religious Reason* (chap. 6: Judaism: The Justice and Mercy of God) on God as Judge in Judaic traditions.

14. The edition used here is that of Marvin Pope (Garden City, NY: Doubleday, 1973). See note on Job 5:3–5 in Pope, p. 42.

15. Job, Pope's edition, pp. 135–136.

16. Job 8:11–13; 4:18:4b, c. See note on Job 18:4b, c, in Pope's edition, p. 134.

17. Outka, "Social Justice and Equal Access to Health Care," *Journal of Religious Ethics, 2* (Spring 1974), 11–32. Outka notes that "entry into the kingdom of heaven" has been connected to merit defined in terms of effort ("energy displayed and fidelty shown") rather than results or achievement. Compare Arthur F. Holmes, "Biblical Justice and Modern Moral Philosophy," *Faith and Philosophy 4* (October 1986), 429–439.

18. For Western views see Gertrude Ezorsky, ed., *Philosophical Perspectives on Punishment* (Albany, NY: State University of New York Press, 1972). See also Rudolph J. Gerber and Patricia C. McAnany, eds., *Contemporary Punishment: Views, Explanations, and Justifications* (Notre Dame, IN.: University of Notre Dame Press, 1972).

19. Judaic and Christian traditions typically insist, however, that reward should not become the *basic* reason or motive for obeying God's morally right commands. See Green, *Religious Reason*, p. 144 ff.

20. That a divinity is conceived of as awarding rewards and punishments, of course, does not mean that this is how divinity should be conceived. See J. Brenton Stearns, "Divine Punishment and Reconciliation," *Journal of Religious Ethics, 9*(Spring 1981), 119 ff. Stearns develops his own view of punishment as the consequence of wrongdoing and argues against the view that the concept of divine punishment has no meaning apart from the idea of suffering imposed by a deity.

21. Alexander Altmann, ed., "The Book of Doctrines and Beliefs," in *Three Jewish Philosophers,* ed. Altmann et al. (New York: Atheneum, 1972), pp. 127, 135, 183.

22. Compare Hick, *Evil and the God of Love.* Compare also Alvin Plantinga, *God, Freedom, and Evil* (New York: Harper and Row, 1974); see the attempt by Marilyn McCord Adams in "Redemptive Suffering: A Christian Solution to the Problem of Evil," in Robert Audi and William J. Wainwright, eds., *Rationality, Religious Belief, and Moral Commitment,* pp. 248–267, to distinguish the sorts of questions which believers can answer and those that remain a mystery. She argues that believers cannot know, say, why God doesn't do more to cut down on evil, but they can affirm that no suffering would be permitted which could not be redemptive and that the final end of the vision of God is a good which, although incommensurate with any other good, is such that one would not complain against God's justice or love (pp. 252, 255, 263).

23. Camus, *The Plague,* trans. Stuart Gilbert (New York: Modern Library, 1948), p. 87ff.; 196; 200.

24. I include in this concept of right and wrong both general moral rules—such as noninjury—and principles of distributive justice which have to do with the production and allocation of the social pie, the fruits of social cooperation. For a famous contemporary theory of distributive justice, see John Rawls' *A Theory of Justice* (Cambridge: Harvard University Press, 1971). In addition to retributive justice and distributive justice (including related forms of redress), some ancient traditions distinguish commutative justice as the justice of exchanges. For our purposes, we can include it as part of distributive justice, those principles which regulate how goods are produced and dispersed.

25. If the deity is the ultimate cause of the evil humans do—either as instruments of punishment or for some other reason—then the classic question is whether the evildoers are truly responsible. This is the problem of determinism, freedom, and moral responsibility.

26. Kant may have included both rewards and punishments and restitution in his notion of happiness proportionate to virtue. For an interpretation, see Allan Wood, *Kant's Moral Religion* (Ithaca, N.Y.: Cornell University Press, 1970), especially pp. 116–132.

27. Some "liberation" theologians, however, object to the idea that God has overcome evil in principle. See the discussion of Sharon Welch ahead.

28. West, *Prophesy Deliverence: An Afro-American Revolutionary Christianity.* (Philadelphia: Westminster Press, 1982). pp. 35, 109. Compare James H. Cone, *The God of the Oppressed* (New York: Seabury, 1975), and William R. Jones, *Is God a White Racist? A Preamble to Black Theology* (Garden City: Anchor, 1973).

29. On notions of the Kingdom of God, see Rosemary Radford Ruether, *The Radical Kingdom: The Western Experience of Messianic Hope* (Paramus, NJ: Paulist Press, 1970).

30. On forgiveness, see Susan Owen, "Repentence and Forgiveness," M. A. Thesis, University of Virginia, 1981; Paul Lauritzen, "Forgiveness: Religious Prerogative or Moral Duty?." *Journal of Religious Ethics*, 15(Fall 1987), 141–154; and Lauritzen, *A Light in the Heart: Religious Beliefs and Emotion,* Brown University dissertation, 1985; Louis Newman, "The Quality of Mercy" *Journal of Religious Ethics,* 15(Fall 1987), 155–172; and Philip L. Quinn, *Divine Commands and Moral Requirements* (Oxford: Clarendon Press, 1978), pp. 146–147. See also Ricoeur on the "ethicojudicial" concept of guilt in The *Symbolism of Evil* (Boston: Beacon Press, 1967), p. 108 ff. Robert Neville distinguishes between guilt as a status (being a wrongdoer), guilt as self-condemnation, and guilt as guilt feelings that are a form of self-punishment. "Suffering, Guilt, and Responsibility," *Journal of Dharma,* 2(July 1977), 251–252.

31. There are a variety of notions of atonement in Judaic and Christian traditions; I do not intend to suggest that quasi-legal metaphors are always employed. The vocabulary of pardon and mercy, however, has biblical roots and is widespread. It would be interesting to compare the various ways in which demerit can be alleviated in Buddhist traditions. Quinn in "Christian Atonement and Kantian Justification", *Faith and Philosophy* 3(October 1986), 440–462 presses the objection that moral debts and moral worth are not transferable against any doctrine of vicarious atonement, for example, Anselm's or Kant's. Quinn concludes that God could forgive and waive or remit debts (conditional upon repentence and amendment of life), but this would not amount to justification in the sense of a verdict of perfect righteousness which we would deserve only if we reached moral perfection. Thinkers in the Christian tradition have I believe sometimes called "justification" the state of affairs that is achieved both by God's forgiveness and by Christ's vicarious atonement, the two both being somehow necessary; this of course does assume that part of the debt at least is transferable to Christ or Christ's merit is transferable to humans. But even justification in this sense which cleared the moral slate does not entail the full righteousness of moral perfection. That state was referred to as sanctification, in place of which Kant offers only moral progress accepted in lieu of perfection. Thus Kant has two problems: aside from the atonement which the new "moral self" does for the old, which can perhaps still be said to be something the individual does for himself or herself. Kant would need a parallel to sanctification, without which the verdict of full righteousness cannot be conferred but since, as Quinn notes, for Kant the "propensity to moral evil is inextirpable by human powers," we can never achieve sanctification and hence never achieve the state of moral perfection (compare Quinn, pp. 257–8).

32. Quinn, *Divine Commands,* p. 161.

33. Quinn, *Divine Commands,* p. 163.

34. Quinn, *Divine Commands,* pp. 162–163.

35. Quinn states (*Divine Commands,* p. 157) that the issue is not how can God spare the wicked at all, but how he can spare some and not others. But the question of how God can spare the wicked at all is answered in the ways Quinn suggests, as well as the question of which sinners are to be saved. One would need to support one of these reconciling views by saying why it should be preferred to a theory that asserts that no relaxation of retribution could be just. See Green—*Religious Reason,* chap. 6, pp. 155–157—on how Judaic traditions relate justice and mercy.

36. See Reeder, "Justice and Benevolence," (unpublished) for an analysis of the ethic of Anarres. George Mavrodes catches exactly what the world of Anarres was supposed to be like when he imagines a situation in which persons no longer buy and sell goods, but simply

receive and give them away in a life of "gift and sacrifice". "Religion and the Queerness of Morality," in ed. Robert Audi and William J. Wainwright, *Rationality, Religious Belief, and Moral Commitment* (Ithaca and London: Cornell University Press, 1986), 225–226. In such a situation, talk of rights and duties would be regarded as a historical curiosity. But Mavrodes refers to this new world which supercedes the present "fallen" world as one in which morality would have withered away. Of course, what Mavrodes presents as beyond morality, I say is beyond "justice," and call it a new morality of "love."

37. On Anarres there is no private property or state property; all goods are held in common, a condition which one can describe as common property or simply common possession. Anarres in this respect is similar to many Western visions of a perfect society that would restore an earlier age before the rise of private property. On Anarres, the justification for this mode of relations lies in an ethic of mutual concern. In many classic theistic visions all property is in reality God's in any case, and the hope is to achieve a state where all could be held in common as originally intended. The necessity for private property is often presented as the result of an unwillingness to use goods in common. See for example, Norman Cohn, *The Pursuit of the Millennium* (London: Paladin, 1970), pp. 181–183, 190–191, 193, 196, 201, 214. Compare Stanley Tambiah's discussion of the origin of property and law in a classic Buddhist text in *World Conqueror and World Renouncer*, (Cambridge: Cambridge University Press, 1976) and O'Flaherty's treatment of Hindu myths in *Origins of Evil*.

38. There are other contrasts between conceptions of justice and love. Two important ones should especially not be confused: (1) Sometimes love or benevolence toward others is contrasted with convictions about distributive fairness; love in this sense could disregard what distributive justice requires, as mercy supplants retributive justice. Although a morality of "love" as I have depicted it is structured by convictions about fairness, I believe it could also provide for actions which on occasion counter fairness; one would not give less justice than it requires (at least not regularly), but one could do more. (2) Sometimes the notion of justice is restricted to a certain sphere of social interaction, for example, the basic arrangements of sexual, economic, and political order; other circumstances such as natural disasters are morally covered by a separate duty of aid, or are left to compassion and benevolence. A morality of "love" embraces both spheres. See Reeder, "Beneficence, Supererogation, and Role Duty," in Earl E. Shelp, ed. *Beneficence and Health Care* (Dordrecht: D. Reidel, 1982), pp. 83–108.

39. Reines, "The Self and the Other in Rabbinic Ethics," in *Contemporary Jewish Ethics*, ed. Menachen Kellner (New York: Sanhedrin Press, 1978), pp. 162–165, 169. Reines links the notion of respect to the idea of all persons being made in the image of God. Reines is concerned to show that ethics in Judaic tradition should not be characterized solely as an ethic of justice in contrast to a Christian ethic of love. To suggest that love is absent from Judaic ethics or to say that Christian notions of love are not guided by a sense of fairness or respect is to miss how both sorts of concepts are integrated in both traditions. See Gene Outka, *Agape* (New Haven: Yale University Press, 1972).

40. See Louis Jacobs, "Greater Love Hath No Man . . . The Jewish Point of View of Self-Sacrifice," in *Contemporary Jewish Ethics*, ed. Kellner, on the role of self-sacrifice in Judaic tradition.

41. See W. K. Frankena, "Love and Principle in Christian Ethics" in *Faith and Philosophy* ed. Alvin Plantinga (Grand Rapids, MI: William B. Eerdman, 1964), pp 203–225.

42. For this theme, see, for example, Stanley Hauerwas, *The Peaceable Kingdom: A Primer in Christian Ethics* (Notre Dame: University of Notre Dame Press, 1983), and Luke T. Johnson, *Sharing Possessions: Mandate and Symbol of Faith* (Philadelphia: Fortress Press, 1981). For a modern statement of the relation between God, trust, and moral growth, see Donald Evans, "Does Religious Faith Conflict with Moral Freedom," in *Religion and Morality*, ed. Gene Outka and John P. Reeder, Jr. (Garden City, NY: Doubleday, 1973), pp. 348–392, and *Struggle and Fulfilment: The Inner Dynamics of Religion and Morality* (Cleveland: Collins, 1979).

43. See, for example, Reines, "Self and Other"; and Jacobs, "Greater Love."

44. Jacobs, "Greater Love," p. 181.

45. See John P. Reeder, Jr., "Assenting to Agape," *Journal of Religion*, 60(January 1980), 17–31.

46. In "Assenting to Agape" I suggested that in the Kingdom of God believers would adopt unrestricted benevolence or concern for others, and that they would prefer to be entirely "devoid of self-seeking" (p. 27). But when resources cease to be scarce, and individuals do not have to put limits on their altruism, it is not necessary that they prefer to be wholly given over to seeking the good of others; what they prefer is to seek their neighbor's good with no restrictions. This does not imply that they will not continue to desire to seek their own good as well. What they want, in sum, is a state where not only is there no psychological or subjective conflict of interest—no conflicting desire to promote the private good of the self—but also no objective conflict, that is, a state where giving and receiving is not a zero-sum game, where my giving will never result in a net loss to myself. Compare the remarks of Dr. J. H. Hertz (quoted in Jacobs, "Greater Love," pp. 176–177) and of Gilbert Meilaender who argues—in *Love and Friendship: A Study in Theological Ethics* (Notre Dame and London: University of Notre Dame Press, 1981)—that in the "community God is preparing" self-fulfilling friendship will be added to the other-regarding concern of agape.

47. See Jeffrey Stout, "Buddhism Beyond Morality: A Note on Two Senses of Transcendence," *Journal of Religious Ethics*, 6(Fall 1978), 319–326. For an account of the dynamics of moral growth as interpreted in the theology of H. R. Niebuhr, see D. M. Yaeger, "On Making the Tree Good: An Apology for an Ethics of Disposition," *Journal of Religious Ethics*, 10(Spring 1982), 103–120.

48. Compare Mark C. Taylor's interpretation of Hegel's view of Abraham, in "Journeys to Moriah: Hegel vs. Kierkegaard," *Harvard Theological Review*, 70(July–October 1977), 313. Hegel opposed to the paradigm of "heteronomous" obedience, not Kantian moral autonomy, but a vision of "love" beyond "morality." Kant transferred the external Lord to the internal moral law and hence perpetuated conflicts between the natural self of inclination, desire, and passion, and the rational self as moral legislator. Hegel in contrast teaches "love" through which moral "law" is "simultaneously fulfilled and annulled. . . . Since the lover wants to fulfill his obligation to the beloved, desire and duty do not oppose one another" (pp. 313–314). Moreover, in "love" self-identity is "fully relational" (p. 314). Self and other have their identity and fulfillment in a whole, in a unity which does not annul difference (pp. 314–316). Taylor notes that Kierkegaard mistakenly took Hegel as proposing a return to nondifferentiation (p. 319). Compare Taylor, *Journeys to Selfhood: Hegel and Kierkegaard*, (Berkeley: University of California, 1980).

49. Marcia Baron suggests that some views of morality include the idea that the good person need not or indeed must not be "governed by a concept of duty." See Baron's "Varieties of Ethics of Virtue," *American Philosophical Quarterly*, 22(January 1985), 47. She objects to this idea on the grounds that it does not allow for what Charles Taylor calls "strong evaluation": Weak evaluation is evaluation in terms of given desires, even higher-order desires (Baron, p. 49); strong evaluation is evaluation based on a reason which is not "desire-based" but reflects a belief about what I should or ought to desire (Baron, pp. 50–51; Taylor, "Responsibility for Self," in *The Identities of Persons*, ed. A. O. Rorty (Berkeley: University of California Press, 1976). Any other view of strong evaluation does not do justice to the "intuition" of a difference between valuing and desiring (Baron, p. 50). The crucial contrast between an ethic of virtue and an ethic of duty in Baron's sense is that on the latter one desires to desire and do what one morally ought to do, whereas on the former one can desire to desire and do *what* is right or virtuous (Baron, p. 48)—that is, what a pattern of character and conduct embodies—but one does not characterize one's desire as a desire to desire and do what one morally ought to do. Even if one accepts Baron's contrast and her account of strong evaluation, I do not see why the perfect person could not *know* what ought morally to be desired, without having that concept do motivational work in the structure of desire (compare her note 23, p. 53). I could reflectively employ such a concept, although it would be motivationally otiose.

50. Gershom Scholem, "Toward an Understanding of the Messianic Idea in Judaism," in his *The Messianic Idea in Judaism and Other Essays in Jewish Spirituality* (New York: Schocken Books, 1971), p. 20; Compare pp. 21, 22–24, Scholem distinguishes Messianic "anarchism" from "antinomian potentialities" (p. 21), which I will discuss in Chapter 3. Scholem distinguishes two strands in the "Messianic idea" in Judaism, the restorative and the utopian; the former envisages a return to an original state, while the latter looks for something new.

Scholem also notes the general tension between *halakhah* and Messianism in Rabbinic literature and subsequent strata of Judaic tradition. Compare David Biale, *Gershom Scholem: Kabbalah and Counter-History,* (Cambridge: Harvard University Press, 1979).

51. Kant as usually interpreted held that the only morally worthy motive is to do
one's duty for its own sake. On the view I sketch here spontaneous goodness is morally superior to acting for the sake of duty. There are possible examples in various Christian traditions. For example, Vigen Guroian—in "Notes Towards an Eastern Orthodox Ethic," *Journal of Religious Ethics 9*(Fall 1981), 236—suggests that the "Kingdom of God is 'beyond ethics'
because the moral law is fulfilled in a free, loving concert of personality which transcends
all experience of duty, right, or obligation. Yet in a world in which the Kingdom is not fully
present, the perfection of men in their social relations is the appropriate goal of human
striving." Compare Stanley S. Harakas, *Toward Transfigured Life: The Theoria of Eastern Orthodox Ethics,* (Minneapolis: Light and Life, 1983). The state "beyond ethics" might be also interpreted to mean the transmoral mode of being I discuss in Chapter 3. But spontaneous
goodness is beyond "justice" while the transmoral state is beyond moral existence altogether.

52. Kant is not usually interpreted as thinking of morally good motives as desires at
all, but I bypass the historical question here.

53. It would be fruitful for example to compare the theme of self-cultivation in Chinese traditions. See Tu Wei-Ming, "The 'Moral Universal' from the Perspectives of East
Asian Thought," *Philosphy East and West 31*(July 1981), 259–267; and his "Further
Thoughts," *Philosophy East and West, 37*(July 1981), 273–277. See also Lee Yearley, "A Com-
parison Between Classical Chinese Thought and Thomistic Christian Thought," *Journal of
the American Academy of Religion, LI* (1983), 427–458.

54. In the novel, *The Dispossessed,* the settlers attempt to go beyond a morality of "justice" but do not conform perfectly to their ideal, as it is one of the burdens of the novel to
show.

55. See James Gustafson, "Religion and Morality from the Perspective of Theology,"
in *Religion and Morality,* ed. Gene Outka and John P. Reeder, Jr. (Garden City, NY: Doubleday, 1973), pp. 142–143.

56. I am grateful to Paul Lauritzen for discussions of this idea. If one's duties were
really only owed to God, then only God's forgiveness would be needed. But if we have direct
duties to others, then it would seem we need human forgiveness as well.

57. Kant evidently held that although the evil maxim (the principle not always to subordinate inclination to duty) is not extirpable in time, human beings can make a decision to
adopt the contrary maxim. The individual is punished by the suffering undergone as the
self moves from the old state to the new; and God will accept the new resolution (always to
subordinate inclination to duty) in lieu of complete goodness and hold the sinner guiltless.
Quinn in "Original Sin" says that Kant's account is inconsistent: Kant cannot hold that one
has two maxims, for that would contradict "rigorism," the idea that one is either at bottom
evil or good (pp. 196, 199); nor can Kant hold that one changes one's maxim, for Kant says
that because the morally evil maxim is adopted "independent of all temporal conditions," it
is inextirpable (p. 199). (Compare Quinn on Wood, note 6, p. 202, and compare Wood,
Kant's Moral Religion p. 223.)

58. The notion of the "end of history" usually connotes the end of natural suffering
or evil; notions of the end of moral and natural evil after death have been combined with
various conceptions of the earthly drama.

59. I emphatically do not intend to suggest that the historical examples discussed in
this chapter hope *only* for moral perfection.

60. John Yoder, *The Priestly Kingdom* (Notre Dame, IN: Notre Dame University Press,
1984), pp. 179–180. This view of his position he sees as a distortion imposed by the
Troeltsch–H. R. Niebuhr school of interpretation.

61. Yoder, *Kingdom,* pp. 11–12, 85.

62. Yoder, *Kingdom,* pp. 34, 61, 91, 115–116, 146, 164–165.

63. Yoder, *Kingdom,* p. 92.

64. Yoder, *Kingdom,* pp. 61, 159, 162–163.

65. Yoder, *Kingdom*, p. 94.

66. *Against Heresies*, chap. 24, quoted in George W. Forell, *Christian Social Teachings* (Minneapolis: Augsburg Publishing House, 1966), p. 40.

67. Kant apparently did not think that humankind on its own could reach moral perfection, although he thought historical progress toward that goal was possible. Human beings can make their disposition to moral goodness dominate their tendency to evil, but the latter will never disappear. See G. E. Michalson, Jr., *The Historical Dimensions of a Rational Faith* (Washington: University Press of America, 1977), pp. 130–132; compare Michel Despland, *Kant on History and Religion* (Montreal and London: McGill–Queen's University Press, 1973), p. 188 ff.; and Carl Raschke, *Moral Action, God, and History in the Thought of Immanuel Kant* (Missoula, MT: Scholars Press, 1975). I tend to agree with Michalson that Kant did not envisage a realization of the Kingdom of God on earth, a community of perfectly moral human beings (Michalson, *Rational Faith*, p. 83). Although some passages seem to envisage an historical realization of the Kingdom of God, others clearly do not (*Rational Faith* pp. 120, 123–124). Raschke argues, however, that Kant shifts from the notion of a proportionment of happiness to virtue achieved by God beyond history to the concept of a morally perfect society in history (Raschke pp. 190, 203–205, 218–219). Despland also believes that in *Religion Within the Limits of Reason Alone* Kant did propound an inner-worldly historical state of moral perfection achieved with divine aid (traditionally conveyed in the notion of a thousand-year reign of the saints on earth (Despland pp. 39, 92, 203–207, 238–239, 273–274, 276–277). But more characteristic of Kant's overall position, Despland has to admit, was a hope for an *approximation* of the Kingdom of ends on earth and a final trust in a transhistorical fulfillment of moral community (Despland, p. 277 ff.). See Terry F. Godlove, Jr., "Recent Work on Kant on Religion", *Religious Studies Review 12*(1986). pp. 229–233.

68. Gustavo Gutierrez, *A Theology of Liberation*, trans. and ed. by Sister Caridad Inda and John Eagleston (Maryknoll, NY: Orbis Books, 1973).

69. See Beverly Wildung Harrison, *Our Right to Choose: Towards a New Ethic of Abortion* (Boston: Beacon Press, 1983), chap. 4.

70. My typology here and in Chapter 3 is indebted to but differs from H. R. Niebuhr's in *Christ and Culture* (New York: Harper and Row, 1951). Some measure of opposition between the new and the old order is assumed, but the typology focuses on whether the new is to be realized or anticipated here and now, must be integrated in various ways with the old order, or is wholly future. Niebuhr's "Christ of culture" seems to me to represent the view that the new order, closely related as it is to the best of the old, can be broadly achieved now, while "Christ against culture" signifies a narrower realization or anticipation in light of a deeper opposition. "Synthesis," "Paradox," and "Conversion" are all modes of integration in my terminology.

71. Jacob Neusner, *Judaism: The Evidence of the Mishnah* (Chicago: University of Chicago Press, 1981), pp. 41–2; compare pp. 27, 37.

72. See, for example, Reinhold Niebuhr, *The Nature and Destiny of Man*, vol. 2 (New York: Scribner's, 1941); also *Love and Justice*, (Cleveland and New York: World Publishing, 1957), ed. D. B. Robertson. According to Niebuhr, agape or Christian love is impossible under the conditions of history, that is, in the realm of conflicts of interest between individuals and groups. But if human nature could be changed, then an Anarres of mutual love would be morally desirable. This may have been part of what Niebuhr meant by agape transcending the conditions of history. On Anarres agents pursue their own good but are concerned for others and care for them. This concern (conjoined with a legitimate concern for the self) is sufficient as a motivation to protect and promote the good of all. But on Anarres, where there is scarcity, distributive limits have to be put on benevolence; whereas in the Kingdom of God these natural limits would be removed, and thus agape could not only exist without any admixture of reciprocity, it would also not need to be limited or restricted—it could be "heedless." See Reeder, "Agape."

73. On Niebuhr, see Gene Outka, *Agape;* and Dennis McCann, *Christian Realism and Liberation Theology: Practical Theologies in Creative Conflict* (Maryknoll, NY: Orbis Books, 1981) Compare Richard J. Mouw, *When the Kings Come Marching In: Isaiah and the New Jerusalem* (Grand Rapids: Wm. B. Eerdmans, 1983) and Nicholas Wolterstorff, *Until Peace and Justice Embrace* (Grand Rapids: Wm. B. Eerdmans, 1983).

74. Richard Rubenstein, *After Auschwitz: Radical Theology and Contemporary Judaism* (New York: Bobbs-Merrill, 1966); compare "Middle Knowledge and the Problem of Evil" in Robert Adams *The Virtue of Faith and Other Essays in Philosophical Theology* (New York: Oxford University Press, 1987) p. 89. On patriarchal conceptions of sin, see e.g. Judith Plaskow, *Sex, Sin, and Grace: Women's Experience and the Theologies of Reinhold Niebuhr and Paul Tillich* (Wash., DC: Univ. Press of America, 1980).

75. Hermann Cohen, *Reason and Hope: Selections from the Jewish Writings of Hermann Cohen*, trans. Eva Jospe (New York: W. W. Norton, 1971), p. 45. George Mavrodes argues engagingly in "Religion and the Queerness of Morality," in Robert Audi and William J. Wainwright, ed., *Rationality, Religious Belief, and Moral Commitment*, pp. 213–216, that it is "'reasonable'" that there should be a moral demand on me "only if there is a moral demand on the world too and only if reality will in the end satisfy that demand." (p. 220). Compare William Lad Sessions, "A New Look at Moral Arguments for Theism," *International Journal for Philosophy of Religion 18* (1985), 51–67; see especially the discussion of A. E. Taylor; John Hick *Philosophy of Religion*, 3E, pp. 28–29.

76. Cohen, *Reason and Hope*, p. 46. I will not try to interpret Cohen. See Wendell S. Dietrich, "The Function of the Idea of Messianic Mankind in Hermann Cohen's Later Thought," *Journal of the American Academy of Religion*, XLVIII(1980), 245–258. See *Religion of Reason out of the Sources of Judaism*, trans. Simon Kaplan (New York: Frederick Ungar, 1972), for Cohen's developed views. Cohen was a Kantian, but he discarded the notions of immortality and happiness proportionate to virtue. He did, however, hold on to the idea of a guarantee of the possibility of a unified moral mankind: God is the guarantor of the duration of the natural and human context of the infinite moral task. See Dietrich, "Messianic Mankind," p. 247.

77. Compare Robert Merrihew Adams' distinction between two sorts of "Kantian" arguments: those which have an ethical premise and purport to "prove the *truth*, or enhance the *probability* of theism, and those which merely advance advantageous reasons for believing"; the former are theoretical, the latter practical. See Adams' "Moral Arguments for Theistic Belief", in *Rationality and Religious Belief*, ed. C. F. Delaney (Notre Dame, IN: University of Notre Dame Press, 1979), pp. 123–124. My distinction is somewhat different, since it divides the arguments into those which suggest that certain religious beliefs function to establish or enhance reasons or motivations and those which suggest that one cannot intend to act upon the moral demand without certain beliefs. The latter I believe is closer to Kant's own argument, although the former appears in certain neo-Kantians, for example, Ronald Green. I do not discuss here one of Adams' major theoretical arguments, the thesis that if a "divine command" theory of right and wrong is true, then God must exist (Adams, "Moral Arguments," p. 117 ff.

78. *Religious Reason*, p. 38. Ronald Green, in the tradition of Judaic and Christian thinkers of the nineteenth century who interpreted morality and religion in Kantian fashion, gives a neo-Rawlsian interpretation of Kant. Green argues that it is in our self-interest to adopt a set of rules which help everyone equally. The difficulty, according to Green, is that while these rules generally advance our self-interest, they may not always do so. What I approve in the abstract as an "impartial legislator," I may balk at as an individual. Moral reason is faced with the problem of the exceptional case where following the moral rules will not advance the individual's happiness in the long run. There simply are cases where society cannot guarantee to the individual the mutual benefits morality is supposed to provide. According to Green, Kant saw this problem and the postulate of a divine being who will proportion happiness to virtue is designed to meet it. Green's version of a Kantian theory of ethics may well leave to "religious reason" the problem of the exceptional case he identifies. Critics of Green have raised the question, however, whether his neo-Rawlsian ethic captures the classic Kantian view that the categorical imperative does not rest on a chain of prudential reasoning but originates in an independent requirement of reason. See Paul Lauritzen, "Kant on Happiness in the Moral Life: A Response to Ronald Green," master's thesis (1980), University of Virginia. Green's reply is that Rawls (or Green's interpretation of Rawls) catches what is true in Kant while discarding what is not. Green makes the notion of agreement or contract the basic form of morality, and thus what moral reason needs beyond the human sphere is a specific type of redress, the fulfillment of the benefits

which one anticipates by adhering to the compact to uphold morality.

79. Donald Evans, *Struggle and Fulfillment: The Inner Dynamics of Religion and Morality* (Cleveland: Collins, 1979), p. 2. Compare the contrast of idolatry and divinely enabled sharing in Johnson, *Sharing Possessions*. Compare also Patricia B. Jung, "Sanctification: An Interpretation in Light of Embodiment," *Journal of Religious Ethics 11* (Spring 1983), 75–95.

80. Evans, *Struggle*, pp. 130, 141, 168. I believe Evans also wants to say that without *divine* forgiveness, moral guilt will continue to inhibit love. Thus forgiveness and trust must be theistically construed to have a morality of love. Compare Adams, "Moral Arguments," p. 134, note 25.

81. The believer who stresses trust in God may include also the notion of hope for compensation, since moral weakness and evil can be acknowledged; perhaps even fear could have a place since it could come into play when love fails. But the harsh, punishing deity seems to be in tension with the benevolent ultimate of Evans' theology. On the integration of the commands to love God and to love thy neighbor, see Robert M. Adams, "The Problem of Total Devotion," in Robert Audi and William J. Wainwright, ed., *Rationality, Religious Belief, and Moral Commitment*, (Ithaca and London: Cornell University Press, 1986), pp. 169–194. See pp. 183–4 on the theme that love reflects trust.

82. Adams argues that the empirical evidence does not show that religious beliefs of this sort reduce crime ("Moral Arguments," p. 131).

83. I have adopted here two arguments in Robert Adams' review of Green's *Religious Reason*, *Religious Studies Review*, 6(July 1980), 183–189; compare also the review by Max Stackhouse, 177–182. See Annette Baier, "Secular Faith," in *Revisions*, ed. Stanley Hauerwas and Alasdair MacIntyre (Notre Dame, IN: University of Notre Dame Press, 1983), pp. 203–221, who argues that it is sufficient if one believes one's action will contribute to the just society for which one hopes; the one who makes a unilateral sacrifice has the satisfaction or "pleasure" of qualifying for a "kingdom of ends." Compare Green, p. 42.

84. Against Green's version of the argument, where moral obedience must turn out to be in one's own self-interest, it might be argued that reason—which is actually prudential in all its operations—could treat cases where following the rules is not in one's self-interest as carefully defined universal exceptions; everyone ought to follow the rules except under conditions a, b, c. Although 20 percent of the country would die, the soldier might live; the general good would be diminished, but the reasoning behind morality would be intact? The contracting agents could agree to this sort of exception?

85. According to Wood, Kant thought that "it is a requirement of rational purposive action that anyone who acts in pursuit of an end accepts a commitment to ground his action towards this end on a belief that the end is at least possible of attainment" (*Kant's Moral Religion*, p. 100). Thus in Wood's words "anyone who denies (or doubts) that the he can conceive the highest good as possible of attainment thereby commits himself not to make the highest good his end, and thus commits himself not to act in obedience to the moral law." (p. 101) But is perfect virtue what the moral law demands of us? Kant evidently distinguished between (1) the goodness that is possible for finite rational creatures (moral evil not extirpable even when the disposition to goodness is dominant)—Wood, *Kant's Moral Religion*, pp. 107–108, 111, 116); (2) the goodness of a holy will which is not achievable by finite creatures but is nonetheless their goal (no moral evil, no effort to overcome obstacles, no experience of the moral demand as constraint)—Wood, pp. 92–93); and (3) the divine holy will (not only does not experience constraint or obligation, but devoid of inclinations or needs, all-sufficient)—Wood, pp. 41–42). Kant apparently did not believe that finite rational creatures could ever reach the moral ideal (Wood, pp. 228–230). Even the person whose supreme maxim is good cannot attain perfection (Wood, p. 231). If the moral law demands perfection, then not only immortality (the opportunity) but something else is necessary to explain how the new good disposition or endless progress in time can take the place of perfection: The doctrine of grace was designed to meet this problem (Wood, pp. 231–233). Now Wood seems correct to say that for Kant justice does not rule out forgiveness, but it is another question whether the "verdict" of forgiveness (justification) can substitute for the attainment of perfect goodness (sanctification). It does not help to cite Kant's own remark that the demand of perfect goodness is an "imperfect" duty after which we need only strive, not attain (Wood, p. 246). If Kant's remark meant that we need not intend the fulfillment

of the moral law, there would be no need to raise the question of what one must postulate religiously. As Wood put it earlier in his book, "If I cannot conceive the attainment of this perfection as a practical possibility, then I commit myself not to make it my end" (p. 231). Kant apparently only said that it was not our duty to achieve perfect goodness in this life (Wood, p. 246. See n. 31.)

86. If for Kant happiness should be distributed according to virtue, then there are two issues: Can we hope for a perfect system of reward or distribution? And can we hope for our own perfect virtue in order to receive it? The issue I take up in this section is whether one must *intend* and believe in the possible realization of perfect states of affairs which fulfill the moral demand; I do not take up Kant's (or anyone else's) views as to what those perfect states would require, for example, God and immortality or Kant's version of grace. Green makes his own neo-Kantian proposal of what one must believe in order to hold oneself morally worthy. One must believe in an agency for whom the "failure always to punish immorality in no way impugns its ability or willingness always to fulfill the moral law," and whose judgment of one's "ultimate acceptability . . . need not always conform to our own self-judgment" (Green, *Religious Reason,* pp. 103, 105). It does not seem necessary, however, to assume that for all finite agents, a willingness to forego punishment "must go hand in hand with the intention to violate the law at some future time or with the belief that the law can and should occasionally be violated" (Green, p. 103). See Adams' review of Green, in *Religious Studies Review* (July 1980). As for acceptance, humans seem able to forgive, although in one sense nothing, not even God, can erase the record of past wrongdoing.

87. Adams notes that Green's argument does not require that agents aim at moral perfection (Adams in *Religious Studies Review,* p. 185). In "Moral Arguments," p. 124, Adams presents the objection I cite here; perhaps we are "obligated to promote only the best attainable approximation of the highest good."

88. See Wood, *Kant's Moral Religion,* p. 25 ff. and passim. I am indebted to Jaime M. Ferreira's paper, "Kant's Postulate: The Possibility of the Existence of God," *Kant-Studien,* 74(1983), 75–80. According to Ferreira, Kant sometimes says that God and immortality must exist; at other points he only says that it must be *possible* that they exist—that is, one can never, from the point of view of moral reason, deny that they exist (not logical, but "real" possibility). Ferreira believes that the latter is consistent with Kant's general epistemology and his view of religious belief. It the Highest Good is to be possible, then so must God and immortality. For a discussion of the Highest Good (moral perfection and the proportionment of happiness to virtue), see Michalson, *Rational Faith,* pp. 158–181; compare Wood, *Kant's Moral Religion,* chap. 3. Compare also Steward R. Sutherland, "Optimism and Pessimism," *Religious Studies 17* (December 1981), 549–558. On the concept of hope, see Louis Pojman, "Faith without Belief," *Faith and Philosophy 3*(April 1986), 157–176.

89. The problem of the absurd in "The Myth of Sisyphus" seems at first to be the loss of a transhuman purpose for existence: ". . . in a universe suddenly divested of illusions and lights, man feels an alien, a stranger. His exile is without remedy since he is deprived of the memory of a lost home or the hope of a promised land." Albert Camus, *The Myth of Sisyphus and Other Essays,* trans. Justin O'Brien (New York: Alfred Knopf, 1955), p. 5, compare p. 24. Thus the "absurd" would seem to be the opposition between the human desire that life have a transhuman purpose and the failure of the universe to provide it. But a critic could reply that even if there is no transhuman significance to existence, one can still have purposes; humans can give life meaning even if God does not. See Kai Nielsen, *Ethics Without God* (Buffalo: Prometheus Books, 1973). But I think Camus has something else in mind. Transhuman canopies of meaning were the basis for the hope that despite earthly suffering, eternal happiness is possible. Without a transhuman canopy, there is no basis for this hope; humans still desire such happiness, but all they can get is bits and snatches (compare Camus' *The Plague,* pp. 270–271—the lost home of happiness). In this sense, Sisyphus' labor is "futile and hopeless" (*Sisyphus,* p. 88). Sisyphus intends not merely to push the rock up the hill, but to push the rock up in such a way that it stays there; he pushes knowing *this* intention is futile. But Sisyphus can revolt, can scorn his fate, and this "lucid" defiance gives existence value (*Sisyphus,* pp. 40–41): "This universe henceforth without a master seems to him neither sterile nor futile. Each atom of that stone, each mineral flake of that night-filled mountain, in itself forms a world. The struggle itself toward the heights is enough to fill a man's heart" (p. 91).

90. Carl Raschke seems to argue that God has no ontological status for Kant and that therefore God is the projected or alienated essence of an ideal moral being. See Raschke's *Moral Action, God, and History in the Thought of Immanuel Kant*, pp. 135, 137, 143, 176 ff.

91. See Kant, *Critique of Practical Reason*, trans. Lewis White Beck (New York: Bobbs-Merrill, 1956), p. 149. Compare Wood, *Kant's Moral Religion*, pp. 182–187. I suggest here a type of justificatory argument that some philosophers call holistic or pragmatist as a way of reinterpreting the Kantian move. For a pragmatist epistemology in ethics proper, see Morton White, *What Is and What Ought to Be Done: An Essay on Epistemology and Ethics* (New York and Oxford: Oxford University Press, 1981); for a pragmatist epistemology applied to questions of morality and religious belief, see Jeffrey Stout, *The Flight from Authority* (Notre Dame, IN: University of Notre Dame Press, 1981).

92. Adams' version of this argument assumes the premise that "what we ought to do must be possible for us to do" ("Moral Arguments," p. 124). Adams also discusses a "practical" version of this argument to the effect that it would be demoralizing—weaken moral motivation—not to believe that moral action will make the world better as a whole (p. 125 ff.). The premise "what we ought to do must be possible for us to do" need not be construed as a matter of definition, but as a moral judgment itself: we ought not to say someone ought to do something unless it is possible for them to do it. But why restrict the occasions on which we can legitimately say ought in a moral sense? Why not say that we can have duties we cannot intend or perform, but *excuse* the agent? In his objection to J. L. Mackie's criticism of moral arguments for God, Plantinga says: "Perhaps I believe that I ought to do something or other, and also see or think I see that I am obliged to do that thing only if I *can* do so: why can't I properly conclude that I can do it?" Mackie, *The Miracle of Theism*, (Oxford: Clarendon Press, 1982); Plantinga, "Is Theism Really a Miracle?," *Faith and Philosophy* 3(April 1986), 121. But what does it mean to say I "see" that I am obliged only if I can?

93. R. M. Hare seems to assume that if we believed we could never carry through *some* moral intentions, then we would have to give them up. See Hare's "The Simple Believer," in *Religion and Morality*, ed. Outka and Reeder, (Garden City, NY: Doubleday, 1973), pp. 393–427. Although he would not permit any belief in transhuman help, Hare construes the belief that we can sometimes carry through our moral projects as a matter of faith, an assumption not grounded in empirical evidence. Hare's argument does not insist on perfection as Kant's does, so it does not require a transhuman power or location. (See the Introduction to *Religion and Morality*, ed. Outka and Reeder, pp. 28–32).

94. Camus, *The Plague*, pp. 118, 122, 262–263, 278.

95. Welch, *Communities of Resistance and Solidarity: A Feminist Theology of Liberation* (Maryknoll, NY: Orbis, 1985), pp. 49–51, 54, 85, 87, 91. I am not suggesting in what follows that Welch or other liberation theologians have not also objected to an anthropocentric ethic; my point is simply to distinguish two sorts of objections to "triumphalism:" the very demand for a guarantee is dropped; the view of what morality demands is changed.

96. See James M. Gustafson, *Ethics from a Theocentric Perspective*, Vols. 1 and 2 (Chicago: University of Chicago Press, 1981, 1984). For interpretations and evaluations of Gustafson's thought, see Harlan Beckley and Charles Sweezy, eds., *Gustafson's Theocentric Ethics: Interpretations and Assessments* (Macon: Mercer University Press, 1988).

III

Salvation

1. THE CONCEPT OF SALVATION

1.1 *Visions of moral perfection.* As we have seen, a religious reality can function to sanction the moral-legal order: to provide rewards and punishments, redress, and finally to provide the basis of a hope for fulfillment. Thus some visions of our end-state picture moral perfection; not only are the burdens of our natural condition relieved or eliminated but our desire to do and be what is morally good is fixed and entirely dominant. It can even be said that we have no need of the concept of moral requirement, insofar as this reflects a psychological condition where the desire to do what is right often conflicts with other desires. The state of moral perfection can also be pictured as a condition where the best form of moral order can finally be attained.

1.2 *Transmoral modes of being.* But in some traditions there is apparently another sort of hope. A state is envisaged where not only is suffering ended but the moral condition itself is transcended. As historians of religion and anthropologists have observed, believers from a variety of traditions seem to hope for a state where the very duality of good and evil is overcome.[1] Either the hope for a transmoral state supercedes the hope for moral perfection or both are in some way expected.

I will call the transmoral state *salvation*. We ask where our morality comes from, how we learn it, and why it should exist; we ask about making it work, overcoming evil, bringing moral goals to fruition; and we can also ask whether there is any release from the moral condition. When we imagine morally perfect beings, we think of beings like ourselves with needs and desires. But in the sort of state I call salvation, the mode of existence hoped for is even further removed from ordinary experience. As I will explain, we would not have needs or desires in the usual sense and we might not even be conscious of ourselves as independent persons.

Why would such a state be desirable?[2] If moral perfection cannot be reached or sustained, then we might long to have done with the tension between the ideal and our imperfect attempts to reach it. Or perhaps we might believe that moral goodness itself is intrinsically flawed because it depends on human agents, and whatever depends on human agents is changeable, and hence insecure. In the moral condition one is still vulnerable and dependent on others. Morally perfect beings, of course, are not instable like the rest of us, but they are still human, still part of the contingent order. And even if moral perfection to a great degree relieved our worries about flaws in human conduct, many traditions have sensed a reality beyond all aspects of the human condition and have longed to attain it; there is a desire to escape the merely human, to reach another mode of being. Thus moral perfection might be seen as the best that can be made of the human condition, but along with natural existence it is a state we might want to transcend.[3]

What would a transmoral state be like? In some visions of natural and moral perfection, as we saw, the condition of human beings would be changed so that there would no longer be any occasion for a number of sorts of moral categories; if there is no sexuality, for example, then there is no need for sexual and familial institutions; if there is no eating and drinking, or exposure to the elements, then there is no need for normative institutions of economic production and distribution. But if human beings protect and promote other dimensions of one another's well-being through normative patterns, then we still have a vision of moral perfection.[4]

In some visions that have appeared in Judaism and Christianity, however, the human condition is more radically changed. In the final relation to God, human needs and desires are satisfied, or perhaps it is more fitting to say that we would not have needs and desires anymore, but simply experience uninterrupted joy or bliss. Either after death or at some climactic end of history, not only are death or specific aspects of the human condition such as sexuality left behind, but we are no longer beings of need and desire. In the final relation to God, our condition is changed;

our needs are met, fulfilled in God; we not only do not face a situation of scarce resources, but it is God, not a human system, which secures our good. Moreover, we are no longer beings whose desires, emotions, and thoughts must be morally shaped. Humans have long dreamed of a time and place—perhaps once lost but some day recoverable—where there is abundance (magic wishing trees or the trees in the Garden of Eden) and humans are no longer evil.[5] The notion of a transmoral state satisfies these longings, but goes a step beyond; God is "all in all" and we would no longer be creatures of need and desire; thus the twin problematic of our relation to nature and our relation to other humans is transcended. In a section of the *Zohar*, a medieval Judaic mystical text, it is said that in the days of the Messiah human beings will not live under the Tree of Knowledge but under the Tree of Life.[6]

Thus as visions of a Kingdom of God or Messianic Age, where natural and moral evil will end, become "dehistoricized," the line can perhaps be crossed between moral perfection and transmoral expectation. No longer beings of need and desire, we "enjoy" a relation to God or other beings. As we are now constituted, our sociality and hence our humanity—our capacity to relate to others in various ways—depends on moral structures that order thought, emotion, and desire, but in the transmoral state we would enjoy bliss without the normative patterns moralities provide. Those who exhibit spontaneous goodness still have their desires and their impact on others structured by a normative pattern although they do not need the desire to be and do what is morally good. But those who no longer have our needs, desires, emotions, and thoughts do not need normative structures. An analogy may help: One pilot flies perfectly by the rule book, doing what is done because that is what is required (dominant desire for the right); a second pilot flies correctly, in a certain pattern, without needing to desire to fly as required (spontaneous goodness); a third pilot just flies (transmoral state). The third pilot need not even fly in a pattern; flying does not need to be structured in order to avoid crashing oneself or hurting others; the pilot and others simply fly in pleasing ways.

The traditions, however, do not usually say much about just what this flying, this new mode of being, is like. It is more a matter of knowing what it is not. In certain visions not only is desire left behind, but we are no longer conscious of ourselves as individual centers of sentience and agency.[7] We can say at least that God (or another representation of the "really real") is the final good, and God, not a moral system, secures that good; we enjoy the good in a way that transcends ordinary desire, and in relation to God we are no longer beings whose desires, emotions, and thoughts are morally structured.[8]

Let me illustrate by focusing on "apocalyptic" visions. On Paul Hanson's view, apocalyptic visions, which look for a divinely produced, imminent end to natural and moral evil, a "new Heaven and a new Earth," express an extreme form of *moral* idealism or visionary hope, which has to be restrained in order to cope realistically with social improvement.[9] Hanson locates the historical origins of these hopes in a struggle between two religious groups, the "visionary" and the "hierocratic," in the period of Israel's history after the return from the Babylonian exile. For the hierocratic group, a rebuilt temple and an attention to cultic law was the key to Yahweh's presence and hence a return to prosperity and political security.[10] For the visionaries, the restoration of Israel as a nation and its future flourishing depended on an act of divine initiation.[11] Gradually as their hopes for supremacy dimmed, the visions of the visionaries became more and more divorced from the realm of history.[12] Hanson argues that this struggle exemplifies a classic conflict between "ideology" and "utopia," between those who are in control of socioeconomic institutions and seek to legitimate them so as to maintain continuity with older structures and those who are alienated or oppressed in some respect and attempt to authorize radical social change.[13] Ultimately, however, says Hanson, the conflict reflects a constant tension between two "elements" that "constitute the heart of all ethical religions."[14] The "visionary" element sees an ideal divine order that exceeds the religiomoral achievements of human institutions; the "realist" element is concerned with the maintenance and legitimation of current structures. When vision is separated from realism, it abdicates responsibility for the social order; when realism loses vision, it sacralizes imperfect human structures. Thus for Hanson apocalyptic is an extreme form of the vision of moral perfection in "ethical religion"; it is the extreme dehistoricized form of the visionary program. For him it needs to be dialectically wedded—here he is arguing for a normative theological and moral position—to a realistic responsibility for social structures, just as realism needs the visionary element in order to criticize and judge itself.[15]

I am not competent to offer a historical interpretation, but it seems worth considering whether apocalyptic hopes always envisage moral perfection. Perhaps some visions look for a transmoral state of being beyond the dialectic of idealism and realism; like some mystical visions, they may look to a new state of being which goes beyond the moral condition. The new existence God is bringing into being could be "dehistorized" (the group to be saved is no longer a sociopolitical unit, the agent of change is the divine being, and the new order incorporates radical improvements in our natural and psychic condition) but still be a vision of moral goodness.[16] To look for a mode of existence in which we are no longer moral beings, however, would give a different sense to the notion of the "end of history." Moral evil would not so much be replaced by moral perfection, rather moral existence is transcended.

But even if we interpret the category of apocalyptic in terms of moral perfection as Hanson does, it does seem that in many versions of Judaism and Christianity a hope is also present for a final mode of existence expressed in terms of concepts such as "heaven" or the "world to come." It appears to be the case in fact that in many Judaic and Christian traditions (including some discussed in Chapter 2) a period of moral perfection in history is envisaged (notions of a Messianic Age or a millenium), which is then *followed* by a new mode of existence which transcends the moral condition.[17] Emil Fackenheim puts it this way:

> ... the "end of days" [the end of evil] was originally conceived as a messianic age in future time, fulfilling the meaning of history. But out of this grew an additional dimension—the notion of a "world-to-come" beyond all time, fulfilling the meaning of each individual life. The one was the realization of peace, justice, and love on earth; the other was an ultimate divine dispensation beyond time and earth. ... To be sure, Jewish belief never achieved clarity as to the relation between these two dimensions, and perhaps could not; for the "world-to-come" was thought to be past human understanding. But it seemed clear that tendencies to reduce either of these dimensions to the other had to be resisted.[18]

A transmoral mode of being, then, secures our well-being through a relation to the religious reality; there is no longer any need to protect and promote well-being through moral norms; our well-being is no longer dependent on the moral relations that structure human interactions. The conditions that make moral systems necessary have to do, as we have seen, with the basic characteristics of human nature and its environment; human beings as we know them are social and hence moral by nature; we depend in our natural condition on patterns of sexual, economic, and political organization. In a word, human desire, emotion, and thought must be ordered in such a way that forms of individual and social flourishing are possible. Even under conditions of natural abundance and moral perfection, well-being is secured through a system of norms which structures thought, emotion, and desire so that some form of social existence is possible. But in a transmoral state, humans are transformed and fulfillment is anchored in the relation to God. The final relation to God transforms *simultaneously* both the external and the internal aspects of the human condition; we no longer depend on external resources, even ones that are always abundant (magic wishing trees), nor are we beings whose internal constitution is such that our interactions must be normatively ordered. We have been freed not only from a dependence on ordinary goods, but from our vulnerability to ourselves and other humans. Whether the final relation is imaged as a mode of existence where individual consciousness is retained or not, the important point is that the new state transcends even the familiar dream of natural and moral perfection.

1.3 Concepts of salvation. The notion of *salvation*, then, I want to reserve for those visions that see a type of transmoral destiny for humankind. A vision of moral perfection rounds out, completes the moral condition; in many religious traditions, however, the destiny of human beings goes beyond this condition; the end-state takes one beyond moral perfection. We move, as Kenelm Burridge puts it, to a different level of being.[19]

It would be possible, however, to use the concepts of sanction and salvation differently. Sanction could signify moral and legal pressures (rewards and punishments) and restoration or compensation for innocent suffering; salvation could be broadened to mean any release from natural and moral evil, including both moral perfection and states that transcend the moral condition.[20] This way of using the concepts would stress the desire for an end to natural and moral evil (for the individual or for humankind in general) and would take moral perfection and a transmoral state as two ways of attaining it.

I have used the concepts as I have because for purposes of this book it seems important to emphasize the difference between visions of moral perfection and transmoral states. My definition of the concepts reflects a distinction between religious interpretations of our moral condition—even its perfection—and visions in which humans, having once emerged into a moral condition, now attain a transmoral level of being. Rudolf Otto was right, in my view, to distinguish what he called a "numinous" goal from a religious destiny conceived entirely in moral terms (he was wrong, however, to extend his thesis to all religions).[21] As Burridge explains, religions often picture humankind as originally a "free-mover," not subject to moral categories but "at one with Creator and Allbeing."[22] Through some primeval process humankind becomes cultural and moral, becomes subject to moral and legal structures. Many traditions also provide us with a way of moving beyond the moral condition. Even if an awareness of the *distinction* between good and evil remains, the new mode of being secures well-being without moral patterns.

1.4 Connections to morality. If the salvific state transcends the moral condition, is it *completely* unrelated to morality? Just the fact that the transmoral state transcends morality is a "connection" of sorts, as I noted in the Introduction; but is the transmoral state linked to morality in any positive way? In seeking and receiving salvific life, or some anticipation of it, does the individual or the religious community forsake the moral-legal order? How are seeking and attaining salvation related to moral existence? In some traditions, Western and Eastern, it does seem that the salvific path and goal have no relation to moral structures whatsoever; moral goodness does not guide, or enable, or in any way characterize those who seek or attain the highest. Sometimes when Otto spoke of a numinous goal he seemed to have this sort of salvation in mind: the numinous is hostile or indifferent to morality. At other times, however, he seemed to have in mind a goal that was beyond moral perfection but which had an organic connection to moral striving.[23]

What I want to do in the body of this chapter is to look at ways in which the numinous is connected to moral striving in some Western traditions. Morality may serve as a framework for salvific striving, as a prerequisite, and in addition, as Otto suggested, the numinous mode of being can fulfill morality in an eminent sense; moral structures are transcended but their requirements also satisfied. Those who taste salvation in this life, moreover, or who live an anticipatory mode of existence, do not always sever all ties with moral structures; indeed Western traditions seem to have devised a number of sorts of relations between the new life and the old. Whereas in Chapter 2 we saw a tension between the old moral world and a new moral order, here in Chapter 3 we will see tensions between the moral life and the goal of transmoral existence. Let us look at some formulations of these ways (framework, prerequisite, eminent fulfillment, life in this world) in which moral systems can be connected to, yet finally transcended by, a transmoral goal.

2. A MORAL FRAMEWORK FOR SALVATION

2.1 *An encompassing structure.* In some traditions it seems that moral structures guide, regulate the salvific path; it could even be said that a moral framework encapsulates, encompasses salvation. Thus seeking is contained within a moral vision, although the salvific state itself is transmoral; the individual is bound to others who also have a transcendent goal. The contrast here is with traditions where the process takes place outside any moral framework. For example, suppose one gained the transmoral state through a process of knowledge which was impervious to the actions of others, which could not be affected negatively or positively by their actions.[24] On this view, moral norms would be irrelevant to the salvific process. Other traditions, however, assert that one can be hurt or helped on the way, although the goal itself transcends the moral condition.

2.2 *The highest or true good.* Now how exactly is it possible that there is a moral framework for the salvific quest? Part of our understanding of the role of moral norms in human life as we know it is that they provide social structures that promote and protect well-being.[25] But it seems clear that a salvific state in which one no longer has needs or desires or even loses personal consciousness is very different from ordinary states or attitudes that we call well-being or happiness. How can creatures who have no desires experience well-being, or those who have no personal consciousness *experience* anything at all? If the object of a morality is to structure relationships in which humans find well-being, then it is hard to see how the salvific path can be encompassed within morality. Yet the religious traditions do speak, say, of the relation to God as "joy" or "bliss."[26] The traditions often apparently take these terms to refer to a kind of satisfaction, related to, even if not identical with, ordinary well-being; the salvific state, in other words, seems to be the supreme good, the supremely valuable state. In some traditions it is even seen as the only true good, in contrast to false or counterfeit goods. Just how there can be this sort of analogy between ordinary well-being and salvation is the problem, but the traditions insist that the analogy is real. Bracketing the issue of a problematic analogy, then, the fact that human beings no longer have desires or even personal existence would not mean that the salvific state is not parallel to other sorts of well-being whose attainment is provided through moral structures in the contexts of ordinary existence. Thus even if the salvific goal is transmoral, it is envisaged as the supreme good and hence it could be encompassed within a moral framework.

The moral system provides a structure, therefore, not only for ordinary well-being but for salvation as well. Some salvation seekers as we will see may not themselves uphold the moral framework as it applies to ordinary life because they expect an immediate consummation and no longer believe themselves responsible for mundane affairs. But the framework still guides their activity; the framework is applied to a transcendent goal.[27] How would this be the case?

2.3 Noninjury. In the first place, we expect to find rules against harm and coercion in moral systems (let us refer to harm and coercion jointly as injury). The definition of these rules and their justification may differ from culture to culture, but part of the function of moral systems is to provide protections of these sorts. Thus we would expect a Judaic or Christian system to include various rules against injuring others in the ordinary course of life.

But the goal of salvation, one's relation to the ultimate, might be thought on occasion to require one to injure someone's temporal well-being. As the story of Abraham and Isaac (Genesis 22) is sometimes interpreted, Abraham is willing to sacrifice Isaac and thus to disregard the ordinary rule against murder, but he does not necessarily injure Isaac at the salvific level. If the deity conforms to the principles or qualities at the heart of the moral order, then nothing Abraham is enjoined to do would finally harm Isaac; what is commanded is loving and just, although perhaps not comprehensible by human beings. Presumably salvation is envisaged in such a way that Isaac's death would not affect his salvific destiny; thus Abraham has not violated morality. On this interpretation God does not violate a basic moral principle, but merely suspends an interhuman prescription; God's command to Abraham is just, for life is God's, and it is also loving, for God will secure Isaac's eternal good.[28]

The contrasting reading of the Abraham and Isaac story, of course, would have it that in being willing to kill Isaac, Abraham departs from the moral framework altogether; it is not that Isaac's final good transcends earthly good, or that it does not depend on Abraham's care, but on God's; rather the moral framework is "suspended" entirely. The moral-legal metaphor in which the incident is couched (God's *command* to Abraham) is precisely what on this interpretation is left behind; Abraham's obedience contravenes basic moral principles or qualities, not just earthly applications thereof. Unless one is prepared to set aside the moral order in this way, so the interpretation goes, the deity one worships is in effect nothing more than morality reified or hypostatized; in the words of Kierkegaard's pseudonymous author in *Fear and Trembling*:

> The ethical is the universal, and as such it is also the divine. Thus it is proper to say that every duty is essentially duty to God, but if no more can be said than this, then it is also said that I actually have no duty to God. . . . If in this connection I then say that it is my duty to love God, I am actually pronouncing only a tautology, inasmuch as "God" in a totally abstract sense is here understood as the divine—that is, the universal, that is, the duty. The whole existence of the human race rounds itself off as a perfect, self-contained sphere, and then the ethical is that which limits and fills at one and the same time. God comes to be an invisible vanishing point, an impotent thought; his power is only in the ethical, which fills all of existence.[29]

The ethical, that is, the moral, cannot be the fulcrum of worship, the link between persons and God, for if it were then the ethical would be the determining factor in the relationship, not God; in effect God would fade away, "his power is only in the ethical . . ." The relation to God cannot be encompassed within a particular moral framework, indeed within any moral framework.[30] If a *moral* framework intervened, one would still be obeying because of one's devotion to morality.[31]

Moreover, on this view just as one does not love and obey God because God has moral qualities, so one does not love and obey God because God transcends morality but somehow still has qualities that are analogous to moral ones. If the relation to God were anchored in these qualities, then we would love God because God's qualities are metaphysically analogous to moral ones; in this sense God's "power" would still lie only in the "ethical." As the pseudonymous author would put it, the relation to God would still be "mediated" or interpreted in terms of the ethical.

The interpretation of the biblical story frequently given in Judaic and Christian traditions, I believe, is not the one enunciated by Kierkegaard's pseudonym (as I have just interpreted it). Nor is it the view that God conforms to basic moral principles even when commanding an exception to interhuman prescriptions. The ultimate is more than moral, but not nonmoral; in its essence it is somehow metaphysically like the qualities or principles of the moral order it creates, although the metaphors and analogies of religious discourse may not allow us to say *how*.

Thus Abraham's devotion to God is not based on his devotion to the moral, but it is based on his devotion to God, as a being with a certain nature, a nature whose characteristics, as I depicted the mainstream model in Chapter 1, shape the created moral order. Thus only in this sense does Abraham's devotion fall "within" the moral. God *creates* the "ethical," so that it is improper to say that moral requirement itself is part of the divine essence. But because of God's nature Abraham knows he would never have been commanded to injure Isaac salvifically.[32]

2.4 Justice and love.   Second, in addition to prohibitions against injury, we can also expect to find in a moral system some notion of distributive justice, some idea of how individuals are to enjoy the fruits and bear the burdens of social existence. In some societies, goods and services are divided in an extremely unequal way; in others there is more equality. Just how the system is set up may be connected, as we saw in Chapter 1, to a vision of creation and the structure of the cosmos. But now our attention is elsewhere: What access and what share do people have in regard to salvific good? Salvation seekers might drop ordinary roles and duties (sex, economy, political order) that institutionalize a view of distributive justice, but the framework of justice might still apply to the salvific path. In some religious traditions there is the assumption that regardless of inequalities of natural talent and socioeconomic status, everyone, at least everyone in a certain moral state, has an equal capacity for the good of salvation. In Theravāda Buddhism, of course, one has to be in a human rebirth in the first place and this might come around more than once; in Judaism or Christianity, one has only one earthly life or perhaps an additional opportunity after death (notions of purgatory in the Roman Catholic tradition, for example). But the natural and social inequalities of life do not affect the ability to seek or receive salvation; one supposedly has religious capacities that are not significantly weakened or strengthened by one's place in ordinary life. Against this background of natural equality of capacity, there still might be ways in which the religious life could be assisted by human actions that stem from the cooperative life of the community. If so, then in a framework where equality is a norm of justice, there would be injunctions to share the *benefits* of such assistance equally.[33]

In contrast, one can imagine an entirely different notion, namely, that religious capacities vary; it might be believed that at least in this life there simply are going to be differences in the capacity for spiritual attainment.[34] Against such a background of natural inequality, we might still find injunctions to give everyone an equal opportunity to realize the capacities they have. But we might find the view that in light of natural differences, inequalities in the distribution of resources were justified. Even where this religious inegalitarianism holds, however, we would still be dealing with a system of distributive justice, a set of beliefs about access to mundane and transcendent good.

Finally, in addition to allocating *benefits,* a system of distributive justice would provide for the sharing of the *burdens* involved. Lay people and religious officials, such as priests or rabbis, share the burdens of the religious community, which is the guardian of tradition and the earthly vehicle of salvation across the generations.[35]

A system of justice, then, against a background of beliefs about human capacities, would link ordinary existence and salvation in a pattern that distributes both benefits and burdens, goods of various sorts and the price of attaining them. In addition to justice, of course, Judaic and Christian traditions appeal to love of neighbor. To teach the truth about salvation, Augustine remarked, is the principal expression of love of neighbor.[36] Some traditions, moreover, as I noted in Chapter 2, work out a morality of "love" as opposed to a morality of "justice." But as I also noted, a morality of "love" is structured by convictions about justice in the sense of distributive fairness. Thus even moralities of "love" will incorporate convictions about how the benefits and burdens of salvific striving are to be allocated and related to mundane well-being. Indeed it might be that one would have to fail to help others at the earthly level in order to promote salvific good. It might be seen as not as important to save others, say, from starvation, as to preach the good news of salvation. As we will see ahead, traditions relate mundane and eternal good in different ways. But the important point now is that even where mundane well-being is downgraded, moral convictions about how we should treat others—specifically how benefits and burdens should be distributed—still guide the lives of believers.

3. THE SALVIFIC PATH

3.1 Moral goodness as a prerequisite.
The moral framework may encapsulate salvific striving, but how does one get or how does one receive salvific life? What condition does one have to be in? How does one prepare? Can one? In particular how is the moral life related to one's state of readiness? Some religious traditions have held apparently that salvation (sometimes imaged as a form of knowledge) is directly attainable no matter what one's moral state. The individual might even be enjoined not to harm and to help others on the salvific path, but salvation might not depend in any way on one's own moral condition. One could propel oneself or be delivered straight to the salvific state without first undergoing a moral transformation. But other traditions, including forms of Judaism and Christianity, seem to have held that a clean moral slate and moral goodness are a prerequisite for salvation.[37] Western traditions that have held out the hope of a transmoral destiny have interpreted the notion of a moral prerequisite in different ways, but something like the vision of

moral perfection sketched in the last chapter seems to emerge in a number of strands. To reach salvation guilt must be assuaged and moral goodness prevail. Let us look at some ways these ideas might be developed.

3.2 The removal of guilt.

The notion of freedom from guilt as a prerequisite might mean simply that all moral debts must be settled. The slate must be cleaned; moral accounts have priority, although not final importance. Another sense of the prerequisite idea is that one cannot come to salvation with punishments outstanding; demerit and the appropriate punishment still to be discharged drag one down, do not permit one to transcend the moral realm. This, of course, assumes that rewards and punishments are attached to merit and demerit; one must clean the moral slate not only for its own sake, but to get rid of its consequences.

3.3 Moral goodness as a stage in self-development.

The achievement of moral goodness—a state of moral growth or even moral perfection—could be seen as a prerequisite above and beyond the removal of guilt. It could be seen as a state in self-development prior to salvation. Perhaps it is said that one must control desire through moral virtue before one can reach the state where desire is transcended in total fulfillment; moral feelings and dispositions can be cultivated as ways of training the mind, readying oneself for the salvific apprehension of the final good.[38]

3.4 Moral goodness and relations to others.

One could also need moral goodness in order to have the qualities necessary to enter a salvific relationship with a deity or other individuals. In some versions of the Christian tradition, for example, a degree of benevolence, concern for the well-being of others, seems to be a prerequisite for the salvific mode of existence where the good of all is affirmed and enjoyed; you are not ready, in other words, to step into the new world unless you are already a certain type of person in this one. Where the final fulfillment is envisaged as a certain sort of relation, in other words, moral goodness points you in the right direction, brings you to the threshold.[39]

3.5 Extrinsic and intrinsic means.

I have been speaking as if moral goodness were necessary in a purely extrinsic sense, either as a state in self-development or as preparation for a salvific way of relating to others; one needs moral goodness in order to do or be something else; it is a launching platform, a ladder to be kicked away. But the qualities of moral goodness are sometimes seen as analogously present in the transmoral state; in this sense they are intrinsic means, ingredient in their end. I will say more about this under the heading of eminent fulfillment.[40]

3.6 Effort and aid.

The achievement of freedom from guilt and the requisite moral goodness can either be seen as due to one's own effort or as a gift of God, or some combination of the two. Protestant Christians have accused Roman Catholics of the view that humans have to "earn" salvation; some Protestants seem to suggest that nothing humans can do on their own, even repentance, is a necessary condition of God's "grace," that is, pardon and forgiveness, moral renewal, and eventual salvation. Catholics have replied that salvation is a "gift" of God, but that humans have a part in preparing for it. But both traditions have usually insisted that forgiveness and sanctification through God's "spirit" are a prerequisite for salvation; many classical debates have occurred about the relation of human effort and divine aid in achieving this prerequisite. The dynamics of moral goodness, the interplay between human striving and divine assistance, become the first act in dramas of salvation.

Another aspect of the classical debates among Christians has not been so much about whether humans must repent or take other steps towards their own moral renewal; even if humans must take these steps, say some Protestants, God can still be selective; God does not necessarily forgive and sanctify all who repent. But this selectivity is still understood as morally justified. Calvin, for example, says that God's mercy is "freely given ... without regard to human worth," and that God's decision is "just and irreprehensible, but incomprehensible."[41] Or as I noted in Chapter 2, other moral considerations can override justice. Thus God, who has qualities analogous to those inscribed in the moral order, completes the process of moral renewal as a prerequisite to salvation, and even if not all who do what they can are selected, the process is said to be morally justified, although not necessarily understandable by humans.[42]

4. EMINENT FULFILLMENT

4.1 A different and better way.   Although the salvific state itself goes beyond the conditions that make morality necessary or even possible, such a state may still be connected to moral experience in another way and I want to call that connection *eminent fulfillment.*[43] By eminent fulfillment, I mean that salvation may negate and yet fulfill moral existence. While salvific striving itself may be encompassed by a moral framework and moral virtue can be a prerequisite, the striver aims at a state that transcends the moral condition. Yet the new state, which finally leaves behind the moral framework, is not entirely discontinuous, but is interpreted as a consummation or fulfillment.

4.2 Negation.   The one who hopes for salvation, as we know, believes in a good that transcends human goods and in a way of realizing that good which does not consist in moral relationships. Thus ordinary goods and moral relations are devalued or negated; they are no longer of final importance. Just how this negation is expressed in this world, as I will try to show ahead, can take many forms, but in one way or another the believer who hopes for a transmoral goal "transvalues" ordinary goods and moral goodness, even the spontaneous goodness of those who do not need to be motivated by moral requirement.

4.3 Fulfillment. Thus the transmoral goal, however much it is encompassed by a moral framework or depends on moral goodness as a prerequisite, is discontinuous with the moral condition and the ties that bind human agents. But at the same time there is continuity. The achievement of the highest good fulfills the search for well-being and the way in which this good is achieved through the deity conforms analogically to the normative relations that provide for the good of self and other under the conditions of moral existence. The transcendent realization of the highest good renders moral systems unnecessary, for it does what they are designed to do in a different and better way.

Let me try to explain this in more detail. Moral relations protect and promote the good of self and neighbor in some pattern; moral notions structure desire, emotion, and thought so that some form of social existence is possible. Even in a state of moral perfection, human agents structure their relations to one another so that an interpersonal pattern of good is achieved. But in a transmoral state which is an eminent fulfillment, moral parameters are achieved analogically in a mode of being which transcends moral perfection and in some versions even ordinary consciousness of self and other. The transmoral state is believed to be, in some sense, *like* moral perfection. The good is achieved in a certain configuration; the flyers do not hurt each other but rather experience joy in their own and each other's flights. But the transmoral state is unlike moral perfection as well because it does not consist in relations between ordinary human agents; the flyers do not have to pattern their flights. The good, moreover, is not only *distributed* in a morally right way, the good is "experienced" in a mode of being that is somehow analogous to moral relations. Salvation which is not eminent fulfillment would be a self-contained bliss or ecstacy that does not involve any relation with another. But in eminent fulfillment (even where ordinary agency and self-consciousness are transcended) each "soul" enjoys the good in relation to God (imagined, say, as love or friendship), or, as is commonly said, self and neighbor share God as final good: a union of self and neighbor in union with God.

In some Christian visions of the Kingdom of God, for example, God secures the good of all. The interests of each self are no longer left to the system that an ethic of "justice" or "love" provides, but God is the Other with the power and the will to respond to all.[44] Thus a happiness open to all who repent is achieved, a happiness that transcends any ordinary good, and it is achieved in a way that exceeds any possible human accomplishment, even moral perfection. The good of self and other is secured without a moral network, even that of spontaneous goodness. The moral framework orders ordinary life and also structures the path to salvation; the moral framework guides access to the highest good but now it is achieved in a way that transcends the structures of human goodness.[45] Believers may not know exactly *what* the new mode of being will be, but they know *that* it will be an eminent fulfillment.

Augustine, for example, was reluctant to say too much about the "incorruptible" bodies of the blessed, although he did insist that the "eyes of the spiritual body" will be able to see God.[46] But he was clear about the basics: perfect happiness and no moral evil for all the saved.

> God Himself, who is the Author of virtue, shall there be its reward; for as there is nothing greater or better, He has promised Himself. . . . He shall be the end of our desires who shall be seen without end, loved without cloy, praised without weariness.[47]

> But the [human] nature . . . , having sinned when it had the ability to do so, it is by a more abundant grace that it is delivered so as to reach that freedom in which it cannot sin. . . . And thus piety and justice shall be as indefeasible as happiness.[48]

> This outgoing of affection [perfect happiness in loving God] . . . shall certainly be, like eternal life itself, common to all.[49]

In visions such as these, the new mode of being could be seen as the telos of the qualities forged in moral experience; detachment from self and identification with others could be realized in a mode of mutual fulfillment; perhaps even the very distinction between self and other does no work, will no longer be necessary. The new mode of mutual joy could be seen as the consummation of the impulse to affirm the good of all and to escape the fetters of self-absorption.

4.4 *Valuation and mode of being.* Thus eminent fulfillment, as it is suggested, for example, in strands of Judaism and Christianity, incorporates two ideas. First, a good is achieved in salvation which is superior to ordinary goods. Second, the salvific mode of existence secures the good of all in a way that is different and better than the way ordinary moral duties and virtues protect and promote human good. The moral framework that structured salvific striving is transcended, but its aims are fulfilled; the final good is realized in a new mode. Salvific attainment and the process of seeking it are justified because salvific good and the mode of its realization go "beyond" yet are in continuity with the moral framework.

5. SALVATION AND LIFE IN THIS WORLD

5.1 *In but not of the world.* In some Western traditions, then, the final destiny is not envisaged as moral perfection, but as a transmoral mode of being. But the struggle for this goal is set within a moral frame-work; moral goodness can even be seen as a prerequisite; and indeed the final goal can be imaged as eminent fulfillment. In this sense, the moral life is not only negated but affirmed. But do believers *achieve* salvation in this life? Western traditions have envisaged a number of possibilities; let me sketch a few.[50]

5.2 Realization. My historical impression is that on rare occasions in Western traditions adherents have claimed that they have been deliv-ered from the moral condition and once and for all completely translated into a transmoral mode of being. Of course, it is extraordinarily difficult to ascertain historically what sorts of claims have been made. But suppose that a group of adherents claimed to have achieved, not merely some form of moral perfection, but a transmoral mode of being. The final transformation is perhaps yet to be fully achieved but the new mode of being has to an important extent already been realized. What would the believer's stance toward the world be while waiting for death or the end of history?

Suppose the transmoral state were not imaged as an eminent ful-fillment, a mode of being which in some analogical way achieves a realiza-tion of moral parameters. Where this was the expectation, then we would not be surprised if the putative realizers feel that they have transcended moral concern altogether; they might feel free to commit or not commit any act; their stance would be amoral, indifferent to moral good or evil.

But if the transmoral state were conceived as eminent fulfillment, then it is not only the highest good, but the highest good as a mode of being which, as I argued, realizes moral relations analogically, a state that transcends but nonetheless fulfills what moral relations demand. Where the goal is understood as eminent fulfillment, then I think the stance of a this-worldly realizer would not be amoral. For the realizers, to be sure, their salvation is not merely de jure (promised by God) but de facto (ac-complished, achieved); in this life, they are already in the relation to God which is the transmoral goal. They do not conceive of themselves as crea-tures of need and desire. In addition, they experience this good in a mode that does not depend on the intentions, desires, and acts of other merely human beings; in short their good does not rest on moral relations. But insofar as the transmoral state is analogous to moral perfection, those saved would not commit just *any* act. It might even be said that they are not able to sin.[51] Thus insofar as they still have or can have an impact on the salvific good of others, they will act according to the framework.[52] Or-dinary institutional norms related to sex, economy, and political order could be transcended; the salvific goal may redefine ordinary duties of not hurting and helping; but the new state would not violate the basic norms of the moral framework.

As far as I can tell from Gershom Scholem's interpretation of Sabbatai Sevi, for example, the so-called "antinomianism" of Sevi or other fig-ures in this seventeenth-century Messianic movement did not reject any continuity with the moral framework. Nathan of Gaza appealed to the tra-ditional concept of special exceptions in Talmudic law, but his real opin-ion, says Scholem, followed the *Raya Mehemna* section of the Zohar: the soul of the Messiah has attained the Tree of Life and passed beyond "the duality and distinctions of good and evil which derive from the Tree of Knowledge."[53] Even the biblical prohibitions of incest are suspended.[54] The redemption Nathan expects is one in which the original and perfect form of the Torah will be reachieved. Says Scholem,

> The Tree of Life symbolizes the paradisiacal unity of the Torah before its separation into the duality of the Tree of Knowledge. In the eschatologic future the dominion of the Tree of Life would encompass the whole cos-mos, and then laws and rules deriving from the Tree of Knowledge, which is the Tree of Death, would pass away.[55]

Thus "antinomianism" could signal the suspension of morality as a human institution.[56] The Tree of Life could signify a state of eminent ful-fillment where the distinction between good and evil is transcended. But this is precisely to affirm that the moral framework is recaptured albeit in a new mode.[57]

5.3 Anticipation.   This view is close to the realization model; the be-liever does not think that salvation has been achieved even partially, but tries to live so far as possible *as if* it had. One is still in the moral condition and the negative and positive injunctions apply to the salvific path, but one casts off a good deal at least of the old code. This is not just a matter of going beyond marriage, property, or the coerce state to a new moral order that would provide alternative sexual, economic, and organizational structures; it is an anticipation of an existence where natural conditions will be altered and one will not need moral structures, even the spontane-ous goodness of moral perfection. Although the framework remains as a moral system that structures the path to salvation, believers cast off the mundane life and bear witness to the transmoral existence to come.

Let me turn to some early Christian sources that may reflect this an-ticipation model. The texts are notoriously difficult to interpret, and many different ideas were evidently going around in the early period, but some of the sources suggest to me an anticipation of the transmoral condition.[58] In Ursula LeGuin's *The Dispossessed,* the utopian settlers on the planet An-arres are motivated by a concern for the good of others, and new sexual, economic, and political institutions are devised. Although New Testament injunctions have been interpreted to signify this sort of society, I think that some sayings can be plausibly viewed as anticipations of a new mode of existence which transcends mutual benevolence; one does not merely reach a stage where "love" is sufficient and "justice" is unnecessary, but in anticipation of mutual and total fulfillment one now abandons any thought of *moral patterns* that preserve the good of the self and others. And even if the sources are best interpreted in their context as part of an expected new world of moral perfection, they have also been *read* in later traditions as anticipations of transmoral existence.

For instance, the injunctions to take no thought for the morrow, to give all you have to the poor, to give one's cloak, to forego self-defense or retributive justice by turning the other cheek could be read as anticipations of a new transmoral existence to come. To give all to the poor, for example, is not only to give one's own goods, to which one has a right according to current notions of property, but it is also to divest oneself of resources that may be necessary to discharge duties to others; one has left the network of ordinary duties and entered upon a new existence; one leaves old duties unfulfilled; one would not be in a position to be a Good Samaritan as one is enjoined elsewhere, at least over a period of time, if one gives *all*.[59] To give all, therefore, could be interpreted as a step beyond even the nonpropertarian moral ideal of the planet Anarres; now one looks to a condition where goods and moral goodness are left behind.[60]

The final fellowship with God is not yet consummated, then, but believers cast off moral and legal traditions that pertain to the major areas of life: personal security, sex, economy, political order. While in some of the New Testament (the texts reflect different communities and forms of early Christianity), love of neighbor is presented as the sum of the "law" or as a new mode of moral existence that replaces the nomos revealed by God to Israel, in other places it seems to embody a way of existing which goes beyond moral perfection.

In this interpretation, then, believers step outside basic aspects of the nomos. This is not a visionary embodiment of a new moral order; that would be a hope for moral perfection. It is an anticipatory leap into a new existence. The task that remains is to bear witness to the consummation that awaits believers. The only adjustments to be made are those absolutely necessary for the maintenance of the religious community and its task in the world.

5.4 Integration with an ongoing social world. In another important motif, some measure of realization or anticipation is envisaged, but these are *confined* in one way or the other and related to life in an ongoing world of moral institutions.[61]

I believe that this provision for an ongoing moral world is what Kenelm Burridge means by "new rules" in his discussion of "millenarianism." According to Burridge, a millenarian movement is one that begins in one or more typical situations: where there is a new source of good or value introduced into a culture, such as, the appearance of Western cargo in the islands of Oceania; where some new measurement of human worth, especially money, is introduced into a primitive economy; where there is an agreed upon set of values but one group is systematically denied access to the relevant goods; where one culture is completely defeated or destroyed by another.[62] Where these situations obtain, a new vision of human good often arises along with a new view of the norms of human community which govern its allocation. An initial phase of growing alienation is followed by a period in which a prophet may announce the new vision and lead the people in various ways designed to prepare for and to enter upon the new order of reality. Here there may occur an experience of "no rules," a throwing off of the old nomos, a release from obligation which in some cultures is expressed in orgiastic sexual activities and the cessation of economic activity. The final phase, if the movement retains any mode of existence, will be characterized by the formation of "new rules," new norms for the production and distribution of the goods that now provide the measure of human worth, the "integrity" or sense of self-worth, which for Burridge is the key to the psychology of millenarianism. He thinks that the stage of "no rules" is invariably followed by the "new rules" phase:

> Through and behind the variety of cultural idioms in which it may be expressed, the millennium points to a condition of being in which humans become free movers, in which there are no obligations, in which all earthly desires are satisfied and therefore expunged. A new earth merges into the new heaven. On the other hand, the phraseology of millenial aspirations *always* envisages a new set of rules, new kinds of obligation, a new earth in which heaven is more brightly mirrored.[63]

As he argues in "Levels of Being," some religious visions provide for a transition that takes one to a "spiritual" level of existence beyond the sphere of culture and morality, but he says there will *always* be a "return to life in time and space."[64]

It seems to me, however, that some traditions seek a *permanent* transition and attempt to achieve realization or anticipation for the community of believers.[65] What Burridge says is always envisaged has often happened nonetheless; there is, on the part of some members of the community or in some aspects of their lives, a reengagement, or rather a continued engagement, of the "redemptive process," the production and exchange of goods through a moral system.

Let us look at some forms of this reengagement or integration in Western traditions. Sometimes realization or anticipation is confined to certain adepts, while others destined eventually for salvation live now in the moral condition and maintain the mundane world; stages or levels of attainment are distinguished; moral practices are seen as a springboard and training ground, and are perhaps also justified as necessary while the world continues; some believers have a responsibility to the mundane order for its own sake, while others focus on salvation. Another form of integration confines realization or anticipation to certain moments of experience (the mystic tastes ecstasy but returns to life in the world), or special contexts (relations within the religious community in contrast to relations with nonbelievers).

The special experience of salvation also may be taken, moreover, to provide a crucial ingredient for ordinary moral relations. One might learn from a "mystical" experience or relations within the religious community some crucial premise about the relation of selves, and one would use this knowledge as one returns to ordinary life; one's salvific and one's ordinary experience are integrated in this way. And one's desires might be transformed so that one is a different person; the "taste" of salvation would function in a fashion similar to the "trust" motif in Evans's theology: an enabling connection or integration is envisaged.

W. T. Stace for example nicely expresses one view of the relation of mysticism and morality:

> The basis of the mystical theory of ethics is that the separateness of individual selves produces that egoism which is the source of conflict, grasping, aggressiveness, selfishness, hatred, cruelty, malice, and other forms of evil; and that this separateness is abolished in the mystical consciousness in which all distinctions are annulled. The inevitable emotional counterpart of the separateness of selves is the basic hostility which gives rise to Hobbes's war of all against all. The natural emotional counterpart of the mystical awareness that there is, in that reality which the mystic believes himself to perceive, no separateness of I from you, or of you from he, and that we are all one in the Universal Self—the emotional counterpart of this is love. And love, according to the theory, is the sole basis, and also the sole command, of morality.[66]

> To say that I love or sympathize with another living being is to say that I feel his feelings—for instance, that I suffer when he suffers or rejoice if he rejoices. The mystical theory will allege that this phenomenon is an incipient and partial breaking down of the barriers and partitions which separate the two individual selves; and that if this breakdown were completed, it would lead to an actual identity of the "I" and the "he." Love is thus a dim groping towards that disappearance of individuality in the Universal Self which is part of the essence of mysticism.[67]

On Stace's view mystical experience would presumably strengthen one's sense of oneness with and love for others when one returns to ordinary consciousness.

Still another mode of integration confines realization or anticipation to inner space. It is not, as in the former model, that one moves back and forth between special experiences or relations and the ordinary world, but that one exists in both the special and the ordinary world simultaneously.

One might live in the "spirit" or "taste eternity" while doing externally what others do.[68] Augustine's thought is notoriously complex, but the following quotations seem to catch the idea of maintaining moral and legal structures while interpreting them as part of a transcendent destiny. For Augustine, believers constitute a "heavenly city" that awaits its consummation; it shares moral and legal structures with the "earthly city" in the meantime:

> The heavenly city, or rather the part of it which sojourns on earth and lives by faith, makes use of this peace [earthly] only because it must, until this mortal condition which necessitates it shall pass away. Consequently, so long as it lives like a captive and a stranger in the earthly city, though it has already received the promise of redemption, and the gift of the Spirit as the earnest of it, it makes no scruple [no objection] to obey the laws of the earthly city, whereby the things necessary for the maintenance of this mortal life are administered; and thus, as this life is common to both cities, so there is a harmony between them in regard to what belongs to it. . . .
>
> This heavenly city, then, while it sojourns on earth, calls citizens out of all nations, and gathers together a society of pilgrims of all languages, not scrupling about diversities in the manners, laws, and institutions whereby earthly peace is secured and maintained, but recognizing that, however various these are, they all tend to one and the same end of earthly peace. It therefore is so far from rescinding and abolishing these diversities, that it even preserves and adapts them, so long only as no hindrance to the worship of the one supreme and true God is thus introduced. Even the heavenly city, therefore, while in its state of pilgrimage, avails itself of the peace of earth, and, so far as it can without injuring faith and godliness, desires and maintains a common agreement among men regarding the acquisition of the necessaries of life, and makes this earthly peace bear upon the peace of heaven; for this alone can be truly called and esteemed the peace of the reasonable creatures, consisting as it does in the perfectly ordered and harmonious enjoyment of God and of one another in God. When we shall have reached that peace, this mortal life shall give place to one that is eternal, and our body shall be no more this animal body which by its corruption weighs down the soul, but a spiritual body feeling no want, and in all its members subjected to the will. In its pilgrim state the heavenly city possesses this peace by faith; and by this faith it lives righteously when it refers to the attainment of that peace every good action towards God and man; for the life of the city is a social life.[69]

In the salvific state, we shall have a "spiritual body feeling no want"; we use the "peace" of earthly law and order in order to provide those minimal conditions that "maintain" mortal life and sustain believers as they aim for salvation. The earthly peace will "bear upon" and each action "refer to" the final good; earthly morality and law are interpreted as a stepping stone to the true peace of the heavenly city.

Whether believers have opted for the realization/anticipation models, or for forms of integration, depends on various elements in their visions of salvation: the relation of mundane to transmundane good (organically connected or sharply distinguished), the path to the highest, the roles of divine and human agency, the timeframe in which the drama occurs. The historical task is to trace the relation of differences of vision to views about the believer's life in this world.

5.5   Wholly future.   One additional option, again dependent on a particular vision of the how, when, where, and who of salvation, is to see the transmoral goal as wholly future. No humans are to attain or to anticipate it, even in any of the integrated forms. The transmoral state is a final consummation to be achieved either after death for the individual or at some climatic end of history. Whatever can be made morally of history, and here opinions will run from optimism to pessimism (see Chapter 2), the final goal transcends earthly experience for all believers. Thus the gamut of options extends from the immediate, to modes of adjustment and compromise, to the wholly future.

6.   CRITICAL DISCUSSION

6.1   *Indifferent or inimical.*   Visions of salvation have to face general metaphysical and epistemological difficulties, of course. The entire idea of eminent fulfillment in a relation to a just or loving deity depends on the notion of analogy. And many moderns believe that traditional religious hopes are groundless; it is a question of evidence and the nature of faith.

But I want to address other issues here. In Chapters 1 and 2 I noted that some religious thinkers have claimed that a sacred source or sanction was required for the validity or the fulfillment of morality. I suggested that this was not the case, although religious beliefs do decisively influence the shape of particular moral systems. In regard to salvation, some opponents and even some proponents of religion have claimed that in contrast to being necessary for morality, the hope of salvation reduces its importance. Even if there are various ways in which moral experience is connected to a transmoral state, does salvation ultimately displace moral concern? Does it divert believers from the social struggle by giving them a reason not to focus their attention on this world? Let us review the links to morality found in some interpretations of salvation.

6.2   *Moral frameworks.*   Suppose indeed that moral norms regarding noninjury, justice, and love encompass a salvific goal. And suppose further that a moral system legitimates earthly inequalities but provides for equal access to the highest good of salvation. A critic might charge that the natural human desire for equal access to earthly goods had been sublimated, that is, repressed, and projected into a transhuman sphere; a false rationale is established for earthly inequalities and hope for all is transferred to some transcendent realm. Although a moral framework does encompass the salvific goal, in contrast to traditions where moral categories have no application to the salvific path, the framework itself is deceptive and oppressive.

This objection is often made by social critics in the Marxist tradition; it is also made by feminists who want to see equality or some new form of moral community in this world.[70] Moral visions that give God the decisive role in the victory of good over evil also sap human initiative, say the critics, but moral hopes at least can be reinterpreted as programs for progress within history; transmoral hopes, however, project a solution beyond moral struggle altogether.[71]

The objection involves at least two sorts of claims. The first is that the metaphysical and moral beliefs that underlie the system of inequality/equality are false. This is straightforward, although adjudicating claims about the reality of the final relation with God or the rightness of a distributive system is extremely complex. On the one hand, there are questions about the nature and existence of the projected salvific state; on the other hand, there are questions about justice, such as, What does equality mean? Are there ever any justified inequalities? I will bypass these metaphysical and moral questions here, but let me observe that the hope for salvation does not commit a system to severe inequality at the worldly level. Traditions that at one time in their history have legitimated non-egalitarian social structures have found ways of justifying social equality while still maintaining a hope for ultimate salvation; inequalities believed to be justified are now seen as illegitimate.

The other sort of claim has to do with how and why the false beliefs arise: People are deceived by their oppressors, or they just deceive themselves, into thinking that the moral order is ineluctably ordained and that the only equality is at the salvific level. I cannot answer this charge in detail, but here is a sketch of a reply. People usually are not just deceived by their oppressors, nor do they deceive themselves, into thinking that earthly inequalities are ordained by the gods and that the only equality is at the salvific level. Their views are part of sets of deeply held factual and moral convictions, convictions that can change over time. I will return to this theme in the Conclusion.

6.3 Prerequisite.   Where moral dispositions are cultivated for transmoral purposes, it may seem that morality is only penultimately important. To be sure, the critic might say, traditions where moral goodness is a prerequisite are to be distinguished from those where it is not, but as a prerequisite goodness is only a means and does not seem important for itself.

This is certainly the case where moral goodness is instrumental, and even where it is analogically realized in the salvific state, it remains only in transmuted form. But where the salvific state fulfills the moral ideal, albeit in a different mode of being, then the moral ideal is an integral part of the final goal.

6.4 Eminent fulfillment.

Thus far from serving as a dispensable prerequisite, the moral framework can be recognized as valid in its own right and the transmoral state can be taken as its consummation or fulfillment. Just as the application of the framework to the path distinguishes some traditions from others, and the necessity of goodness as a prerequisite is a distinguishing feature of some transmoral visions, so the end-state can be pictured as analogous to moral perfection and thus seen as eminent fulfillment. In this sort of vision, the moral framework remains at the heart of the system, although the moral condition itself is transcended. To be sure, as we have seen, in some traditions the realization of the moral ideal on earth is put aside or downgraded in favor of the salvific path. This judgment, however, does not reduce the significance of the fact that *morality* is to be fulfilled in another mode of being.

6.5 Life in this world.

The salvific state may indeed provide an eminent fulfillment, the highest good in a transmoral mode of being. But does this sort of hope remove any reason for improving the social order? Even if hopes for salvation do not necessarily imply ineluctable inequalities in earthly society, is it the case that one does not have a reason to work for earthly justice and love if one looks to a transmoral goal?

I have noted that realizers and anticipators presumably do believe themselves justified in shucking off institutional responsibilities and ordinary duties. Here we have a straightforward collision between eternal and earthly good. The opposition is between those who believe such a departure is justified and those who don't. While a Kantian, for example, would not object in itself to a salvation that eminently fulfilled the moral demand, he or she would presumably balk at a devotion to the eternal which did not treat earthly moral progress as equally important.

In addition, critics of realization and anticipation have argued that some forms of salvific experience (often called "mystical") are inherently incompatible with morality. Certainly if in the ultimate mode of being, moral good and evil are both included or in some mysterious way *combined* (the so-called "coincidence" of opposites), then it would seem that salvation is not an eminent fulfillment of moral good, but a fusion of good and evil. This is an interpretation that a defender of eminent fulfillment would have to reject. But the notion of participation in an undifferentiated Unity that *transcends* the world of distinctions, however, does not seem to be equally objectionable.[72] To be sure, as Arthur Danto and Wayne Proudfoot argue, if the capability to distinguish between self, others, and objects is lost, then one is not able to make distinctions between right and wrong courses of action;[73] indeed one is no longer capable of action. Suppose that the mystic can do things, though we don't call it action: Will the mystic behave in a way that is morally indifferent to good and evil? No, for it is not the case that the mystic's behavior can be either good or evil just because a mode of being has been reached where these categories no longer apply. As I suggested earlier, the crucial issue is whether the mystical state is seen as eminent fulfillment. If it is, then the realizer will *behave* in ways that accord with the basic framework even if agency, action, and ordinary duty are transcended.

In addition to realization and anticipation, I also observed that some traditions have complex patterns of integration that maintain the world. Perhaps there are levels of attainment or one needs to keep ordinary structures for their own sake while history continues; in one way or other the religious vision may provide for pockets of realization or anticipation and an ongoing moral world at the same time; the two are related or connected in some way. An anthropologist or historian might, of course, argue that ordinary existence just does continue and despite the telos of a salvific goal, traditions are forced to work out patterns that sustain and structure ordinary existence; it is not that their own worldview initially provides say, for a synthesis of roles and responsibilities, but the tradition is forced to adjust, and along the way the ideology is altered to legitimate what was historically necessary.

Criticisms, in any case, can be brought against the adequacy of the integration. Take the notion that the "mystic" who returns from a transmoral experience to the ordinary world manifests an ethic of "love," (Stace's notion of the "mystical theory of ethics"), for example. It is not at all clear that merely thinking of oneself as a separate center of sentience *leads* to selfish, aggressive behavior; nor does it seem obvious, if this is what Stace meant, that the dissolution of difference in the One *produces* sympathy and benevolence in ordinary life.

For instance, William J. Wainwright discusses the "mixed life" of certain Western mystics who *return* from contemplation to active life; in the words of Gregory, with Christ as the model believers live so "that the love of their neighbor may not interfere with the love of God; nor again the love of God cast out, because it transcends, the love of their neighbors."[74] Wainwright examines justificatory claims that may underlie the return and offers objections to each in turn.

First, since we are all one (something learned in the mystical experience), we should treat others in a loving way (when we return). The basic objection to this argument is that if we are all literally one, then we would really just be loving ourselves; love requires difference as well as union.[75]

The second justificatory argument claims that if in the salvific state, "ego and self" are abolished, only love will remain. To this argument,

Wainwright objects that even if with the loss of self one loses the desires that furnish reasons for selfishness, one does not necessarily gain any reasons against it, or any reasons to love.[76]

Thus the "we are all one" argument would prove too much, for it would seem to eliminate the possibility of love of others, and the argument from the unreality of the self proves too little, for while selfish desire is gone, there is no guarantee that reasons *for* altruism are provided.

Despite Wainwright's criticisms, it may be that some sorts of experiences labeled "mystical" could provide a crucial ingredient for some moralities. Wayne Proudfoot, for example, suggests that a possible way to "construe" such experience is to believe that it has the "implication" that some contemporary philosophers have called "universalization" or "universalizability."[77] The requirement that moral judgments apply or should be acceptable to all individuals is somehow based on the perspective one gets in mystical experience.[78]

I think Proudfoot's point can be interpreted as follows: Some sorts of experiences labeled "mystical" could include crucial cognitions about the nature of the self which have a moral role.[79] That is, perhaps experiences of "unity" consist in a radical new awareness of what the self is and how it is related to others. For example, the contemporary philosopher Thomas Nagel has argued that the corollary of seeing ourselves simply as one person—one strand of consciousness, sentience, and agency among others—is the moral idea that anyone's suffering should be as much a reason for us to act as our own would be; if we truly see ourselves in this sense as part of a larger whole, then we must acknowledge that someone else's pain is as much a reason for us to act as our own would be; not to acknowledge the moral corollary would be to look at ourselves in one way some of the time (one person among many) but to look at ourselves differently on other occasions (only *my* pain is a reason for me to act). In this sense, then, if I believe my pain should be relieved, then I believe anyone's should.[80]

Now whatever the merits of Nagel's argument, I think we can see how it could get recast into a religious form. Only in the so-called "mystical" experience do we *see* ourselves as we truly are—as strands or elements of consciousness in a larger whole—and only when armed with this insight will we return with the proper moral stance towards the neighbor; mystical "union" with God gives us the insight on which love of neighbor rests. This is not to suggest a dichotomy between reason and desire or emotion; the new cognition is affective; it would somehow both guide and shape our dispositions. I do not intend to defend such a view of mystical experience and love here, but it is one important way in which transmoral experience could be said to be connected to earthly morality.

Where the religious vision holds together earthly moral existence and salvific life, it is often asumed in the overall system of thought and practice, however, that the superiority of the final goal warrants the devotion of greater resources to salvation than to the improvement of the present order; this can be so even where salvation is not even partially realized or anticipated but seen as wholly future; the lion's share of the community's effort goes to preparation. It is very important to note, therefore, that in one *sense* or another and to one *degree* or another, many classic forms of Western traditions seem to be *both* world-affirming and world-renouncing (it is too simple to say that one tradition or subtradition is world-affirming and another world-renouncing).[81] Many forms of Judaism and Christianity relate a continued existence in this world to a longed-for World-to-Come or Kingdom of God.[82] Whether aspects of ordinary existence are cast in very negative terms, as in some versions of Christianity, or integrated in a relatively more positive way, the present order can be *subordinated* to the eventual consummation of the Kingdom of God or the World-to-Come.[83]

What we can tentatively conclude, therefore, is that where there is a transmoral salvific goal moral structures have secondary value *and* are often subordinated.[84] Sexual-familial, economic, and political structures may be "affirmed" within one type of adjustment or another, but this affirmation is relative; efforts related to salvation are not only more important, it is believed they should get greater overall attention.[85]

Thus the opposition between temporal and eternal good is most apparent in realizers and anticipators, but even in many classical forms of integration there is subordination. What contemporary Roman Catholic liberation theologians have against traditional syntheses of temporal and eternal good is that the temporal is not seen as the first, organically connected stage in the realization of a unified process of "liberation," which begins on earth and is fulfilled transmorally in eternity; the struggle for social justice is integrated with "spiritual" concerns only as a subordinate partner. And contemporary feminists as I have noted would also reject a theology that subordinated the struggle for a new order here and now. These critics would insist that even if a transmoral goal is envisaged, earthly good must not be subordinated. Previous thinkers, say the critics, not only bifurcated temporal and eternal good, but were too pessimistic about the possibilities for earthly improvement. Even the most optimistic of the integrationists thought that only limited improvements were possible on earth. Beyond the traditional forms of integration, therefore, a new definition of "liberation" must be devised, which has a temporal dimension and gives equal importance to earthly moral progress.

Even my interpretative category of "salvation," which signifies the transmoral state itself, these critics might argue, reflects the traditional separation and subordination of temporal to eternal good. But I have tried to use the notion of salvation in such a way that while it signifies a state that transcends human good and moral relations, the concept itself does not imply that earthly good should be *subordinated*. That salvation is *superior* in value does not entail the present *subordination* of earthly good. One could look to a mode of being beyond the moral condition while believing that moral progress was the place to begin; LeGuin's Anarres (or something like it) could be the first stage of the Kingdom.

Finally, however, we must confront the charge of moral anthropocentrism which James Gustafson has leveled against the Christian tradition, but more broadly against the underlying Western assumption that God's goal is the ultimate well-being of the individual.[86] Whether that state is envisaged solely in moral terms (happiness and perfect goodness), or is also seen ultimately as a transmoral mode of being, the individual is preserved. Even where personal identity is replaced by a supraindividual consciousness, the individual is still part of the new mode of being (individual identity is not lost but becomes part of a larger identity), in contrast to the final oblivion which Gustafson portrays as the destiny of us all. However the purposes of the Creator for the good of the whole take shape (whatever that good and whomever it involves), human individuals simply return to matter: "dust unto dust."

But in Chapter 2 I noted that Gustafson has confidence that the Creator's moral purposes will be achieved. Can Gustafson allow for an analogue to the traditional hope for a transmoral mode of being? Not as individuals, of course, but it seems to me that one could look to such a future for the cosmos. One does not know of course exactly what the Creator's purposes are but one is confident they are for the good of the entire cosmos. That ultimate good could take the form of a transmoral state in which human, or if humanity if extinct, nonhuman beings will have evolved beyond morality. Insofar as one approves the Creator's purposes and insofar as even after death one is still part of the cosmos which evolves, one could hope for a transmoral goal.

7. CONCLUSION

Visions of salvation, then, can be connected in various ways to morality; the charge that they are necessarily inimical or indifferent to moral structures is false. But despite all the ways in which moral goodness can encompass, prepare, and even find eminent fulfillment in salvation, in the end, as Burridge put it, the final state means another "level of being." Religious visions may provide an account of the origins and structure of the moral order (source), relate ultimate powers to its maintenance and fulfillment (sanction), and they may tell of a new mode of being beyond morality (salvation). How this new being can be positively related to the earthly struggle and how it is related to individual identity are questions at the heart of many contemporary efforts to appropriate the ancient traditions.

NOTES

1. See Kenelm Burridge, "Levels of Being," in *Religion and Morality*, in ed. Gene Outka and John P. Reeder, Jr. (Garden City, NY: Doubleday, 1973), pp. 78–107. Compare Mircea Eliade, *Patterns in Comparative Religion* (New York: World Publishing, 1963), p. 424. If the end-state or final destiny is negatively valued, not desired as good, then I would not call it salvation; it could be a part of a *religious* vision, however. See the concept of "holy nothingness" in Richard Rubenstein, *After Auschwitz: Radical Theology and Contemporary Judaism* (New York: Bobbs-Merrill, 1966).

2. Compare Stephen Theron, in "Happiness and Transcendent Happiness," *Religious Studies*, 21 (September 1985), 349–368, who argues that if we desire happiness, we must desire an atemporal state "in which we can possess all we desire without any risk of loss (p. 366)." Grace M. Jantzen distinguishes in regard to diverse notions of salvation: "antecedent condition (from what we are saved), . . . method (how we are saved), or . . . goal (to what we are saved)." Jantzen, "Human Diversity and Salvation in Christ," *Religious Studies*, 20, (Dec. 1984) pp. 579–592. On Aquinas, see Jean Porter, "Desire for God: Ground of the Moral Life in Aquinas," *Theological Studies*, 47 (1986), 48–68; especially p. 63–65 who notes that for Aquinas, "moral goodness remains even in the beatified." And compare John Langan, "Beatitude and Moral Law in St. Thomas," *Journal of Religious Ethics*, 5 (1977), 183–195. The final state need not be disembodied; see Margaret R. Miles on Aquinas' view that the body must be reunited with the soul for perfect happiness. *Fullness of Life: Historical Foundations for a New Asceticism* (Philadelphia: Westminster Press, 1981), pp. 132–4; 128–9.

3. As I understand it, Jonathan Z. Smith's distinction between visions which are locative (one's place in a given order) and those which are open (escape from limits and patterns) does not correspond to my contrast of moral perfection and salvation. Visions of moral perfection as well as salvation could fall into the "open" category. See Smith's "The Influence of Symbols upon Social Change: A Place on which to Stand," *Worship 44* (1970), 457–474.

4. Just how moral perfection would be specifically envisaged depends on the morality of the tradition or culture in question; I am talking now about visions which attempt to go beyond any conception of good and evil.

5. See Frank E. and Fritzi P. Manuel, *Utopian Thought in the Western World* (Cambridge: Harvard University Press, 1979). One can imagine partial accomplishments of these goals: natural perfection without moral perfection, or moral perfection without natural. The difficulty with the former is illustrated in a film I once saw about chimpanzees: there were plenty of bananas to satisfy every desire, but some individuals simply prevented others from getting any. The difficulty with the latter is illustrated in Le Guin's Anarres *(The Dispossessed)*. Even aside from the moral imperfections the novel reveals, there are the remaining hardships of a planet where resources are at best scarce.

6. See the discussion of the section called "Raya Mehemna" in Manuel and Manuel, *Utopian Thought*, pp. 54–55. See Gershom Scholem, *Major Trends in Jewish Mysticism* (Jerusalem: Schocken Publishing House, 1941), p. 308; and *Sabbatai Sevi: Mystical Messiah* (Princeton, NJ: Princeton University Press, 1973), p. 809. "Raya Mehemna" is characterized as an "imitation" printed as part of the *Zohar*—see Introduction to *Zohar: The Book of Enlightenment*, trans. and intro. by Daniel Chanan Matt (New York: Paulist, 1983), p. 10. See Gershom Scholem, *Kabbalah* (New York: Quadrangle, 1974), pp. 218–219. Scholem, commenting on this work and another associated with the Zohar, the *Tikkunei Zohar*, says that in the time of redemption "dominion will pass to the Tree of Life and all will be as before Adam's sin. . . . The future abolition of the commandments mentioned in the Talmud (Nid. 61b) was taken by the Kabbalists to refer to the complete spiritualization of the commandments that would take place under the dominion of the Tree of Life" (pp. 166–167). The Tree of Knowledge and the Tree of Life, it is said in the Zohar, had been bound together; but Adam separated them, "giving substance to evil" which had been "contained within the Tree of Knowledge of Good and Evil" but is now materialized in the evil instinct *(yezer ha-ra)*" (p. 124). The Manuels also discuss another text, the *Sefer ha-Temunah*, where the notion of a succession of creations (and relations) is outlined. We once lived in an era of Benevolence *(Hessed)*, but now we live under an era of law, where evil desires require prohibitions. In a

coming era of Compassion *(Rachamim)* there will be one real family, people will eat manna, and all will be equal *(Utopian Thought,* pp. 55–56). Some of these texts or parts of them may suggest moral perfection, not a transmoral state. See chapter 2, n. 50, p. 90.

7. Arthur Danto argues in *Mysticism and Morality* (New York: Harper and Row, 1973) that self-consciousness is a necessary condition of having a moral system. Compare David Little and Sumner B. Twiss, *Comparative Religious Ethics* (San Francisco: Harper and Row, 1978). This is not to adopt a particular metaphysical or sociological notion of the individual; it merely points to a capacity to be aware of oneself and others as centers of sentience and agency.

8. One critical issue in the interpretation of Theravāda Buddhism is whether in the realization of *Nibbāna* (the salvific state) one is conscious of oneself or others as selves. Another disputed point is whether *Nibbāna* signifies a transformation in our experience of reality or whether it represents a new sort of reality; on both questions, see Donald Swearer, "Bhikkhu Buddhadasa on Ethics and Society," *Journal of Religious Ethics*, 7(Spring 1979), 54–64. For extended treatments of interpretations of *Nibbāna*, see Guy Welbon, *The Buddhist Nirvana and Its Western Interpreters* (Chicago: University of Chicago Press, 1968); David J. Kalupahana, *Causality: The Central Philosophy of Buddhism* (Honolulu: University Press of Hawaii, 1975), p. 180 ff.; and Donald Swearer, *Buddhist Ethics: A Modal Interpretation*, unpublished. G. L. Doore argues that if "mystical union can be seen not to involve annihilation of personality," then Eastern conceptions of final liberation and Kantian notions of the "highest good" could be compatable. G. L. Doore, "Religion Within the Limits of the Quest for the Highest Good," *Religious Studies, 19* (September 1983), 345–359.

9. Paul Hanson, *The Dawn of Apocalyptic: The Historical and Social Roots of Jewish Apocalyptic Eschatology*, rev. ed. (Philadelphia: Fortress Press, 1979), pp. 62–63, 127–134, 150–152. Natural evil is removed by the partial or complete transformation of nature. See Hanson on Isaiah 65 (p. 138 ff.; compare pp. 155–161). And moral evil is removed by the judgment of the wicked and the vindication of the righteous, or in some visions, by the judgment, forgiveness, and recreation of the chosen (Hanson, pp. 377, 397, 405). See Hanson's helpful appendix on the definition of apocalyptic (p. 427 ff.). What I am talking about here is Hanson's second "level of definition," a distinctive eschatology or view of divine plans in relation to history; this distinguishes a "perspective" (p. 431) from a literary genre or a socioreligious movement in which the eschatological perspective is at the heart of the symbol system. For a contrasting view see John Collins who argues that it is not the idea of a definitive climax or the notion of two ages but a specific sort of hope which distinguishes apocalyptic, namely, a hope for a "heavenly" life, in particular, the transcendence of death. See Collins' "Apocalyptic Eschatology or the Transcendence of Death," *Catholic Biblical Quarterly, 36*(1974), 21–43; his "The Symbolism of Transcendence in Jewish Apocalyptic," *Biblical Research, 19*(1974), 5–22; and his *The Apocalyptic Imagination: An Introduction to the Jewish Matrix of Christianity* (New York: Crossroad, 1984). In *Daniel, With an Introduction to Apocalyptic Literature* (Grand Rapids: Eerdmans, 1984), Collins discusses two types of apocalypse, the historical and the other-worldly journey. Compare also the essays in *Apocalypticism in the Mediterranean World and the Near East,* ed. David Hellholm (Tübingen: J. C. B. Mohr (Paul Siebech), 1983. For a helpful guide to the general subject and later Christian traditions, see Bernard McGinn's Introduction in his *Visions of the End: Apocalyptic Traditions in the Middle Ages* (New York: Columbia University Press, 1979); and Bernard McGinn's Introduction in *Apocalyptic Spirituality*, trans. and ed. Bernard McGinn (New York: Ramsey; Toronto: Paulist Press, 1979).

10. Hanson, *Dawn of Apocalyptic*, pp. 177–178, 182, 249–250.

11. Ibid., p. 62 ff., 71–77, note 44, 71–72; compare p. 276.

12. Ibid., pp. 393–395.

13. Ibid., p. 212 ff.; Hanson cites Mannheim, Weber, and Troeltsch.

14. Ibid., pp. 29–31.

15. Ibid., p. 210, 259–60, 280–281, 410–411.

16. Ibid., p. 29, 71–76. Hanson claims that in ancient Israel visions of the end-time are progressively "dehistoricized." The notion of Israel as an object of divine deliverance is replaced by a particular group within Israel or by the righteous of all humankind. A restora-

tion tied to contemporary historical events and personages, for example, the Persian King Cyrus, gives way to divine achievement. In addition, the substance of what is expected is not cast primarily in terms of a historical kingdom but takes the shape of a new natural and human order.

17. On the relation between the Messianic Age and the salvation of the soul in the thought of Maimonides, see Gershom Scholem, *The Messianic Idea in Judaism and Other Essays on Jewish Spirituality* (New York: Schocken Books, 1971), pp. 24 ff., especially pp. 30–31. Maimonides apparently conceived of the Messianic Age as part of history; Israel would have her own king and live in peace but the natural order would not be modified; the telos of existence is the World to Come. For this interpretation, see Gershom Scholem and Manuel and Manuel in *Utopian Thought*, p. 53. For a brief survey of Judaic traditions about the Messianic age and the World to Come, see Louis Jacobs, *A Jewish Theology* (New York: Behrman House, 1973), chaps. 22, 23.

18. "The Jewish Concept of Salvation," in *Quest for Past and Future: Essays in Jewish Theology* (Boston: Beacon, 1968), pp. 167–168. An early Christian theologian Lactantius (3–4 C.E.) expressed his hope as follows: After God has vanquished the evil "nations,"

> . . . then the just will go forth from their hiding places and will find everything covered with corpses and bones. Every wicked nation will be rooted out and God's people will be the only nation in the world. For seven uninterrupted years the forests will remain untouched and no wood will be cut from the mountain, but rather the arms of the nations will be burnt. There will be no more war, but peace and eternal rest. When the thousand years shall have been completed, God will renew the world, heaven will be folded up, and the earth will be changed. God will change men into the likeness of angels. They will be white as snow and always live in the sight of the Most High. They will sacrifice to their Lord and will serve him forever. (McGinn, *Apocalyptic Spirituality*, p. 77)

19. Kenelm Burridge, "Levels of Being," in *Religion and Morality*, ed. Outka and Reeder, Jr., pp. 92, 102. Basil Mitchell, in "How Is the Concept of Sin Related to the Concept of Moral Wrongdoing," *Religious Studies, 20* (1984), 165–173, argues that although the boundaries of the concept of moral responsibility can be stretched quite wide, there are other aspects of experience which the theologian calls sin. Even when we have connived at evil, we would not necessarily extend the "rigour" of moral blame, and there may be aspects of our condition which we confess as sin which separate us from God but which strictly speaking we did not choose (pp. 169, 173). See the other essays on these themes in *Religious Studies* 20. Otto saw "sin" as the state of being alienated from or in opposition to the numinous; sin is a negation of numinous, not moral value. See "What is Sin?" and other essays in *Religious Essays: A Supplement to the Idea of the Holy*, trans. Brian Lunn (London: Humphrey Milford, Oxford University Press, 1931). See, e.g., pp. 23, 27–9.

20. Compare my concept of salvation with Obeyesekere's in "The Rebirth Eschatology and Its Transformations: A Contribution to the Sociology of Early Buddhism—in Wendy O'Flaherty, ed., *Karma and Rebirth in Classical Indian Traditions* (Berkeley, Los Angeles, and London: University of California Press, 1980): no suffering, perfect bliss, ultimate status, final goal. I want to reserve the concept of salvation for states where, to be sure, freedom from suffering is achieved, but where the moral condition is also transcended. For other interpretative purposes, however, Obeyesekere's broader definition may be preferable. On various meanings of salvation, liberation, or redemption within traditions, and various attempts to construct concepts of salvation and related notions for scholarly purposes, see S. G. Brandon, ed., *The Savior God: Comparative Studies in the Concept of Salvation: Presented to E. O. James* (Manchester: Manchester University Press, 1963); R. J. Zwi Werblowsky and C. Jouco Bleeker, eds., *Types of Redemption* (London: E. J. Brill, 1970) (see especially the Introduction by Gershom Scholem and "Types of Redemption: a Summary," by Werblowsky); and Eric J. Sharpe and John R. Hinnells, eds., *Man and His Salvation: Studies in Memory of S. G. F. Brandon*, (Manchester: University of Manchester Press, 1973) (especially Willard G. Oxtoby, "Reflections on the Idea of Salvation," pp. 15–37). For the view that "salvation is essentially the *overcoming* of evil," see Kenneth Surin, "Revelation, Salvation, the Uniqueness of Christ, and Other Religions," *Religious Studies, 19* (September 1983), 323–343.

21. *The Idea of the Holy* (New York: Oxford University Press, 1958). See the helpful *Rudolf Otto: An Introduction to His Philosophical Theology* (Chapel Hill and London: University of North Carolina Press, 1984), by Philip C. Almond.

22. Burridge, "Levels," p. 102.

23. See John P. Reeder, Jr.,"Otto's Notion of the Holy," in *Religion and Morality*, ed. Outka and Reeder, pp. 255–292. Otto tried to show that the numinous aspect of the Holy is the metaphysical "ground" of the moral. (Philip Almond argues that Otto posited the Holy in both its aspects as the ground of morality; Almond, *Otto*, pp. 102–106). Charles Lewis, in "Divine Goodness and Worship Worthiness," *International Journal for Philosophy of Religion*, *14*(1983), 143–158, argues in the tradition of Otto that the Holy has a special numinous claim or goodness that cannot be assimilated to moral obligation or goodness. Sin refers to nonmoral aspects of our alienation from God. But although God's will "cannot be fathomed by the measure of moral standards of conduct," as Job finally realized, the believer submits to God out of gratitude for his mysterious and unconditioned love" (152). I think Lewis means that God as the numinous is a mysterious loving and hating nonmoral power, whose nature is not even in some nonconceptualizable sense metaphysically analogous to qualities such as love and justice. I think Otto did speak this way, but he also argues that the numinous is the "ground" of the moral; the Holy does not have two natures. Thus as I read Otto his point is not metaphysical but semantic and epistemic: the holy is partly capturable and known in moral categories (albeit metaphorically or analogically), but is also nonconceptualizable and nonknowable. I admit however that there is evidence for Lewis' reading. See Reeder, "Otto's Notion." Even if my reading is wrong, then what I present here would be an alternative way of understanding God and salvation as transmoral. Compare Scott Dunbar, "On God and Virtue," *Religious Studies*, *18*(December 1982), 489–502, who says the transcendent ground of being "lies beyond morality," yet is also the "source" of morality (p. 497).

24. This view may be held in certain Gnostic forms of Christianity. Compare Gene Outka, "On Harming Others," *Interpretation* Vol. 34 (October 1980), 381–393.

25. Kantian theories of ethics do not derive the right from the good, but even a Kantian morality protects and promotes the good of self and other.

26. In some translations of Buddhist sources, *Nibbāna* is rendered as "bliss." It would be interesting to compare the use of terms such as these in Western and Eastern contexts. What terms are used and how is their use in reference to salvation related to their meaning in ordinary contexts?

27. Little and Twiss in *Comparative Religious Ethics* limit moral frameworks to mundane well-being. This move is useful for some interpretive purposes, but we also need to understand how moral frameworks can structure paths to salvation. See the Introduction in Outka and Reeder, *Religion and Morality*.

28. For an analysis of Thomas Aquinas on the command to Abraham and other biblical examples, see Giles Milhaven, "Moral Absolutes and Thomas Aquinas," in *Absolutes in Moral Theology?*, ed. Charles Curran (Washington: Corpus Books, 1968), pp. 154–185.

29. Kierkegaard, *Fear and Trembling and Repetition* (ed. and trans. Howard V. Hong and Edna H. Hong (Princeton: Princeton University Press, 1983), p. 68. Philip Quinn in "Moral Obligation, Religious Demand, and Practical Conflict", in *Rationality, Religious Belief, and Moral Commitment*, Robert Audi and William J. Wainwright eds. (Ithaca: Cornell University Press, 1986), says that Kierkegaard's view of the Abraham incident might be interpreted as an indefeasible (nonoverridable) requirement from God and a prima facie moral requirement which would be overriden (201). But the view Quinn labels Kierkegaardian (without claiming historical accuracy for his interpretation) is this: there is an indefeasible religious requirement and a moral requirement that is not overridden and hence is "actual" (202ff;205). To show that this sort of conflict is possible, Quinn assumes that God is essentially good, but that God's goodness is not exclusively moral; "because the requirements imposed by divine command spring from a realm of value not wholly coincident with the moral realm, they are not exclusively moral requirements at all" (204). Of course says Quinn, it could be held that the nonmoral requirement imposed by God overrides a moral requirement (206–7), but he does not think that this possibility best catches the conflict of nonoverridable requirements in Kierkegaard's treatment and other examples (207). In my

interpretation of the pseudonymous author's view, the important point is that the religious demand is taken as nonmoral, as a distinct realm of value as Quinn puts it, whether or not it is also said that such a demand overrides the moral requirement or stands in conflict with an actual moral requirement. The Kierkegaardian story does, however, seem to suggest that it was justified for Abraham to obey God, as opposed to Quinn's picture of conflicting incommensurable values (207–208). Quinn refers to Gene Outka, "Religious and Moral Duty: Notes on *Fear and Trembling*" in Outka and Reeder, eds., *Religion and Morality,* for a different view of what the appearances are that need to be accounted for. For essays on *Fear and Trembling,* see Robert L. Perkins, ed. *Kierkegaard's Fear and Trembling: Critical Appraisals* (Alabama: University of Alabama Press, 1981); for a recent essay which notes a great deal of the secondary liteature, see Joseph A. Magno, "How Ethical is Abraham's 'Suspension of the Ethical?' ", *Faith and Philosophy,* 2 (January 1985), 53–65. On Judaic traditions, see Shalom Spiegel, *The Last Trial: On the Legends and Lore of the Command to Abraham to Offer Isaac as a Sacrifice: The Akedah* (New York: Schocken, 1969) and Ronald Green, "Abraham, Isaac, and the Judaic Tradition," *Journal of Religious Ethics,* 10 (Spring 1982), 1–21.

30. On some interpretations the issue in *Fear and Trembling* is the question whether the command to Abraham contravenes not a particular moral order but any morality. If moral systems do certain jobs, then they have certain features, for example, they pertain to well-being and they are governed by norms such as consistency. The question would be whether the religious relation Kierkegaard envisages these features and whether therefore, although a certain moral system is "suspended," morality per se is not. Edmund Santurri—in "Kierkegaard's *Fear and Trembling* in Logical Perspective," *The Journal of Religious Ethics,* 5(Fall 1977), 225–247—argues that the religious relationship does not accord with formal features or criteria of moral duty; Gene Outka in "Religious and Moral Duty" in Outka and Reeder, *Religion and Morality,* pp. 204–254—argues that it could. I believe that the text takes the "universal" or the "ethical" as a substantive moral system which exhausts the sphere of the moral.

31. See Larry K. Nelson who focuses on Kierkegaard's psuedonym's statement that ". . . if one cannot say more [that what God wills is right], then one affirms at the same time that properly I have no duty toward God"; in other words, if I obey God because God commands what is right, then in effect I am obeying the "ethical," not God. See Nelson's "The Independence of Moral from Religious Discourse in the Believer's Use of Language," *Harvard Theological Review,* 68(April 1975), 183. Thus to avoid this "reductionism," Kierkegaard's author develops the idea of an "absolute duty to God" for which one cannot give moral reasons. God's will as moral can come into collision with God's will as "absolute," and when that happens the moral gives way (Nelson, pp. 184–185). But according to Nelson on this account, Abraham would not really be violating the moral rule against killing (pp. 186–187); "by virtue of the absurd" this killing if commanded by God cannot be a moral transgression (p. 187); Abraham acknowledges the fallibility of his own judgment. Nelson thus makes the problem one of moral trust; Abraham does not doubt the moral principle, but acknowledges that his own judgment in this case is fallible. But if the moral gives way, then how can it be a matter of moral trust? On my interpretation, Abraham acknowledges a nonmoral duty which conflicts with the ethical. Kierkegaard's author may also teach that faith negates but fufills *(aufheben)* the ethical. At one place in *Fear and Trembling,* the author asks "Is there a Teleological Suspension of the Ethical?" and the response seems to be that if the ethical is the highest, then the ethical is the same as "eternal salvation," which is the final telos, and thus the ethical could not be teleologically suspended for anything else (p. 54). But if the ethical is not the highest, then, that which is teleologically suspended is not "relinquished" but is "preserved" in the highest, its telos. If this is the pseudonymous author's view, then it resembles the position I will present next where one relates to God on the basis of God's qualities independent of their role as the defining standards of the moral order. As I will argue ahead (eminent fulfillment), the moral is negated but fulfilled in a final relation to God; as Gene Outka put it in "Religious and Moral Duty," Abraham remains confident of God's love. But despite the use of the *aufheben* motif here, I believe that the pseudonym would reject the view I identify as mainstream; if there is an *aufheben,* it is not "mediated" by faith in qualities which somehow metaphysically correspond to the standards of the moral order; even this would be to try to encompass Abraham's faith within the moral once again; if there is *aufheben,* it remains "paradox," unfathomable to reason. Compare Re-

eder, "Otto's Notion," and Mark C. Taylor, "Journeys to Moriah: *Hegel vs. Kierkegaard,*" *"Harvard Theological Review,* 70(July–October 1977), p. 322 ff.

32. Compare Moritz Lazarus who said that in Judaism the "moral principle" is not independent but is part of the divine essence. See Lazarus' *The Ethics of Judaism*, vol. 1 (Philadelphia: Jewish Publication Society of America, 1900), pp. 130–131; quoted in Louis Jacobs, "The Relationship between Religion and Ethics in Jewish Thought," in *Religion and Morality,* ed. Outka and Reeder, p. 162. Lazarus (pp. 125–132), commenting on Eduard von Hartmann, said:

> "The moral principle is, indeed, not above and not beside the Divine Being; it is *in itself*. Precisely for that reason it is at the same time *in God*—in God inasmuch as he is the prototype of morality. To repeat: not because the principle is in God is it the moral principle, but because it is the moral principle, in itself and absolutely, therefore it is necessarily in God." (Lazarus, p. 131)

Otto also discussed similar issues raised by Nicolai Hartmann; see "Freiheit und Notwendigkeit," reprinted in Otto, *Aufsätze zur Ethik*, herausgegeben Jack S. Boozer (München: Verlag C. H. Beck, 1981), pp. 215–226. It should be noted that when I say the deity in its essence is like or analogous to qualities such as love and justice, I am making a *metaphysical* point, not a point about religious language. As I say in the text above, believers affirm this metaphysical point even though they may not believe that the metaphors and analogies of religious discourse can express the similarity. Some believers have held that analogies give us some information about God; this is roughly what Otto meant by the rational-moral side of the Holy. Other believers have held that human analogies do not really give information about God (at least without a special act of empowerment by God) but point to a truth which is not humanly conceptualizable; this is perhaps what Otto meant by the nonconceptualizable numinous aspect of the Holy. On senses of analogy, see Victor Preller, *Divine Science and the Science of God: A Reformulation of Thomas Aquinas* (Princeton: Princeton University Press, 1967). Compare Ralph McInerny, "Analogy and Foundationalism in Thomas Aquinas," in Robert Audi and William J. Wainwright, eds., *Rationality, Religious Belief, and Moral Commitment: New Essays in the Philosophy of Religion* (Ithaca and London: Cornell University Press, 1986), pp. 271–288.

33. See Gene Outka, "Religious and Moral Duty," "On Harming Others," and "Equality and Individuality: Two Thoughts on Themes in Kierkegaard," *Journal of Religious Ethics*, 10(Fall 1982), 171–203.

34. Louis Dumont argues in *Homo Hierarchichus* (Chicago: University of Chicago Press, 1980) that in the Hindu tradition the direct search for salvation is classically assigned to the *samnyāsin*, the renouncer, who leaves the world to seek liberation or salvation (Dumont, especially p. 435, note 24). This is often represented as the fourth goal (in addition to *dharma, artha, kāma*) and the last stage of life for the three highest varnas (the twice-born) (Dumont, pp. 274; 432, note 18; 433, note 19). The renouncer gives away his goods and loses rights to family property; he completes his own funeral ceremonies (Dumont, p. 433, note 18). Thus the *samnyāsin* sets himself over against the entire structure of class and caste, the order constituted and regulated by *dharma*. But if the fourth class, the *shudra*, is excluded from salvific attainment, does that mean that there is still salvific inequality in the system as a whole? The doctrine of *karma*, however, provides for the eventual possibility of a twice-born existence. There are matters which should be studied historically in dialogue with contemporary discussions of distributive justice.

35. On reciprocity between monks and laity in Buddhist traditions, compare Phra Rajavaramuni, "Foundations of Buddhist Social Ethics in Contemporary Thailand," *Ethics, Wealth, and Salvation: A Study of Buddhist Social Ethics*, ed. Russell Sizemore, and Donald Swearer (forthcoming).

36. In the Theravāda Buddhist tradition, although everyone deserves their place in life, it seems to be wrong not to help others, not only in regard to food or a more fortunate rebirth, but also in regard to attaining *Nibbāna*, hence the importance of teaching the truths taught by the Buddha. The Buddha and his disciples came into the world as an expression of benevolence. See David Little on the "interpersonal teleological" pattern of reasoning in

Buddhist tradition, "Ethical Analysis and Wealth in Thervāda Buddhism: A Response to Frank Reynolds," in Sizemore and Swearer, *Ethics, Wealth, and Salvation.* On the view that in some Buddhist traditions the search for salvation is not other-regarding, see Little and Twiss, *Comparative Religious Ethics,* chap. 8.

37. The idea that freedom from guilt and goodness are not prerequisites should be carefully distinguished from another idea, namely, the notion that the one who has attained salvation is free from moral responsibility. I will deal with the latter ahead.

38. On moral virtue as prerequisite, see Jeffrey Stout, "Buddhism Beyond Morality: A Note on Two Senses of Transcendence," *Journal of Religious Ethics,* 6(Fall 1978), 319–325; see also Gananath Obeyesekere, "Theodicy, Sin, and Salvation in a Sociology of Buddhism," in *Dialectic of Practical Religion,* ed. E. R. Leach (Cambridge: Cambridge University Press, 1968), p. 19.

39. See John Hick on this life or a training ground for becoming the sort of person capable of the final relation to God—*Evil and the God of Love,* rev. ed. (San Francisco: Harper and Row, 1978).

40. Compare David Little in "Ethical Analysis and Wealth" on extrinsic and intrinsic means.

41. *Institutes of the Christian Religion,* Vol. 2 (Philadelphia: Westminster Press, 1960), Books III, xxi 7, p. 931; quoted in Forell, *Christian Social Teachings* (Minneapolis: Augsburg Publishing House, 1966), p. 179.

42. See Max Weber in H. H. Gerth and C. Wright Mills, eds., *From Max Weber* (New York: Oxford University Press, 1958), pp. 275, 359; *The Sociology of Religion,* trans. Ephraim Fishoff (Boston: Beacon Press, 1963), pp. 201–202 ff. Some Protestants may have said that God's selection is not guided by any moral (or morally analogous) considerations. Compare Brian Hebblethwaite in *The Christian Hope* (Grand Rapids, MI: William B. Eerdmans, 1984) on moral objections against anything less than universal "salvation."

43. I follow up here an idea of Otto's which has Hegelian roots. See *The Idea of the Holy,* p. 75. Compare W. K. Frankena—"The Concept of Social Justice," in *Social Justice,* ed. R. R. Brandt (Englewood Cliffs, NJ: Prentice Hall, Inc., 1962), p. 2; and "Love and Principle in Christian Ethics" in *Faith and Philosophy,* ed. Alvin Plantinga (Grand Rapids, MI: William B. Eerdman's, 1964), p. 221 ff.—on the use of this idea in the moral sphere as the claim that "love fulfills justice." See Chapter 2 on "justice" and "love."

44. Kant's God did not have needs and desires (inclinations) and thus transcended even the ideal of moral perfection. But this being nonetheless embodied the moral demand. The transmoral mode of being as eminent fulfillment fulfills Kantian hopes: moral perfection *of* the individual and realization of the moral demand *for* the individual (happiness proportionate to virtue).

45. I would like to compare eminent fulfillment in Western traditions with views of the achievement of *Nibbāna* in forms of Buddhism, where it is apparently said that the liberated one transcends ordinary concern but manifests a special sort of benevolence toward all.

46. Augustine, *The City of God,* trans. Marcus Dods (New York: Random House, 1950), XXII.29, p. 859 ff.

47. *City of God,* XXII.30, pp. 864–865. I assume Augustine meant that justice is *analogically* present, that is, "indefeasible," or no longer contingent or subject to change.

48. *City of God,* XXII.30, pp. 865–866.

49. *City of God,* XXII.30, p. 865.

50. The sketch of types of relations to "this world" that follows is indebted to H. R. Niebuhr's categories in *Christ and Culture* (New York: Harper and Row, 1951). Niebuhr brilliantly categorized some of the major trends in Christian tradition, but did not, in my view, explain them adequately because he downplayed the significance of apocalyptic eschatology in early Christianity and did not distinguish between moral perfection and salvation. Niebuhr's book is structured around the degree of tension felt between the possibilities of human experience as we know it and the new possibilities created by the refashioning, "redeeming" acts of the deity. My treatment here assumes that there are degrees of tension (expressed either in terms of moral perfection or a transmoral goal) but locates the historical options on an immediacy–adjustment–futurity continuum. Compare Chapter 2.

51. Compare Augustine, *City of God*, XXII.30 pp. 865–866. Augustine insists that this is the "superior" form of freedom of the will.

52. Cohn discusses in *The Pursuit of the Millenium: Revolutionary Millenarians and Mystical Anarchists of the Middle Ages* (London: Paladin, 1970). the idea that the believer has become identical with God (p. 179, for example) and thus has God's *right* to all of creation; the believer then can appropriate anything, regardless of earthly norms of property (p. 182). This view seems to me a development of the medieval idea that God is not bound by interhuman norms but can give commands to the contrary; for example, since all is God's, God can command someone to "steal." No injustice is done since God as creator has a right to everything. (See Giles Milhaven, in "Moral Absolutes and Thomas Aquinas".) One adept is quoted as saying, "This soul has no will but the will of God who makes it will what it ought to will" (p. 184). As God, the believer is no longer in the moral state, but since God is just (in an analogous sense), so is the believer. Some adepts of the "Free Spirit" even thought evidently that it was permissible to use violence, but this may be traceable to other currents of thought in the matrix Cohn discusses (p. 183).

53. Gershom Scholem, *Sabbatai Sevi* (Princeton, NJ: Princeton University Press, 1973), pp. 809–810; compare pp. 319–320, 323–324.

54. Ibid., p. 810.

55. Ibid. pp. 809, 319–324. See David R. Blumenthal, *Understanding Jewish Mysticism: The Merkabah Tradition and the Zoharic Tradition* (New York: KTAV 1978) for texts and helpful interpretations.

56. More difficult to interpret is the idea that the Messiah must do evil (even apostasy) in order to overcome it (Scholem, *Sabbatai Sevi*, pp. 801–810; Scholem, *Major Trends*, pp. 307, 311–312; this evidently could mean truly sin or only apparently sin (compare *Major Trends*, p. 312; compare pp. 314–315). In any case, some followers held that the old law should be kept until redemption is complete and that ordinary believers shouldn't imitate the Messiah; others held he should be imitated now (*Major Trends*, pp. 309 ff.).

57. Sholem, *Major Trends*, p. 308; Scholem, *Sabbatai Sevi*, pp. 319–321: As the Tree of Life, the Torah does not exist as specific commandments but in a "spiritual" form; the categories of "permitted and forbidden, pure and impure" are left behind, (*Sabbatai Sevi*, p. 321).

58. See John Gager, *Kingdom and Community: The Social World of Early Christianity* (Englewood Cliffs, NJ: Prentice-Hall, Inc., 1975). Compare Susan Niditch in *Chaos to Cosmos* (Chico, CA: Scholars Press, 1985) who interprets Paul's view of the new life in Christ as the recapturing of Eden.

59. See Luke T. Johnson, *Sharing Possessions: Mandate and Symbol of Faith* (Philadelphia: Fortress Press, 1981).

60. In "Assenting to Agape"—*Journal of Religion*, *60*(January 1980), 17–31—I argued that agape should be understood as an anticipation of the coming Kingdom of God; in that Kingdom, God would be the all-sufficient and eternal good, and individuals would unrestrictedly affirm the good of others. I did not make clear, however, the distinction between an ethic of love as an ideal of moral perfection and a transmoral relation. Where natural goods are not scarce, individuals do not have to impose any limits on their actions for others as the settlers on Anarres did; each individual can trust the benevolence of others, and there is an abundance such that the individual seeks and receives what he or she desires; this would be the ideal of natural and moral perfection discussed in Chapter 2. Insofar, however, as believers are no longer creatures of need and desire, their relation to each other and to God will only be analogous to moral perfection; it will achieve the moral ideal but in a different mode.

61. Stanley Tambiah argues that the social order maintained by the king is integrated with the salvific path in some classical forms of Theravāda Buddhism. In early Buddhist doctrine and practice kingship—more broadly economic and political order—was designed for the well-being of the people; in this sense, the king's primary motive was benevolence:

> Monks, these two persons born into the world to the profit and happiness of many, to the profit, happiness and welfare of many folk. What two?

A Tathagata, an Arahant [*arhat*] who is a Fully Enlightened one, and a world-ruling monarch. These are the two so born.

Nonetheless, as Tambiah himself shows, the social order is maintained and various forms of suffering ameliorated in order to help people practice *sila* (morality) and to provide a context in which those capable of it could strive directly for *Nibbāna*. The order the king provides not only establishes a context in which people can earn merit and a better rebirth, but enables some to seek *Nibbāna*:

> The dharma of a king does not require him to show the way to nirvana but to act, just as a canopy gives shade, as the provider of general conditions of a prosperous and virtuous society in which the sāngha [order of monks] and its dhamma . . . [teachings and actions directed to *Nibbana*] may flourish.

See Tambiah, *World Conqueror and World Renouncer* (Cambridge: Cambridge University Press, 1976), pp. 45, 54; compare pp. 38–49, 58, 60, 62. Frank Reynolds, however, argues that Tambiah elevates to primacy only one Buddhist view of the relation of the Sangha and the monarchy, and neglects another view which stressed the Sangha/laity relation and deemphasized the actual political order. See Reynolds, "Totalities, Dialectics, and Transformations," *History of Religions*, 18(February 1979), 264–265.

62. Kenelm Burridge, *New Heaven and New Earth: A Study of Millenarian Activities* (New York: Schocken Books, 1969), p. 143 ff.

63. Ibid., p. 165 (italics mine).

64. Ibid., pp. 102–103.

65. Burridge himself suggests that some religious traditions look not merely for a *change* in the "redemptive process"—the system for the production and distribution of goods which is regulated by a moral-legal order and based on a view of the ultimate powers that bear on human well-being—but for a final transition. See "Levels of Being," 102 following.

66. Stace, *Mysticism and Philosophy* (Philadelphia and New York: J. P. Lippincott, 1960), p. 324. Eckhart apparently thought that in union with God one doesn't love as a subject loves an object, but " 'Everything that loves what is indistinct and indistinction hates both what is distinct and distinction. But God is indistinct, and the soul loves to be indistinguished, that is, to be and become one with God' " Quoted by McGinn in Edward College, O.S.A., and Bernard McGinn, trans. and introduction, *Meister Eckhart: The Essential Sermons, Commentaries, Treatises and Defense* (New York: Ramsey; Toronto: Paulist Press, 1981), p. 49.

67. Stace, *Mysticism*, p. 329. Otto—in *Mysticism East and West*, trans. Bertha L. Bracey and Richard C. Payne (New York: Macmillan, 1932)—says that mystical experience does not lead to good works for Sankara, whereas they do for Eckhart (pp. 207–209). For Sankara, says Otto, the one who has attained unity with Brahman "leaves all activity and reposes in oneness"; for Eckhart, the human will is merged with the divine will but contemplation leads to love. Is Sankara's view closer to what I called realization? Otto's interpretation and comparative hypothesis need reexamination. Moreover, no general "East–West" conclusions should be drawn in any case.

68. Compare Donald Swearer, "Transformational Ethical Pattern of the Bhagavad-Gita, *Journal of Religious Studies*, IV(Spring 1972), 132–142. What Arjuna is enjoined to do (go to war) and the detachment with which he is urged to do it mirror Krishna-Vishnu's action and mode of being:

> The four-caste system did I generate with categories of 'constituents' and works; of this I am the doer, (the agent),—this know,—(and yet I am) the Changeless One who does not do or act. (4.13)

> Works can never affect Me. I have no yearning for their fruits. Who so should know that this is how I am will never be bound by works. (4.14) [R. C. Zaehner, ed. and trans., *The Bhagavad-Gita* (New York: Oxford, 1969).]

Arjuna is to be as nonacting as Krishna is. But also like Krishna he is to *work* to maintain the world through action. In himself Krishna-Vishnu is uncreated and changeless. He is the author and maintainer, however, of material nature and the nomos. Why the world continues to be created and maintained (through countless cycles of emanations and reabsorptions) is unclear, but the counsel to Arjuna parallels Krishna-Vishnu's own ultimate "sameness and indifference" coupled with his creative-sustaining activity (compare 5.7).

69. Augustine, *City of God*, xix.17. pp. 695–697.

70. See, for example, Beverly Wildung Harrison, *Our Right to Decide: Toward a New Ethic of Abortion* (Boston: Beacon Press, 1983) chapter 4, especially p. 100. See the discussion in Sharon D. Welch, *Communities of Resistance and Solidarity: A Feminist Theology of Liberation*, (Maryknoll, NY: Orbis, 1985). See also Brian Hebblethwaite, *The Christian Hope*, pp. 169–172.

71. See Frank Reynolds on similar criticisms of Buddhist hopes for *Nibbāna*, "Ethics and Wealth in Theravāda Buddhism: A Study in Comparative Religious Ethics," in *Ethics, Wealth, and Salvation*, Sizemore and Swearer, eds.

72. See William Wainwright, *Mysticism* (Madison: University of Wisconsin Press, 1981), pp. 222–223. Wainwright links the first argument to "cosmic consciousness" and the second to "monistic consciousness." Wainwright argues that only some cosmic consciousness or "nature" mystics proclaim the coincidence of *all* distinctions or the inclusion of evil as well as good in the divine (*Mysticism*, pp. 223–224); nor do all monistic consciousness mystics assert the unreality of *all* distinctions or the phenomenal world. Wainwright also argues that the experience of "union" or the "dissolution of boundaries" is not equivalent to the thesis that we are all "literally one entity." Wainwright seems to suggest that there are certain core experiences which are then *interpreted*. See George A. Lindbeck's critique of this model of explanation in *The Nature of Doctrine: Religion and Theology in a Postliberal Age* (Philadelphia: Westminster Press, 1984). Wainwright, of course, could simply speak of various sorts of experiences. Compare Steven Katz, "Models, Modeling, and Mystical Training," *Religion*, *12*(1982), 247–275 and Wayne Proudfoot, *Religious Experience* (Berkeley: University of California Press, 1985).

73. Arthur C. Danto, *Mysticism and Morality* (New York: Evanston; San Francisco and London: Harper and Row, 1972); and "Ethical Theory and Mystical Experience: A Response to Professors Proudfoot and Wainwright," *Journal of Religious Ethics*, *4*(1976), 37–46. See Wayne Proudfoot, "Mysticism, the Numinous, and the Moral," *Journal of Religious Ethics*, *4*(1976), 3–28; and Wainwright's "Morality and Mysticism," *Journal of Religious Ethics*, *4*(1976), pp. 29–36. Compare James R. Horne, *The Moral Mystic* (Waterloo, Ontario: Wilfred Laurier Press, 1983).

74. Wainwright, *Mysticism*, p. 201. One could contrast Stace and Wainwright by saying that the former has in mind a purely causal thesis about how sympathetic benevolence is produced, whereas the latter is talking about reasons for desiring the good of others, not whether we do or not. But Stace does not say exactly what he means by love as the emotional "counterpart" of mystical awareness, and reasons or insights can have transforming effects on desire and emotion. I will assume therefore that Stace and Wainwright are talking about how something called mystical awareness could "lead" cognitively and affectively to love of neighbor.

75. Wainwright, pp. 219–220.

76. Pp. 220–222. Wainwright also argues that the metaphysic of "emptiness" is not strictly speaking a state of mystical consciousness, and besides, the mystic may remain in the world.

77. Proudfoot, "Mysticism," pp. 10–12.

78. The criterion of universalizability presupposes a world of selves and objects, whatever one's metaphysic of them is. There are several senses of universalizability, of course; at one place Proudfoot says it signifies "independence of particular persons or ends" (p. 11). See J. L. Mackie, *Ethics: Inventing Right and Wrong*, (London: Penguin Books, 1977); and Paul Taylor, *Principles of Ethics: An Introduction* (Belmont, CA: Dickenson, 1975).

79. Proudfoot also discusses ways in which the experience of a "numinous" reality can be construed; on the one view, moral reflection is precluded, but on the other the reality can make claims on us (Proudfoot, "Mysticism," pp. 12–18). See his constructive suggestions on pp. 18–25. Note that Proudfoot uses "numinous" to signify a type of religious experience, in contrast to Otto who used the term to refer to the nonconceptualizable element in

the holy, whether imaged as an object or reality over against the self, or as undifferentiated unity.

80. Nagel, *The Possibility of Altruism* (Princeton, NJ: Princeton University Press, 1970). Steven Collins in *Selfless Persons: Imagery and Thought in Theravāda Buddhism* (Cambridge: Cambridge University Press, 1982), pp. 193–5 compares Nagel's ideas to themes in Theravāda Buddhism.

81. Contrary to Max Weber and his followers, Stanley Tambiah and others make the point that in many forms of traditional Theravāda Buddhism the search for *Nibbāna* on the part of monks is not divorced from social involvement. See also the introduction and essays in the *Journal of Religious Ethics*, 7(Spring 1979). Various authors make the point that the notion of a radical disjunction between karmic existence and striving for *Nibbāna* does not characterize the thought or practice of Theravāda Buddhism. For the contrary point of view see Winston L. King, *In Hope of Nibbāna* (LaSalle, IL: Open Court, 1964); and Melford Spiro, *Buddhism and Society: A Great Tradition and Its Burmese Vicissitudes* (New York: Harper and Row, 1970).

82. See Louis Jacobs who argues that "Rabbinic Judaism is *both* this-worldly and other-worldly . . ."—*Jewish Theology*, p. 309.

83. Frank Reynolds draws attention to the complex ways in which Theravāda Buddhists have related "path action" and *kammic* action, *Sangha* and "laymen." See "Four Modes of Theravada Action," *Journal of Religious Ethics*, 7(1979), 12–26. He notes four modes of action: path-winning monks or *bhikkhus, puthujjana bhikkus* whose actions remain within the kammic sphere, laypersons who focus on kammic action within ordinary social structures, and laypersons who enter the path and practice as Stream-winners, Once-returners, or Non-returners, or remain as *bodhisattas* (especially as *bodhisatta* kings). These four modes have been related in various ways in Buddhist societies and reveal that although Buddhists make a distinction between *lokiya* (this-worldly) and *lokuttara* (other-worldly) action, various overlapping categories have emerged.

84. Reynolds has charted a series of contrasts between classical Christianity and Theravāda Buddhism which parallels—with a broader canvas and different emphases—my effort in this chapter. See Reynolds' "Contrasting Modes of Action: A Comparative Study of Buddhist and Christian Ethics," *History of Religions*, 20(August and September 1980), 128–146. He identifies a common "pattern," a distinction between this-worldly and other-worldly action (see his note 9, p. 140) and finds similarities and differences in the ways the traditions see this-worldly activity, the transition or transformation through which it is transcended, and the "dynamics of supra-worldly attainment" (p. 135). Reynolds also discusses differences in the ways Christians and Buddhists have structured their communities and defined themselves in relation to the outside world.

85. I am talking about the way worldviews are linked, as Geertz would put it, to moods and motivations in a system of meaning, the *manifest* links between belief and patterns of conduct and character. The unintended or *latent* effect of religious thought and practice is another matter. Max Weber is interpreted as holding that the goal of election produced a worldly focus which was not explicitly enjoined in Protestant theology. See *The Protestant Ethic and the Spirit of Capitalism*, trans. Talcott Parsons (New York: Scribner's, 1958).

86. Gustafson, *Ethics from a Theocentric Perspective*, Vols. 1 and 2 (Chicago: University of Chicago Press, 1981 and 1984). On the notion of salvation as a relation to "Ultimate Reality" and on the "transcending" of personal consciousness, compare John Hick, *Death and Eternal Life* (London: Collins, 1976), chapter 22, especially pp. 459 ff.

Conclusion

We naturally try to place morality, the constitutive institution of society, in the context of ultimate reality, the basic structures and powers that affect our struggle to live and flourish. We naturally ask about the causal source of all human experience, including morality; about how we come to apprehend right and wrong, to have moral beliefs; about how the beliefs we have are justified, whether their rationale has anything to do with the ultimate context of existence. Some cultures have answered these questions by postulating forms of a transhuman reality as the source of morality—the source not only of specific norms, but of the very meaning of rightness and moral goodness. Taking such a reality as the source of morality will make a difference in one's life depending on how that reality and its relation to human existence is understood: Do we really stand under a divine legislator? Visions of ultimate good and moral duty will vary according to the framework of values, factual beliefs, and moral norms in particular cultures.

The way we understand our lives will also be different depending on how we diagnose and prescribe for moral evil. Believing in a divine judge adds a superstructure to the mechanisms of moral pressure and legal enforcement that humans devise. If we could believe in divine redress, then Jews or blacks or American Indians or women or any of the countless others who have been oppressed could believe in ultimate justice. They could believe that having tried to do what is right, right will ultimately be done to them. In addition, we wonder about our own and humankind's moral flaws: is there any hope for improvement or perhaps even moral perfection? Can I progress? Can the species? I may be able to carry through a moral project—my doing of my duty is not always frustrated by others or by natural events—but if most people including myself often succumb to evil then maybe overall moral defeats will equal or even out-number moral achievements.

Finally, human beings in many cultures have envisaged, beyond moral perfection, a transmoral goal. If we have a vision of a mode of life that takes us out of the moral sphere, we may adopt a way of life which will distinguish us from those who do not share our beliefs. Believing that the moral demand is to be eminently fulfilled in a new mode of being, individuals will face the world in a way that in one way or another ex-presses this vision. The believer structures existence in light of a vision of salvation.

Thus like Otto I would say that it is a mistake for Kantians to locate the hope for moral perfection at the heart of *all* religions.[1] Otto was right to identify a longing for a transmoral mode of existence. Otto, however, went astray when he claimed that the experience of the numinous was a part of all fully developed religions. There are simply different sorts of religious visions, some that aim at a transmoral goal and some that don't. Moreover, where a transmoral goal is postulated, it is sometimes entirely cut off from morality; but in some traditions, particularly mainstream forms of Judaism and Christianity, the transmoral destiny, as Otto himself suggested, eminently fulfills the moral demand.

One question has only received partial attention here: In what sense are religious beliefs about source, sanction, and salvation the products of human imagination? Have human beings invented fictitious explanations of how their moralities came about? Peter Berger, in the tradition of Emile Durkheim, said that notions of divinity tend to be nothing more than the normative social order reified and projected as divine; something that is a human product is "thrown out" and characterized as a reality ex-ternal to and independent of humankind.[2] Kant, in order to meet the problems of moral unfulfillment, "postulated" God, immortality, and grace. But are these beliefs justified or is the evidence insufficient? Finally, Otto thought that we have a special capacity to experience the numinous. But are visions of an existence beyond the duality of good and evil, be-yond even moral perfection, anything more than fictive representations of a state we long for, plunged as we often seem to be in moral despair?

Although I did not try to settle these issues, there is a point that ought to be made again at the conclusion of this volume. Berger claimed that religious ideas were not only products of the human imagination but tend to be fictions invented to quell anxiety. But even if we assume that religious questions arise out of anxiety about well-being, that does not mean that one just invents a comforting answer. Religious beliefs are more like *theoretical* models that describe and explain (or even justify) the human condition.[3] Religious ideas may express hopes of one sort or another, but it is too simple to say that they help us forget what we know is really true. As views of the human condition, they do not let us turn our back on what is evil or unsatisfactory in the real world as a fantasy does, but they purport to deal with both what is positive and what is negative in human experience; and they are not "immune," as Freud apparently thought, to evidence.[4] As I noted in Chapter 2, believers could admit that in one sense their beliefs are wish-fulfillments, but they have not ignored or suppressed evidence, and they often change their views in light of new beliefs.

Religious models or theories, furthermore, are built up from images or metaphors drawn from ordinary experience. Obviously human beings would tend to model ultimate reality and its connection with themselves on what they already know: social relations, machines, their bodies. Thus mis-named primitives work out subtle and comprehensive accounts of their experience.[5] For example, the notion of a divine king who legislates a nomos is not a dreamlike divinization of a familiar political pattern, produced to quell anxiety about the precariousness of social reality. It is part of a vision of the origin, apprehension, and justification of the nomos.

There is still the question of whether models such as these are true or justified by the evidence. They are the product of human efforts to understand and explain our existence; they purport to account for experience and they are subject to change and refutation as the history of religions demonstrates. Once we see sets of religious ideas as interpretations of our condition, we can acknowledge that they are the products of the human imagination. To acknowledge this, however, is not to assert, for example, that a deity has not spoken to or encountered human beings (concepts of revelation in Judaism and Christianity); it is to say that the thesis that a god manifests itself and the thesis that it hasn't are both interpretations, both are theories of human existence; in this sense, both are products of the human imagination. The traditional Judaic or Christian thinker, who believes the deity has disclosed itself, has interpreted human existence in one way, just as Camus does when he images human beings over-against an implacably indifferent universe.

NOTES

1. See Michel Despland, *Kant on History and Religion*, (Montreal and London: McGill–Queen's University Press, 1973), p. 11.

2. Emile Durkheim, *Elementary Forms of the Religious Life* (New York: Free Press, 1965); Peter Berger, *The Sacred Canopy*, (Garden City, NY: Doubleday, 1969). Berger's notion of religious "cosmization" builds on Durkheim.

3. Ian Barbour, *Myths, Models, and Paradigms* (New York: Harper and Row, 1974). On metaphor, see Sallie McFague, *Metaphorical Theology: Models of God in Religious Language* (Philadelphia: Fortress, 1982); see also Mary Gerhart and Allan Melvin Russell, *Metaphoric Process: The Creation of Scientific and Religious Understanding* (Fort Worth: Texas Christian University Press, 1984); on theological construction see Gordon D. Kaufman, *The Theological Imagination: Constructing the Concept of God* (Philadelphia: Westminster Press, 1981); David Tracy, *The Analogical Imagination: Christian Theology and the Culture of Pluralism* (N.Y.: Crossroad 1981); and Ronald Thiemann, *Revelation and Theology: the Gospel as Narrated Promise* (Notre Dame, IN: University of Notre Dame Press, 1985). On the notion of narrative as a distinctive methodological category in theology and ethics, see James McClendon, "Narrative Ethics and Christian Ethics," *Faith and Philosophy, 4* (October 1986), 383–396; for evaluations, see Paul Nelson, *Narrative and Morality: A Theological Inquiry* (Pennsylvania State University Press, 1987) and Paul Lauritzen, "Is 'Narrative' Really a Panacea? The Use of 'Narrative' in Metz and Hauerwas," *The Journal of Religion, 67*(July 1987), 322–339. In my view, the category of narrative can help to provide a richer phenomenology of moral and religious experience; it may also play a substantive role in some views of morality, for example, Hauerwas' and MacIntyre's ethics; but I do not see that it resolves or bypasses traditional metaphysical or epistemological issues (how does God act, for example, promise things; how are moral and religious beliefs justified, and if they need evidence, what sort).

4. Freud did not say that religious ideas were inherently untrue; it is science which shows them up. See *The Future of an Illusion*, trans. W. D. Robson-Scott and ed. James Strachey (Garden City, NY: Doubleday, 1969). They arise because of emotional need and they are adhered to with no regard for evidence, but it takes the vision of science to show that they are false. But Berger suggests that religions by their very nature tend to obscure the knowledge of what is really true, namely, the human origin and precarious nature of the social order. In this sense religion alienates, obscures, mystifies. Because of the need to quell our anxiety, we tend to sacralize—render unchangeable—our purely human heritage. See *The Sacred Canopy*, pp. 85–86.

5. See Godfrey Lienhardt, *Divinity and Experience: The Religion of The Dinka* (Oxford: Clarendon Press, 1961).

Name Index

Subject Index